Understanding and Using

Microsoft® Windows™ 3.1

Steven C. Ross
College of Business and Economics
Western Washington University

Ronald W. Maestas
Department of Business
New Mexico Highlands University

WEST PUBLISHING COMPANY
Minneapolis/St. Paul • New York
Los Angeles • San Francisco

Production, Prepress, Printing and Binding by West Publishing Company
Project Management by Lisa M. Labrecque

 *Printed on 10% Post Consumer Recycled Paper*

Microsoft® and Windows® are registered trademarks of Microsoft Corporation.
Screens are reprinted with the permission of Microsoft Corporation,
copyright ©1983–1993 Microsoft Corporation.
All rights reserved. Reprinted by permission.

Library of Congress Cataloging-in-Publication Data

Ross, Steven C.
    Understanding and using Microsoft Windows 3.1 / Steven C. Ross,
Ronald W. Maestas.
        p.   cm. — (Microcomputing series)
    Includes index.
    ISBN 0-314-02589-8
    1. Windows (Computer programs)   2. Microsoft Windows (Computer file)
I. Maestas, Ronald W.   II. Title.   III. Series.
QA76.76.W56R662   1994
005.4'3—dc20   *93-8665*
                                                       CIP

Contents

UNIT 3 / PROGRAM MANAGER   34

Windows Applications 95

…never cease to wonder when men say that only the wise are beautiful, with what physical senses they have seen that particular beauty, and with what eyes they have beheld the form of the flesh and the loveliness of wisdom.

St. Augustine

Understanding and Using Microsoft Windows 3.1 presents an operating system environment that can be used to replace the "usual" MS-DOS/PC DOS environment—specifically, with the use of the hugely popular program Microsoft Windows 3.1. Windows 3.1 is an attempt to make the computer more "user friendly."

Its drop-down menus, dialog boxes, and graphic symbols called icons provide an extremely efficient manner to execute commands. As technology changes, software like Windows and advanced hardware provide faster and ever more efficient methods of working with a personal computer. Operating systems provide the foundation for business students and professionals alike to become skillful users.

Why This Book?

There are many books available that discuss Microsoft Windows 3.1. Why, then, would anyone write another book? We decided to do so because both our students and our colleagues at several universities desired a book tailored to the way personal computing is taught at the college and professional level. We saw that there was no book designed for use in academic or workshop settings. We saw a need for a text that would present concepts and skills as well as provide activities, applications, and questions for practice and teaching purposes. *Understanding and Using Microsoft Windows 3.1* is such a book.

Our goal was to support the efforts of the instructor by providing the essential facets of the software, together with activities and exercises, to reinforce and evaluate the student's learning experience. Examples are drawn from the fields of business administration and economics to illustrate how the software can be used in other course work as well as in the daily tasks performed by business professionals. The instructor's manual provides supplementary materials and suggestions for integrating this book with other course materials.

This book serves a different role than the reference manuals furnished with the Microsoft Windows 3.1 software. Those manuals are quite comprehensive, but often are difficult to read and fail to provide adequate examples. Accordingly, we sought to provide instruction in fundamental, intermediate, and advanced operations, supporting it with substantial reference material. When more detailed information is required, the user will have a significant foundation for finding and using it.

Finally, *Understanding and Using Microsoft Windows 3.1* serves as a member of THE MICROCOMPUTING SERIES published by West Publishing Company. It can be used alone, in combination with other books in the series (listed in the Publisher's Note on pages xvi-xx), or to supplement any other book in a course where a knowledge of Microsoft Windows 3.1 is required.

How to Use This Book

You should complete the first four units in the order presented. With that background, the material in the remainder of the book can be covered in the order that suits you best—although several units do assume that you have completed earlier units and build upon that knowledge base. The more work you do on the computer, the better you will learn the topics. At a minimum, you should complete the Guided Activities with each unit. Each activity is designed to illustrate points made in the current and previous units, and many contain additional material that is best presented during a computer session.

Each unit includes the following features:

LEARNING OBJECTIVES the knowledge and skills addressed in the unit.

COMPUTER SCREENS figures depicting the steps and illustrating the results of most commands.

GUIDED ACTIVITIES step-by-step, hands-on exercises guiding the reader through operations discussed in the unit.

REVIEW QUESTIONS questions designed to test your understanding of the material presented. The answers to selected Review Questions are contained in Appendix C.

KEY TERMS a list of the important terms and concepts discussed in the unit. This list is designed for review and self-test.

DOCUMENTATION RESEARCH exercises that require you to use the software publisher's documentation to learn more about the commands and functions discussed in the unit.

Additional features of this book are as follows:

WINDOWS SETUP This appendix, Appendix A, contains a short discussion of setting up Microsoft Windows 3.1.

KEYBOARD COMMANDS This appendix, Appendix B, contains a list and short discussion of Microsoft Windows 3.1 keyboard commands.

INDEX The index covers commands, functions, symbols, and other topics. This is designed to allow you to locate the relevant information quickly.

A Note of Thanks

From Steve Ross

- to Ron Maestas—getting a friend to write a book with you is tough, but finding one who will stay a friend throughout the process is even more difficult;

- to Greg Foy, Floyd Lewis, and T. J. Olney, my colleagues at Western Washington University with whom I have discovered the joys of Windows;

- to Meredith, Kelly, and Shannon, still in love and having fun after all these years.

From Ron Maestas

- to Steven C. Ross, whose friendship, collegiality, and guidance helped me maintain my sanity;

- to Max Baca, Field Services/LAN Manager at New Mexico Highlands University, for getting me out of trouble; he has one of the brightest minds I know;

- to Sylvia Quintana Baca, a graduate of New Mexico Highlands University, who assisted me in the preparation of the manuscript;

- to Jim Odom, PC Technician at New Mexico Highlands University, who consistently gave me encouragement;

- to Raymond B. Maestas, a graduate from the University of New Mexico, who first encouraged me to write a book and who put his heart and soul into the manuscript; he gave the book a student's perspective in the Guided Activities and Review Questions;

- to Dominic Maestas, a student of the United States Air Force Academy, whose intelligence, enthusiasm, and curiosity for computers are contagious;

- to Lisa Maestas, a graduate from New Mexico State University, School of Accountancy, whose dedication, determination, and organization have taught me how to persevere;

- to my beautiful wife, Monica, whose love and support have *always* been with me in all of my endeavors, starting in Alamosa, Colorado, to Tempe, Arizona, Minneapolis, Minnesota, Bloomington, Indiana, Seoul, South Korea, and finally to Las Vegas, New Mexico; I love you very much!

- to Monica, Lisa, Raymond, and Dominic Ron Maestas: I hope that I have made you as proud of me as I am of you—each of you has been an inspiration to me.

From Both of Us...

- to the many students and teachers who adopted the first edition of *Understanding and Using Windows 3*;

- to the reviewers of the previous version of this manuscript—John Nicholson of Johnson County Community College, Michelle Lenox of Nashville State Technical

College, Joseph Franklin of Asheville–Buncombe Technical Community College, and Cliff Layton of Rogers State College—whose comments and careful reading of the manuscript helped us immensely as we labored to write about this exciting technology;

- to Rick Leyh and Jessica Evans of West Publishing, for pushing this project through to completion…with a gentle touch;

- to Lisa Labrecque, Lisa Auer, Jeanette Brinker, Curtis Philips, Mark Rhynsburger, and Mark Woodworth for producing this book.

S.C.R & R.W.M.
Bellingham, Washington, and Las Vegas, New Mexico
June 1993

This book is part of THE MICROCOMPUTING SERIES. This popular series provides the most comprehensive list of books dealing with microcomputer applications software. We have expanded the number of software topics and provided a flexible set of instructional materials for all courses. This unique series includes five different types of books.

1. *West's Microcomputing Custom Editions* give instructors the power to create a spiral-bound microcomputer applications book especially for their course. Instructors can select the applications they want to teach and the amount of material they want to cover for each application—essentials or intermediate length. The following titles are available for the 1994 Microcomputing Series custom editions program:

Understanding Information Systems	*Lotus 1-2-3 Release 2.2*
Understanding Networks	*Lotus 1-2-3 Release 2.3*
DOS (3.x) and System	*Lotus 1-2-3 Release 2.4*
DOS 5 and System	*Lotus 1-2-3 Release 3*
DOS 6 and System	*Lotus 1-2-3 for Windows Release 4*
Windows 3.0	*Microsoft Excel 3*
Windows 3.1	*Microsoft Excel 4*
WordPerfect 5.0	*Quattro Pro 4*
WordPerfect 5.1	*Quattro Pro for Windows*
WordPerfect 6.0	*dBASE III Plus*
WordPerfect for Windows (Release 5.1 and 5.2)	*dBASE IV Version 1.0/1.1/1.5*
Microsoft Word for Windows Version 1.1	*dBASE IV Version 2.0*
Microsoft Word for Windows Version 2.0	*Paradox 3.5*
PageMaker 4	*Paradox for Windows*
Lotus 1-2-3 Release 2.01	*Microsoft Access*

For more information about *West's Microcomputing Custom Editions*, please contact your local West Representative, or call West Publishing Company at 512-327-3175.

2. General concepts books for teaching basic hardware and software philosophy and applications are available separately or in combination with hands-on applications. These books provide students with a general overview of computer fundamentals including history, social issues, and a synopsis of software and hardware applications. These books include *Understanding Information Systems*, by Steven C. Ross.

3. A series of hands-on laboratory tutorials (*Understanding and Using*) are software specific and cover a wide range of individual packages. These tutorials, written at an introductory level, combine tutorials with complete reference guides. A complete list of series titles can be found on the following pages.

4. Several larger volumes combining DOS with three application software packages are available in different combinations. These texts are titled *Understanding and Using Application Software*. They condense components of the individual lab manuals and add conceptual coverage for courses that require both software tutorials and microcomputer concepts in a single volume.

5. A series of advanced-level, hands-on lab manuals provide students with a strong project/systems orientation. These include *Understanding and Using Lotus 1-2-3: Advanced Techniques Releases 2.2 and 2.3*, by Judith C. Simon.

THE MICROCOMPUTING SERIES has been successful in providing you with a full range of applications books to suit your individual needs. We remain committed to excellence in offering the widest variety of current software packages. In addition, we are committed to producing microcomputing texts that provide you both the coverage you desire and also the level and format most appropriate for your students. The Acquisitions Editor of the series is Rick Leyh of West Educational Publishing; the Consulting Editor is Steve Ross of Western Washington University. We are always planning for the future in this series. Please send us your comments and suggestions:

Rick Leyh
West Educational Publishing
1515 Capital of Texas Highway South
Suite 402
Austin, Texas 78746

Steve Ross
Associate Professor/MIS
College of Business and Economics
Western Washington University
Bellingham, Washington 98225
Electronic Mail: STEVEROSS@WWU.EDU

We now offer these books in THE MICROCOMPUTING SERIES:

General Concepts

Understanding Information Systems
by Steven C. Ross

Understanding Computer Information Systems
by Paul W. Ross, H. Paul Haiduk, H. Willis Means, and Robert B. Sloger

Operating Systems/Environments

Understanding and Using Microsoft Windows 3.1
by Steven C. Ross and Ronald W. Maestas

Understanding and Using Microsoft Windows 3.0
by Steven C. Ross and Ronald W. Maestas

Understanding and Using MS-DOS 6.0
by Jonathan P. Bacon

Understanding and Using MS-DOS/PC DOS 5.0
by Jonathan P. Bacon

Understanding and Using MS-DOS/PC DOS 4.0
by Jonathan P. Bacon

Networks

Understanding Networks
by E. Joseph Guay

Word Processors

Understanding and Using WordPerfect for Windows
by Jonathan P. Bacon

Understanding and Using Microsoft Word for Windows 2.0
by Larry Lozuk and Emily M. Ketcham

Understanding and Using Microsoft Word for Windows (1.1)
by Larry Lozuk

Understanding and Using WordPerfect 6.0
by Jonathan P. Bacon

Understanding and Using WordPerfect 5.1
by Jonathan P. Bacon and Cody T. Copeland

Understanding and Using WordPerfect 5.0
by Patsy H. Lund

Desktop Publishing

Understanding and Using PageMaker 4
by John R. Nicholson

Spreadsheet Software

Understanding and Using Quattro Pro for Windows
by Larry D. Smith

Understanding and Using Microsoft Excel 4
by Steven C. Ross and Stephen V. Hutson

Understanding and Using Microsoft Excel 3
by Steven C. Ross and Stephen V. Hutson

Understanding and Using Lotus 1-2-3 for Windows Release 4
by Steven C. Ross and Alan H. Bauld

Understanding and Using Quattro Pro 4
by Steven C. Ross and Stephen V. Hutson

Understanding and Using Lotus 1-2-3 Release 2.01
by Steven C. Ross

Understanding and Using Lotus 1-2-3 Release 2.2
by Steven C. Ross

Understanding and Using Lotus 1-2-3 Release 2.3 and Release 2.4
by Steven C. Ross

Understanding and Using Lotus 1-2-3 Release 3
by Steven C. Ross

*Understanding and Using Lotus 1-2-3: Advanced Techniques
Releases 2.2 and 2.3*
by Judith C. Simon

Database Management Software

Understanding and Using Microsoft Access
by Bruce J. McLaren

Understanding and Using Paradox for Windows
by Larry D. Smith

Understanding and Using Paradox 3.5
by Larry D. Smith

Understanding and Using dBASE III Plus, 2nd Edition
by Steven C. Ross

Understanding and Using dBASE IV Version 2.0
by Steven C. Ross

Understanding and Using dBASE IV
by Steven C. Ross

Integrated Software

Understanding and Using Microsoft Works 3.0 for the PC
by Gary Bitter

Understanding and Using Microsoft Works 3.0 for the Macintosh
by Gary Bitter

Understanding and Using ClarisWorks
by Gary Bitter

Understanding and Using Microsoft Works 2.0 on the Macintosh
by Gary Bitter

Understanding and Using Microsoft Works 2.0 on the IBM PC
by Gary Bitter

Combined Books

Essentials of Application Software, Volume 1: DOS, WordPerfect 5.0/5.1, Lotus 1-2-3 Release 2.2, dBASE III Plus
by Steven C. Ross, Jonathan P. Bacon, and Cody T. Copeland

Understanding and Using Application Software, Volume 4: DOS, WordPerfect 5.0, Lotus 1-2-3 Release 2, dBASE IV
by Patsy H. Lund, Jonathan P. Bacon, and Steven C. Ross

Understanding and Using Application Software, Volume 5: DOS, WordPerfect 5.0/5.1, Lotus 1-2-3 Release 2.2, dBASE III Plus
by Steven C. Ross, Jonathan P. Bacon, and Cody T. Copeland

Advanced Books

Understanding and Using Lotus 1-2-3: Advanced Techniques Releases 2.2 and 2.3
by Judith C. Simon

Steven C. Ross holds a B.S. degree in History from Oregon State University and M.S. and Ph.D. degrees in Business Administration from the University of Utah. He is an Associate Professor of Management Information Systems at Western Washingon University, Bellingham. His previous positions were as Associate Professor of Information Systems at Montana State University, Bozeman, and Assistant Professor of Management at Marquette University in Milwaukee. His responsibilities include the introduction of microcomputers into the primary computer courses and the integration of computer applications throughout the curriculum.

Dr. Ross is the Consulting Editor for THE MICROCOMPUTING SERIES. In this capacity he advises both West Publishing Company and the authors on pedagogical, creative, editorial, design, and marketing issues. He is the author or coauthor of a dozen articles dealing with information management and education, and this is one of 25 books on microcomputing that he has written or edited. Two of his books in this series have been translated into French. He also consults with businesses of all sizes to integrate microcomputers into their managerial operations. His teaching and consulting experiences have provided ample material for this book.

Ronald W. Maestas holds a B.A. and an M.A. degree in Business Education from Adams State College as well as an Ed. D. degree in Business Education from Arizona State University. He successfully completed the AACSB Information Systems Faculty Development Institute at the University of Minnesota and the Advanced Institute at Indiana University. He is a Full Professor of Management Information Systems at New Mexico Highlands University, Las Vegas, New Mexico. His previous appointments include Department Head and Cross Country Coach at New Mexico Highlands University; his 1987 team were the NAIA runner-up champions. He served as the national distance coach for the Swaziland Olympic team at the 1988 Summer Olympics in Seoul, South Korea. His current responsibilities include the introduction of microcomputers into the business curriculum and the integration of computer applications throughout the business school.

Dr. Maestas is the coauthor, with Steven C. Ross, of *Understanding and Using Microsoft Windows 3*. He has received a National Science Foundation grant to integrate computers into the Information Analysis class. He has served as a reviewer for several books on microcomputers and has been a beta tester for Ashton-Tate's Digital VAX/VMS version of dBASE IV. He has made several presentations at regional and national conferences. His 20 years of teaching have provided him with a good foundation for this book.

Fundamental Windows Operations

■ **PART ONE** In this part we introduce Microsoft Windows 3.1. Unit 1, "The Windows Environment," illustrates concepts and features of the program, describes starting Windows and the Program Manager application, and provides an overview of the Windows family of products. Unit 2, "Basic Skills," contains a series of discussions and activities that provide practice in dealing with the different types of windows, using both the mouse and the keyboard for input.

Unit 3, "Program Manager," deals with the fundamental aspects of the default shell of Windows. Here we discuss how to move among program groups and how to start application programs. Unit 4, "File Manager," explores the numerous techniques available in that program for administering storage of data and programs in files, in directories, and on disks.

Unit 5 presents the "Control Panel," a program that allows you to change the visual and mechanical aspects of the Windows interface. You can, for instance, change both the colors of window borders and the background of your windows screen. Finally, Unit 6 discusses "Print Manager," the program that manages the printing of the output of most Windows programs.

Which Version of Windows Are You Using?

Windows 3.1 is a substantial improvement over previous versions of Microsoft Windows, but, as with any software product, further improvements are probable.

The major differences among versions of Windows have been behind-the-scenes performance improvements (for example, the latest program release runs faster and is less susceptible to certain types of errors) rather than differences in the manner in which the program is operated. In version 3.1 some visual differences are found in the File Manager program, while new menu items were added to many of the Windows applications.

This book should serve you well, however, regardless of which version of Windows you use. If you have an older version, compare the commands on your menu (for, say, Program Manager) with those presented in this book. We believe that there will be very few differences in technique from one version of Windows to the next.

The Windows Environment

For you to appreciate Microsoft Windows 3.1, you need to become acquainted with some basic concepts that are unique to the program. Since Windows has become extremely popular, you should learn, understand, and utilize its features to better prepare yourself for using personal computers in your career.

Learning Objectives

At the completion of this unit, you should know

1. the concepts and features of Microsoft Windows 3.1,

2. what a graphical user interface (GUI) is,

3. some of the applications available with Windows 3.1.

At the completion of this unit, you should be able to

1. start Windows 3.1,

2. exit Windows 3.1,

3. describe the Main Menu,

4. describe Windows and non-Windows applications.

Windows Concepts

Windows is a ***graphical user interface***[1] (abbreviated as ***GUI***, pronounced "gooey") that provides its users with more intuitive methods for working on personal computers and more visual cues than offered by traditional ***character-based user interfaces*** (***CUI***). These permit a wide range of operations using a mouse or other pointing device. Those who are not good typists appreciate being relieved of the necessity of entering commands by typing—since a simple point, drag, or click of the mouse can perform sophisticated operations that require several keystrokes in a CUI environment.

In Windows, the computer screen is referred to as a ***desktop***. The Windows desktop is similar to the surface of the desk you use at work or at home. The desktop displays information in rectangular areas, or frames, called ***windows***. You work with applications and documents within these windows.

Figure 1.1 illustrates a desktop with various key terms noted.

Across the top of each of the two windows is the ***window title***, which tells you what the window contains. The thin frame around the window is called the ***window border***. Windows usually contain ***applications***, computer programs used for a particular kind of work, such as word processing, spreadsheets, or databases. Some applications programs allow you to have more than one ***document*** active at a time; for instance, you could be working on a term paper in one document window and a letter to a friend in the other. Windows can be arranged on the desktop, just as you can move work items around on an actual desk. For example, to review a spreadsheet and a report from two separate applications, you can change the size of the windows so that you view each side of the desktop simultaneously. Figure 1.1 shows two windows, one in the background containing the program Microsoft Word for Windows (a full-featured word processor) and one in the foreground containing Program Manager, the usual starting place for Windows operations.

In most cases, the window containing an application or document is not large enough to display the entire document. ***Scroll bars*** are used to move parts of a document into view when the entire document will not fit in a window. The ***menu bar*** at the top of each window contains a number of commands that are standard across Windows applications, as well as commands that are specific to the application contained in the window. (These menu names and commands will be printed in initial caps in this text.)

Icons are small pictographs that appear on some screens. Icons are used to represent running applications, documents, and program groups in Program Manager. For example, a graphic of a clock represents the Clock application. If you should choose to leave an application for a while, you can ***minimize*** the window to an ***application icon***. The application will continue to run even though it does not appear in a window. After you minimize an application, Windows will place its application icon at the lower edge of the desktop until you ***restore*** it to window size

---

1 In this section, we introduce a number of terms, typeset in ***boldface italic***, that deal with the operation of Windows. Some are defined here, while others are defined elsewhere in the book. As you read the text and work on your computer, develop your own definitions for these terms and concepts. The Key Terms section near the end of each unit lists the terms introduced in that unit.

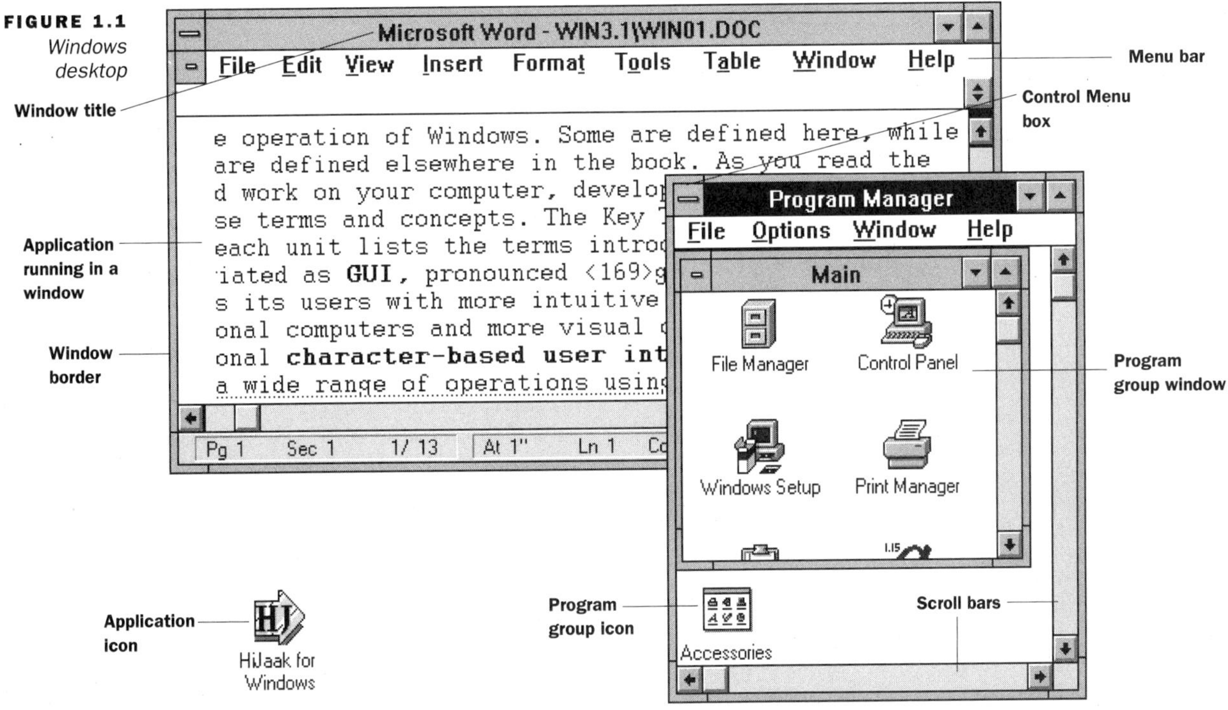

again. In Figure 1.1, you see the icon for HiJaak for Windows, a screen-capture program, on the bottom of the desktop. If you wish, you can *maximize* a window so that it occupies the entire screen. Maximized windows allow as much information as possible from a single application to be displayed on the screen.

The Program Manager window contains two kinds of objects. The window labeled "Main" in the figure is a *program group window*, a window that contains a set of programs. The Program Manager window also contains *program group icons*, such as Accessories, which represent program groups that have been minimized, or "put away", for the moment.

With Windows, you can run several applications at once and switch quickly among them. For example, you can switch from a database application to a spreadsheet and then to a word processor with a few simple commands and without having to wait while you quit one application and start another.

When you work with two or more applications, whether they are designed specifically for Windows or not, you can transfer information from one to the other. You select the information you want from one application, *cut* or *copy* it to the Windows Clipboard (a temporary storage area), and *paste* it into another application. By moving information in this manner, you can combine into one single document the work you have done in a number of different applications.

Windows comes outfitted with a collection of useful accessory programs to help you manage the various tasks that are part of your daily work. These are contained in the Accessories program group, illustrated in Figure 1.2. These accessories include a clock, an appointment calendar, a notepad, a card file, and a macro recorder. Windows also includes three full-featured applications: Write, Paintbrush, and

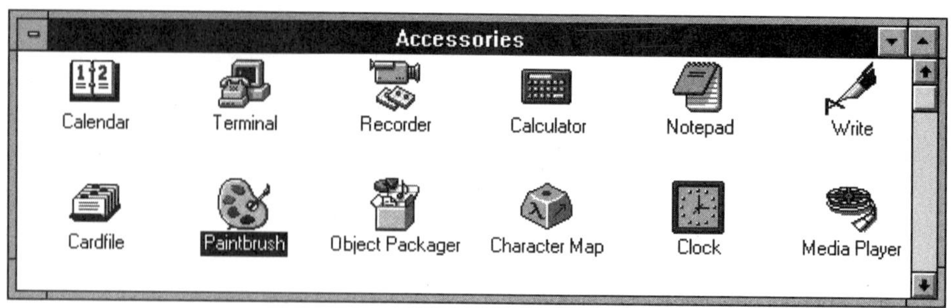

FIGURE 1.2
*Windows
Accessories*

Terminal. These applications are useful when preparing and editing documents, creating illustrations, and connecting to computers and on-line information services.

As you work with an application, you can pause at any time to take care of other tasks. For example, you might need to make some additions to the card files, schedule another meeting on your calendar, or pull together some quick totals with Windows' electronic calculator. Additional accessories include a character map, a media player, an object packager, and a sound recorder, which will be discussed later in the text.

Windows Features

Microsoft Windows 3.1 is the most popular graphical user interface program to exploit the advanced features of computers introduced since the original IBM PC. With it, users of DOS computers have at their command a control program that is flexible and powerful enough to support applications of many kinds, at virtually all levels of complexity and ambition. With more than 10 million users since its initial release in May 1990, Microsoft Windows has become the new standard for personal computing. Customers are choosing Windows because it is easy to use and because the most powerful new applications (over five thousand now available) are the focus of development activity and innovation at every major independent software vendor. There are several reasons for Windows' success.

First, an enormous range of Windows applications is available now. Windows users do not have to wait years for the kinds of applications promised, but not yet delivered, for other advanced operating systems.

Second, unlike some other systems, with relatively small numbers of computers sold and expensive hardware, Windows runs on tens of millions of DOS-based machines. In fact, Windows can run on virtually any DOS-based machine with a suitable graphics adapter and monitor. Optimal performance requires extra memory and a speedy microprocessor, but Windows 3.1 makes its appearance at an ideal historical moment, since RAM (a computer's primary working memory) is inexpensive and 386SX, 386, and even 486 machines are far less costly than ever before.

Third, Windows 3.1 is able to push any PC to its limit in ways that few other programs can. It exploits the power of a 386 or 486 machine (with at least 2MB of RAM, since Windows 3.1 runs better with a minimum of 4MB of RAM) by letting you *multitask* (operate more than one) DOS sessions while you run multiple

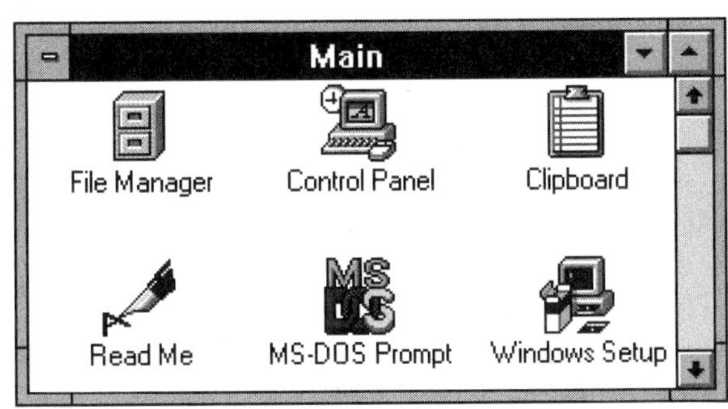

FIGURE 1.3
Windows' Main program group

Windows applications. On a 286 machine, Windows lets you multitask Windows applications and access up to 16MB of RAM.

Windows allows your computer to operate with greater efficiency, unhampered by memory restrictions of previous operating environments. Windows makes efficient use of all the memory installed in your computer, enabling you to execute several programs simultaneously. Windows also allows for the easy transfer of information from one program to another.

Windows is in effect the computer cockpit that allows you to control all of your computer's capabilities with the push of a button. Like the pilot of a modern, sophisticated aircraft, you are guided quickly through Windows' numerous functions by graphic symbols. You use Windows applications in the same intuitive way that you use Windows itself. With little effort, you can master high-powered, Windows-based programs for desktop publishing, spreadsheets, word processing, and graphics, such as PageMaker, Excel, Word, and Paintbrush.

The Main program group (most of which is illustrated in Figure 1.3) lists some of the other features found in Windows 3.1. These include:

File Manager, which allows a full range of mouse-driven operations to copy and move both files and directories, by dragging their icons with your mouse.

The Control Panel, which lets you connect to network printers, switch or add ports, set multitasking options, and customize the appearance of your desktop.

MS-DOS Prompt, which allows you to use many of the commands familiar to users of MS-DOS.

Print Manager, which provides information about files that are printing and allows the operator to pause or cancel print jobs and view network print queues.

Clipboard, which is the temporary storage place for information being transferred from one application to another.

Windows Setup, which is used to change settings for the keyboard, the mouse, and the video display screen.

Read Me, a document that contains late-breaking information not available in on-line help screens or printed manuals.

A Quick Introduction to Working with the Mouse

If at all possible, use Windows on a computer with a mouse or other pointing device. In this book we will tell you how to give the commands using the keyboard, but many operations are far easier using the mouse. The following terms are used to describe mouse operations. When we refer to "the mouse button" we mean the left button on those mice that have more than one button. If you are left-handed, you can change a multibutton mouse so that the right button functions as "the mouse button." Instructions for doing this are in Unit 2.

POINT Means to move the mouse pointer—often an arrow but sometimes another symbol—to an object. You will be instructed to *point* to an icon, a window title, the border of a window, a menu item, or various objects in a window, such as a spreadsheet cell.

CLICK (Also *choose* or *select*) means to press and then quickly release the mouse button after you have pointed to the object to be selected. With most mice, this produces a "click" sound. *Clicking* is used to instruct Windows to activate a window, open a menu, execute a command, or pick an item from a list.

DRAG Means to point to an object, then press the mouse button and hold it down while you move the mouse. *Dragging* is used to move objects such as windows and icons and to change window size. Dragging is also used in applications programs to *mark* or *highlight* a range of objects (for example, words, spreadsheet cells) before executing certain commands. For instance, you can highlight a group of words, then use a command to italicize them.

DOUBLE-CLICK Means to press the mouse button twice after you have pointed to an object. *Double-clicking* is a shortcut method for selecting and executing some commands. Throughout this book, we tell you where to use double-clicking.

Starting Windows 3.1

You have now been introduced to the basic concepts and terminology of Windows 3.1. This section shows you how to start and end a Windows session. The manner in which you load (run) Windows will depend on your system configuration.

The procedure for starting Windows varies from place to place and perhaps even from computer to computer. In this section we discuss a typical procedure for hard disk systems. If necessary, your instructor or system manager can assist you with any differences within your school or organization. To use Windows, you need a computer that has Windows installed on the hard disk or network as well as a formatted disk to save the files you create. If Windows has not been installed on your system, consult Appendix A for installation procedures.

Once Windows has been installed on your system, you may begin. The following Guided Activity assumes that your system *does not* have a "shell" or "menu" program that is executed when the computer is started. If this assumption is incorrect, your instructor or system manager will have to give you additional instructions in starting Windows.[2]

GUIDED ACTIVITY 1.1

Starting Windows

1. Turn on your PC and monitor. Enter the appropriate date and time if your computer asks for them.

2. The monitor will display the DOS prompt C>.

3. At the DOS prompt, type WIN or win and press ⏎Enter to start Windows 3.1.

4. The Microsoft Windows 3.1 copyright screen appears.

5. After a short pause, the Windows desktop appears. This might be a solid color, a design, or a picture, depending on your computer and your organization's preferences. On the desktop, you might see icons representing one or more programs, or you might see one or more windows that contain icons. We can't predict how your organization has set up Windows, so our instructions at this point are a bit equivocal.

   Windows usually begins with the Program Manager window open.[3] This window is identified by the words "Program Manager" in the window title bar. If you see an icon at the bottom of the screen with the words "Program Manager" underneath it, you should open the Program Manager window using the instructions in the following Guided Activity. Program Manager will serve as the basis for all of your work in Windows.

GUIDED ACTIVITY 1.2

Opening the Program Manager Window

Program Manager

1. Locate the Program Manager icon, which looks like the icon to the left.

2. If you are using a mouse, point to the Program Manager icon. Double-click on the icon—that is, press the left button twice quickly. Or, press the left button once, then choose Restore from the list of commands presented. The Program Manager window will be activated.

   If you are not using a mouse, hold down the Alt key while you press the Tab key until Program Manager and its icon are displayed in the center of the screen. Release the Alt key and the Program Manager window will be activated.

---

2 In many cases, starting Windows from a shell is simple: Highlight the "Windows" entry using the arrow keys and press ⏎Enter. Many organizations are now setting up their computers to automatically start Windows, making this exercise unnecessary.

3 Some schools and organizations use programs other than Program Manager as the basic window. Your instructor or lab manager should tell you if this is the case and should inform you how your local program differs from the Program Manager instructions given throughout this book.

GUIDED ACTIVITY 1.3

Exiting Windows

1. Close any active windows (except Program Manager) before leaving Windows. You will learn how to close active windows in later units as we discuss the Windows software.

2. If you are using a mouse, click twice on the Control Menu box at the upper-left corner of the Program Manager window. Or click once on the Control Menu box, then click on the word Close.

   If you are using the keyboard, press [Alt][Spacebar], use the arrow keys to highlight the word Close, and then press [Enter].

3. Respond to the dialog box to confirm your desire to exit. With a mouse, you can click once on the OK button. With the keyboard, use the arrow keys to highlight the button (notice that the edges of the highlighted button are darker and wider), then press [Enter].

Additional Microsoft Software

Microsoft Windows 3.1 is capable of running many other programs, including drawing packages, "smart" utilities, and project and data managers. Some programs, written especially for Windows, are called ***Windows applications***. These include software published by Microsoft Corporation as well as software from other publishers. At the time this book was written, Microsoft had published several Windows applications, the most prominent of which are Project, PowerPoint, Word for Windows, Excel, and Access. Following is a brief description of each of these. See Unit 11 for examples of how these products are used and more complete discussions of their features.

Project takes full advantage of the graphical capabilities of the Windows environment, which makes project management easier, more powerful, and far more flexible to use. Project management is an inherently graphical application, since project time-lines, for example, are more comprehensible as charts than as text. Microsoft has used the Windows environment to create entirely new techniques for handling task relationships, resource management, reports, and data entry. Project goes beyond the arbitrary structures of conventional text-based project managers such as Time-Line and Harvard Project Manager.

Microsoft PowerPoint, another program designed for Windows, offers a fast, easy way for you to create and manage your own high-quality overhead projections and 35mm-slide presentations. The uniqueness of PowerPoint software lies in its approach, for it addresses the needs of the business person, not the graphic designer. Microsoft PowerPoint is also unique with respect to its guiding principle: "A better process yields better results."

Capitalizing on the Microsoft Windows graphical environment, PowerPoint software makes the process of creating presentations simple, beginning with ***WYSIWYG*** ("what you see is what you get") technology. WYSIWYG lets you create slides or overheads directly on-screen. Add to that the ability to store all your presentation visuals in a single file, special presentation-management features that make organizing your presentation easy, plus a complete set of tools. In essence, PowerPoint gives you virtually all you need to produce a professional-looking presentation yourself. It lets you remain in control of your presentation from start to finish.

Word

Word for Windows is the word processing package developed by Microsoft for the Windows environment. It is a sophisticated program that includes a spell checker, a thesaurus, mail merge, and many other utilities. Word permits the importing of pictures, charts, and stylized text directly into a document. It provides a variety of character styles, including bold and italic character sets, single and double underlining, strike-through, superscript, subscript, and hidden text.

Word contains a number of paragraph formats that are helpful as you set up your text. A document can contain multiple formats, permitting you to have a standard format for most text—say, double-spaced and justified—but also to reserve special formats for headings and important paragraphs. These special formats can have left, center, or right alignment; a unique typeface; extra spacing before, after, or in the middle of the paragraph; and numerous other characteristics. The possibilities for arranging text are as many and varied as your imagination will permit, while the graphical user interface makes it easy for you to see the effect immediately.

Microsoft Excel

Excel is a state-of-the-art spreadsheet package from Microsoft and the first popular package to use the graphical user interface extensively. Excel provides a broad range of formatting options, allowing you to enhance the visual appeal of your product with multiple fonts, borders, shading, customized number formats, and color. Excel is designed to allow you to construct powerful models, displaying and linking multiple spreadsheets on your screen. You can check your figures as well with an array of advanced, built-in auditing tools. Excel has over one hundred built-in worksheet functions and more than two hundred macro functions. For graphic display of numbers, a gallery of more than forty built-in chart types, plus customization, is available in Excel.

Excel uses the standard GUI features of user-defined menus, dialog boxes, and on-line help to facilitate your work. You can record macros as you work, store them on separate sheets, and apply them to any worksheet. Excel is compatible with Lotus 1-2-3, dBASE III Plus, and Microsoft Multiplan, supplementing these data analysis packages with its own set of features.

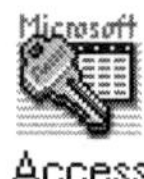

Access

Database management systems have traditionally split into two camps: those that are so complex that only a professional programmer can make them work, and the so-called "easy-to-use" database management systems that in reality are so underpowered that they sacrifice speed or skimp on critical features.

With Microsoft Access, however, you don't have to scrap your existing and valuable investment in data. Microsoft Access directly reads and writes in all of the popular file formats--even across a network, simultaneously with other users. You can easily share data, passing it back and forth with others in your workgroup who use Paradox®, dBase®, or other database management systems. Access allows you to get your data quickly by using *graphical query by example (QBE)*. With a mouse, just drag and drop tables, join fields, and specify criteria. Forms are built in minutes by using *visual form-generation* tools. Access allows you to quickly access database tools with the *dynamic toolbar*, create reports and forms using *ReportWizard* and

FormWizard. Cue Cards provide a step-by-step, on-line help screen alongside the database task you are working on. Finally, Access macros allow you to easily automate routine database management tasks, such as printing out a series of monthly reports. They provide an easy, fill-in-the-blank programming model for those who do not want to immerse themselves in Access Basic code.

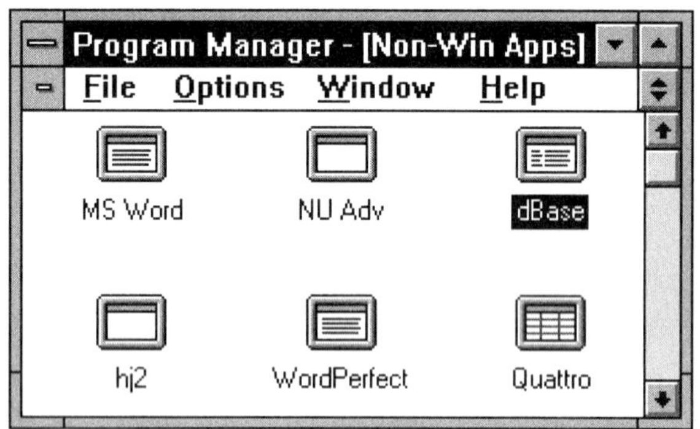

FIGURE 1.4
Typical non-Windows applications program group

Finally, Windows permits you to use *non-Windows applications*, such as Lotus 1-2-3, Quattro Pro, dBASE III Plus, HiJaak, WordPerfect, Norton Utilities, and the like, without exiting from Windows. If Program Manager shows an icon or window named "Non-Windows Applications" as shown in Figure 1.4, or something similar, it probably contains this kind of application program.

Overview of This Book

This text is designed to teach the basics of Windows applications. Basic skills will be practiced and fundamental concepts will be illustrated to help you master Windows. You will learn how to operate within the Windows environment. Windows includes all the programs you need to manage your software applications and files easily and efficiently. Furthermore, you will learn ways to increase your computing power and knowledge. With its emphasis on essentials and its practice-oriented instructions (Guided Activities, Review Questions, and Key Terms), this book will help you learn how to use Windows for your daily work.

Additional topics to be covered in this book include other Windows applications—such as Word, Excel, Project, and PowerPoint. This book deals with the programs included with Windows—Write, Paintbrush, and Terminal—as well as Windows accessories (calculator, calendar, card file, clock, notepad, recorder, and PIF editor). You will soon be exploring the Wonderful World of Windows!

Review Questions

The answers to questions marked with an asterisk are contained in Appendix C.

1. There are many ways that Windows 3.1 applications parallel items on your desk. Describe as many of these as you can.

*2. Discuss the factors leading to the recent success of Microsoft Windows 3.1.

*3. Briefly, state and describe the features and capabilities of Windows 3.1. (*Hint:* Review the icons in this unit.) Where applicable, state the advantages gained by using these features.

*4. List the steps for starting Windows 3.1.

Key Terms

The following terms are introduced in this unit. Be sure you know what each of them means.

Application	Graphical user interface	Program group icon
Application icon	(GUI)	Program group window
Character-based user	Graphical query by	ReportWizard
interface (CUI)	example (QBE)	Restore
Choose	Highlight	Scroll bar
Click	Icon	Select
Copy	Mark	Visual form-generation
Cut	Maximize	Window
Desktop	Menu bar	Window border
Document	Minimize	Window title
Double-click	Multitask	Windows application
Drag	Non-Windows application	WYSIWYG
Dynamic toolbar	Paste	
FormWizard	Point	

Documentation Research

We would be remiss if we did not stress the importance of your using software documentation. The *Microsoft Windows User's Guide* is a very helpful learning resource that supplies additional information not included in this text. One of the best habits you can develop in this course is to refer often to the documentation supplied by the software manufacturer. If your school or organization makes that documentation available to you, then use it to determine the answers to the following questions. Documentation Research sections are at the end of most units; answers can be found in either the on-line Help facility or the manual.

For the following questions, read *Getting Started with Microsoft Windows.*

1. List the minimum software and hardware requirements your computer needs to run Windows successfully.

2. Several on-line documents are copied onto your hard disk when you install Windows. What is the purpose of these text files?

3. How does the *User's Guide* represent keyboard formats? For example, what is the difference between the plus sign and the comma?

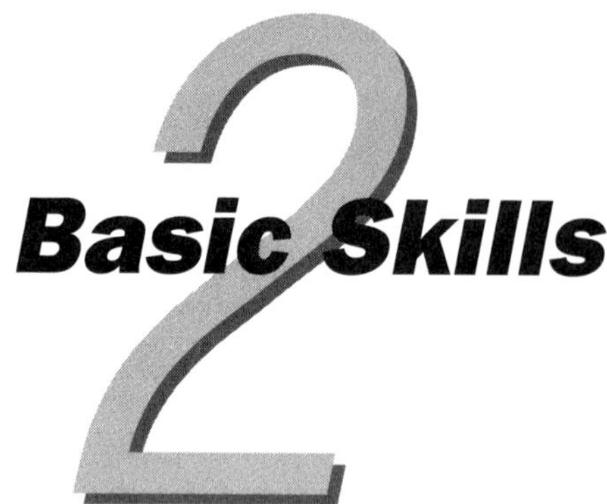

Basic Skills

Mastering basic concepts and skills is extremely important as you proceed to learn new software. This is particularly true of Windows, which is unique since it utilizes specialized terminology as well as different approaches to execute commands. This unit introduces you to the use of both mouse and keyboard for entering commands, then discusses the advantages and disadvantages of each method. In addition, you will learn the types of windows (application and document) that are used with Windows 3.1.

Learning Objectives

At the completion of this unit, you should know

1. the terminology of Windows,

2. advantages and disadvantages of using the mouse for input,

3. advantages and disadvantages of using the keyboard for input,

4. the difference between an application window and a document window.

At the completion of this unit, you should be able to

1. use both mouse and keyboard to enter commands,

2. open and close drop-down menus,

3. open dialog boxes and make entries in them,

4. move windows, icons, and dialog boxes,

5. change the size of a window,

6. minimize, maximize, and restore a window,

7. close an application window,

8. switch among application windows,

9. access and use the on-line Help facility.

Two Types of Windows

Throughout this book we will refer to various types of windows. The two most important types are application windows and document windows. Other types of windows are variations on these. An ***application window*** contains a program, such as Excel or Word. A ***document window*** contains a specific spreadsheet or graph in Excel, a document file in Word, and so on. Many Windows applications allow you to work with more than one document (whether spreadsheet, graph, or document) at once. The program group windows (for example, Main) in Program Manager are also classified as document windows.

Using a Mouse

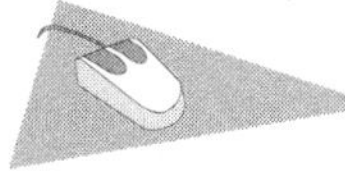

Microsoft Windows 3.1 can be operated most efficiently by using a mouse. The mouse offers an easy way to work with Windows because it enables the user to quickly move the cursor on the screen. When the mouse is rolled over a flat surface, such as a desktop or mouse pad, the cursor moves in the same relative direction on the screen. Instructions are given to Windows using the mouse control functions introduced in Unit 1: pointing, clicking, choosing, selecting, dragging, marking, and double-clicking.

Normally, the left mouse button is the "active button," which is convenient for right-handed users. The mouse can be configured for left-handed users, making the right mouse button the active button. Double-click on the Control Panel icon (in the Main Program group in Program Manager), then double-click the mouse icon. The mouse dialog box will appear. Place an X in the box adjacent to Swap Left/Right Buttons by clicking inside the box, then click on the OK button (using the right mouse button) to exit. Click on the arrow pointing down to minimize the Control Panel window.

Using a Keyboard

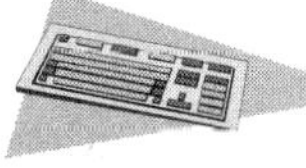

This unit and all subsequent units contain activities that require you to enter information from the keyboard. Your input must be accurate or the results will vary from what is described in the text. We have established a number of typographical conventions that will make it easier for you to know exactly which keys to press.

The word *Press* is used whenever you are instructed to push a single keystroke. For instance, after highlighting a command option, you will be instructed to

Press [Enter].

or

Press the [Enter] key.

This means you press the Enter or Return ([Return]) key on your keyboard once. On older PC keyboards, the [Enter] key is unlabeled except for a broken (crooked) arrow. In this text, that key is always referred to with the symbol [Enter].

Other keys that you press are listed below with their symbols shown in the first column.

[Alt]	Alt or Alternate key
[Backspace]	Backspace key
[CapsLock]	Caps Lock key
[Ctrl]	Ctrl or Control key
[Del]	Del or Delete key
[↓]	Down arrow key
[End]	End key on numeric or cursor movement pad
[Esc]	Esc or Escape key
[F1]	Function key labeled F1
[F2]	Function key labeled F2
[F3]	Function key labeled F3
[F4]	Function key labeled F4
[F5]	Function key labeled F5
[F6]	Function key labeled F6
[F7]	Function key labeled F7
[F8]	Function key labeled F8
[F9]	Function key labeled F9
[F10]	Function key labeled F10
[F11]	Function key labeled F11
[F12]	Function key labeled F12
[Home]	Home key on numeric or cursor movement pad
[Ins]	Ins or Insert key
[←]	Left arrow key

NumLock   Num Lock or Numeric Lock key

PgDn   PgDn or Page Down key

PgUp   PgUp or Page Up key

PrtSc   PrtSc or Print Screen key

→   Right arrow key

Shift   Shift key

Spacebar   Spacebar key

Tab   Tab key

↑   Up arrow key

Three of these keys (Alt, Ctrl, and Shift) are used in combination with a second key. For example, if instructed to press Alt Tab, you would hold down Alt, press the Tab key once, and then release Alt.

When keys are pressed one right after another, as opposed to the first key being held and the next pressed, the key notations are separated by commas. For example,

Press Alt H, I

In this case, you would press Alt then H, release both, and then press I once.

The word *Type* is used to indicate that multiple keystrokes must be entered on the keyboard. The specific keys to be typed are shown in the following typeface:

Type `Good Morning, Good People.`

In this example, you would type "Good Morning, Good People." (without the quotation marks but including the period).

Keyboard operations (commands) are generally the same from one Windows application to another. Sometimes the keyboard allows you to use a single-key shortcut, which replaces any mouse movements.

When you wish to obtain menu names in the menu bar, press the Alt key or the F10 (function key). Each menu or command name contains an underlined letter and is chosen by pressing that letter on the keyboard. In rare cases, the underlined letter is duplicated and you can select the second instance only by using the arrow keys to highlight that command and then pressing Enter.

For instance, Program Manager's File menu can be opened by pressing Alt F; Options menu Alt O; Window menu Alt W; and Help menu Alt H. Figure 2.1 shows the File menu after it has been opened. The Options menu for Program Manager contains the choice to Save Settings on Exit. The Windows

FIGURE 2.1
File menu of Program Manager

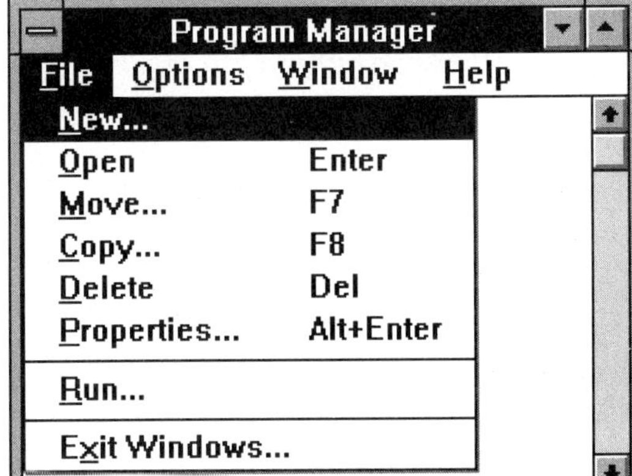

Control menu can be accessed by pressing [Alt][X] if you are in an application window, or [Alt][-] (hyphen) if you are in a document window (or by clicking on the Control Menu box).

There are times when using the mouse will not be efficient or even possible. In some instances, you might find it easier to use a combination of keyboard commands and mouse functions, or, if you prefer to keep both hands on the keyboard, to use just the keyboard commands alone. In any case, becoming familiar with both the mouse and keyboard will enhance your ability to use Windows.

NOTE *A list of keyboard commands for all applications included with Windows 3.1 is contained in Appendix B to this book.*

GUIDED ACTIVITY 2.1

Starting the Clock

Most of the concepts discussed in this unit can be illustrated using the Clock program. The Clock program is normally located in the Accessories program group. Your instructor or lab manager should tell you if it is elsewhere. In this Guided Activity, we start the program so it will be available for subsequent operations.

1. If you have not done so already, start Windows and open the Program Manager window. Instructions for this are in Unit 1.

2. Open the Accessories program group window:

    If you see an icon labeled "Accessories…"

    Double-click on the icon.

    Press [Ctrl][Tab] until the icon title is highlighted (watch the screen as you press the keys and you will notice that one window or icon at a time has a highlighted title); then press [Enter].

    If you see a window labeled "Accessories…"

    Click (once only) on the window title bar.

    Press [Ctrl][Tab] until the window title is highlighted (watch the screen as you press the keys and you will notice that one window or icon at a time has a highlighted title); then press [Enter].

3. Start the Clock program:

    Double-click on the Clock icon.

    Use the arrow keys to highlight the Clock icon title, then press [Enter].

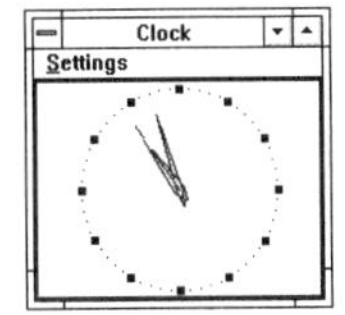

4. You should see a window like the one at the left on your screen. We will experiment with the clock window throughout this unit.

Menus

Windows commands are listed on menus. Each application has its own menu, with a Control menu common to all applications. The Control menu opens from the small box (the Control Menu box) in the upper-left corner of each window, as shown in Figure 2.2. Other menus are represented by names in the menu bar at the top of each application window. In Windows, you select a menu, then choose a command from that menu. Choosing the command usually closes the menu.

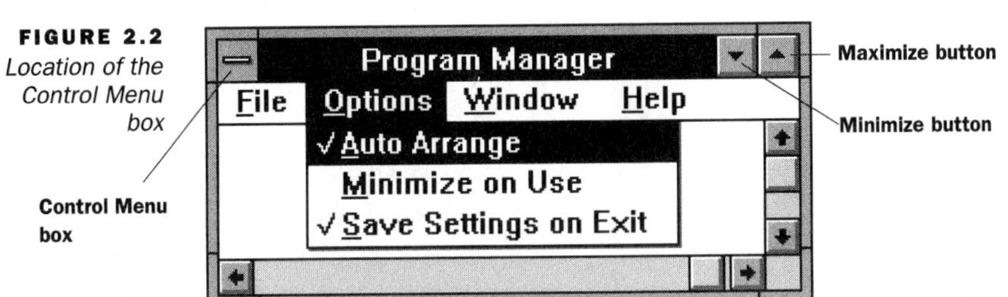

FIGURE 2.2
Location of the Control Menu box

Control Menu box

Opening and Exiting Menus

To open a menu using the mouse, point to the name of the menu on the menu bar and click the name to open the menu. Figure 2.3 shows the Help menu after it has been opened.

To open a menu using the keyboard, press [Alt] (or [F10]), then press [←] or [→] to select the menu you want. When the menu name is highlighted, press [↓] to open the menu. A shortcut is to press both [Alt] and the underlined letter in the menu at the same time. For instance, you could open the Help menu illustrated in Figure 2.3 by pressing [Alt][H].

To exit a menu using the mouse, click the menu name or click on an area outside the menu. If you are using the keyboard method, press [Alt], [F10], or [Esc] to exit the menu.

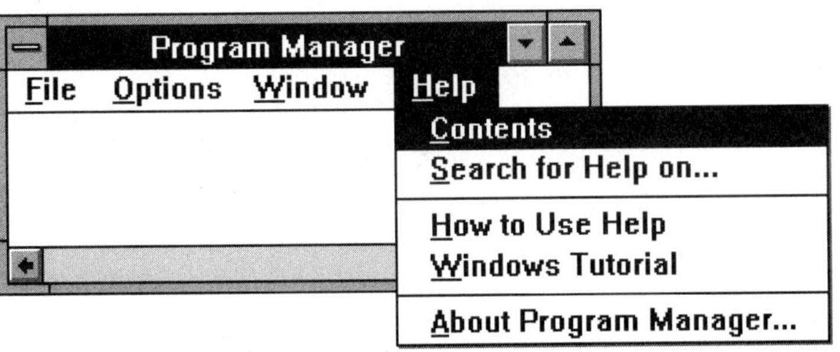

FIGURE 2.3
An open Help menu

Selecting Menu Commands

Items listed on menus are often commands that represent choices. You select one of these to carry out a desired task. In addition, items listed on menus can be formatting effects for text (such as bold or centered), a list of open windows or files, or the names of *cascading menus*, which are menus that list more commands.

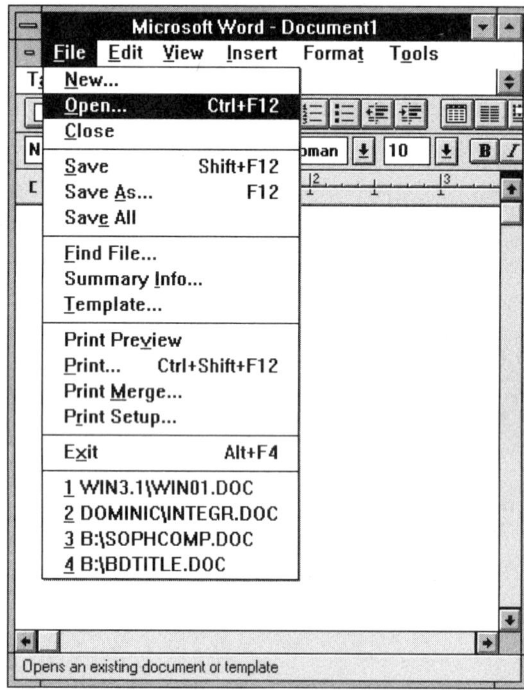

FIGURE 2.4
The File menu for Word for Windows

To choose an item from a selected menu, click on the item name. For example, if you wish to open a file within Microsoft Word for Windows, click on File, then select Open. If you are using the keyboard for command selection, press [Alt], then arrow to File, then arrow down to Open, and, finally, press [Enter]; see Figure 2.4.

When choosing menu commands, you will notice that some menu items appear gray instead of black, some have check marks next to them, several have ellipses (…), and others have key combinations listed across from them. Windows applications all follow certain conventions when listing items on a menu. These conventions signal extra information about the menu commands that follow.

Menu Convention	*What It Means*
Command name in gray	The command is not available at the moment. You might have to select something (such as a paragraph or a spreadsheet cell) before you can use the command, or it may just be that the command cannot be used with your particular application.
An ellipsis (…) after the name	A dialog box will appear when the command is chosen, asking for information the application needs to carry out the command.
A check mark next to the name	The command is active. This convention is used for commands that toggle (switch) between one state and another. For instance, the Clock can be set to analog or digital display.
A key combination after the name	The key combination is a shortcut for this command. Use this key combination to choose the menu command without first opening the menu.

An arrowhead at the right side of a menu command

The command leads to a cascading menu, which lists additional commands that are available.

GUIDED ACTIVITY 2.2

Using Menus

1. If you do not have the Clock program in operation, follow the instructions in the previous Guided Activity. If Clock is open but is not the active window (the one with the highlighted title), either click on the title with the mouse or press [Alt][Tab] until it is highlighted.

2. Open the Settings menu:

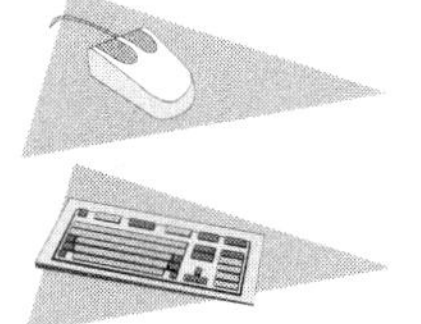

Click on Settings in the menu bar.

Press [Alt][S].

3. Change the display to Digital:

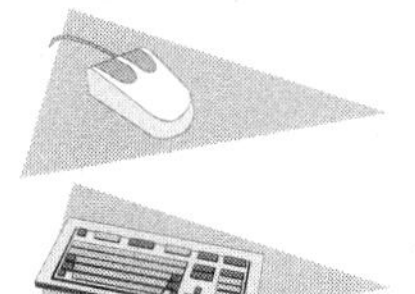

Click on Digital.

Press the letter [D] (which is underlined in Digital).

This command causes the display to shift to numbers instead of hands.

Dialog Boxes

Windows uses ***dialog boxes*** to request information from you as well as provide information to you. Whenever you see an ellipsis (…) after a menu command, a dialog box follows. For example, when you select Character from the Word for Windows 2.0 Format menu, the program displays a dialog box asking for details on how you want the character(s) to appear. You complete the dialog by providing the requested information. The dialog box illustrated in Figure 2.5 appears after the user requests that a character be formatted in Word for Windows.

If you are using a mouse, you can click the various features you desire. The fonts are contained in a ***drop-down list box***. To choose a font, click on the arrow next to the font box (which has been done in Figure 2.5 to show the font choice of Times New Roman). To see additional choices, click on the arrows at the top and bottom of the scroll bar. Click on the choice you want. The square boxes are ***check boxes***; you can choose more than one of these (you could format text as both bold and underlined). Some boxes, called ***text boxes***, allow you to enter information directly; for instance,

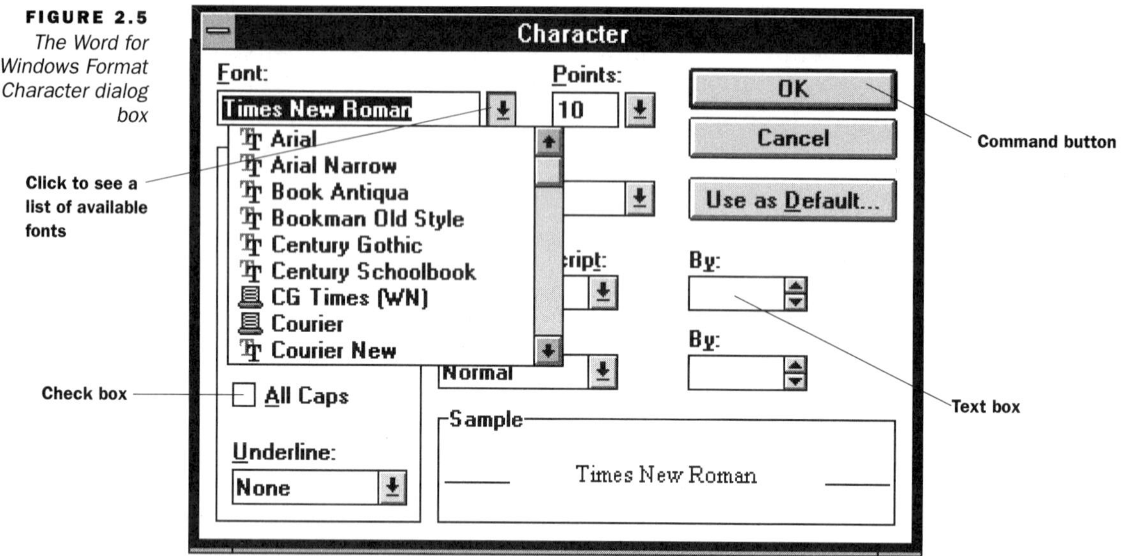

FIGURE 2.5
The Word for Windows Format Character dialog box

you can designate the precise amount by which text is to be raised in a superscript. *Command buttons*, such as OK, Cancel, and Use as Default, are self-explanatory and usually exit the menu or call additional menus. To make an entry in a text box, simply type. To delete an existing entry, press [Del] or drag the mouse across the entire entry before starting to type.

Entering information and selecting choices using the keyboard is fairly easy. Use the [Tab] key to move around the dialog box. Press [Spacebar] to enter or remove a check in a check box. Press an arrow key to select a different *option button*. Press [Alt][↓] to open a drop-down list box, use [↑] and [↓] to locate your choice, and then press [Enter] to select that choice.

Working with Windows

When you work with an application or create a document, you will most likely have several different windows open on your desktop. Windows can be moved, changed, shrunk, enlarged, restored, and ultimately closed. Using and understanding the elements of windows will help you arrange and control your workspace. For example, the Clock window can be enlarged, compressed, or moved, depending on your wishes. You can accomplish these tasks with the mouse or by using the arrow keys.

Clock maximized:

Clock minimized:

As you know by now, a window is a rectangular area where applications are run, documents created, and other activities conducted. A window is composed of a frame, scroll bars, Control Menu box, title bar, menu bar, maximize-minimize box, the actual workspace, and the mouse pointer. Most of these terms have been introduced earlier in this book. Locate each element and familiarize yourself with each of them. Learning to navigate through the window is important! The next several Guided Activities illustrate the use of these Windows control features.

Switching Among Application and Document Windows

At times, when you have more than one application window open on your desktop, you may want to switch to a window other than the *active window*. The active window is distinguished from the inactive windows by a title bar of a different color or intensity. In Figure 2.6, Program Manager is the active application window and Main is the active document window (program groups are "document windows").

FIGURE 2.6
*Active window
and icons*

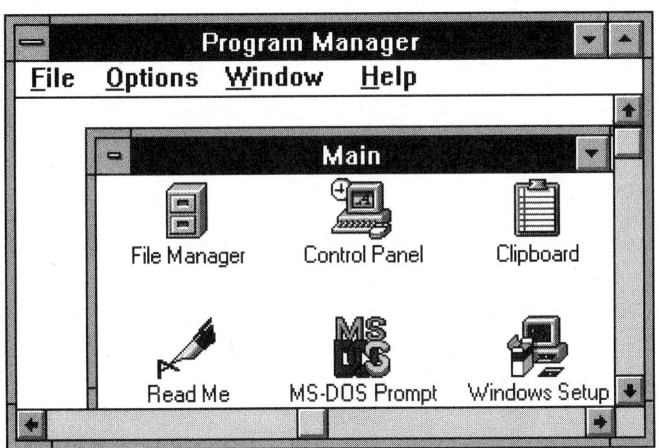

An active window will be placed in the foreground (in front of the other windows that are open), covering all or portions of any *nonactive windows*. Part of the application window can be moved beyond the borders of the desktop, placing some of the windows contents outside your view. To switch to an application window, simply click any area within the window with your mouse, or press [Alt][Tab] on the keyboard repeatedly until the window you want is active. To switch to a document window, click any area within the window with your mouse, or press [Ctrl][Tab] on the keyboard repeatedly until the window you want is active.

Task List

Another method of switching to an application window is to use the *Task List*, a window that shows you all applications currently in use. To use Task List to switch application windows:

1. Click on the Control Menu box in the upper-left corner of the active window.

2. Click on the *Switch To* command. The dialog box illustrated in Figure 2.7 will open, but your list of tasks will probably be different from that illustrated here. (Another method for calling the Task List is to double-click on an area of the desktop that is not covered by a window.)

3.   Double-click on the application to which you wish to switch.

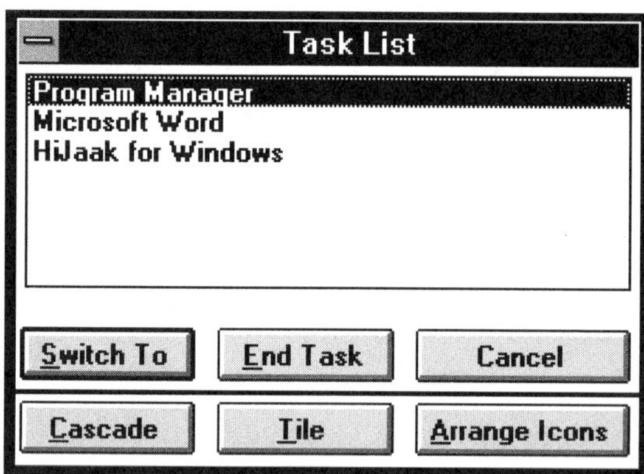

FIGURE 2.7
The Task List

1.   Press Ctrl Esc, which calls the Task List dialog box.

2.   Use the arrow keys to highlight the application to which you wish to switch.

3.   Press Enter.

Window List

When you are working in an application that allows multiple document windows, the Window menu usually allows you to switch between the documents. Click on Window, or press Alt W, and a list of available windows will be displayed, as shown in Figure 2.8. Press the number of the desired window or click on its name, or use the arrow keys to highlight it and press Enter.

FIGURE 2.8
The Window menu list

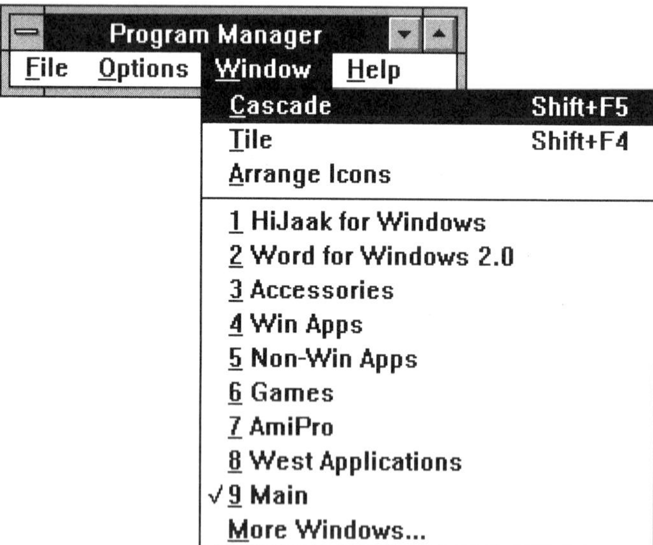

GUIDED ACTIVITY 2.3

Switching Applications Using the Mouse

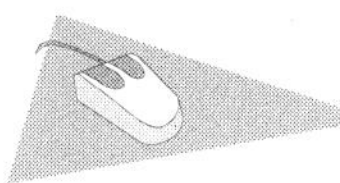

1. Call the Control menu from the active application window by clicking on the Control Menu box at the upper-left corner of the window.

2. Click on Switch To to display the Task List.

3. Choose Clock by double-clicking the application name in the list box in Task List; or click the name of the application in the list box, and then click on Switch To.

GUIDED ACTIVITY 2.4

Switching Applications Using the Keyboard

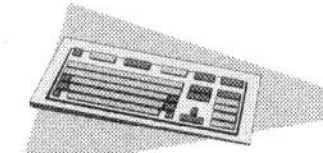

1. Press Ctrl Esc to display Task List.

2. Choose Clock by pressing ↑ or ↓ to select the application in the list box.

3. Press Enter.

Moving Windows and Icons

As your work with Windows becomes more complex, you will probably feel the need to rearrange the windows and icons on the desktop so that you can see more at one time. The following Guided Activity gives simple instructions for moving objects on the desktop.

GUIDED ACTIVITY 2.5

Moving a Window or Icon

1. Point either to the title bar of the window or dialog box, or to the center of the icon you wish to move. Select the Clock window for this activity.

2. Press and hold the mouse button to drag the title bar (or icon) to a new location. As you move a window or dialog box, an outline of the window or dialog box moves with it. As you move an icon, the mouse pointer changes to a black-and-white outline of the icon, which moves as you slide the mouse.

3. When the window, icon, or dialog box is in the desired location, release the mouse button. You can press Esc anytime before you release the mouse button to cancel the move.

Try the next Guided Activity to practice the keyboard method, for a comparison.

GUIDED ACTIVITY 2.6

Moving a Window or Icon

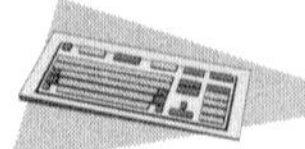

1. Decide which window or dialog box you want to move. For this activity, use the Clock window. If necessary, press [Alt][Tab] to cycle through the window and application icon titles until you reach the one you want to move. If you wish to move one of the Program Manager program group windows (say, the Main group), press [Ctrl][Tab] until the proper window is highlighted.

2. Open the Control menu by pressing [Alt][Spacebar] for an application window or dialog box. Press [Alt][-] (hyphen) for a document window (for example, the Main program group window).

3. Choose the Move command. The pointer changes to a four-headed arrow.

4. Press the arrow keys to move the window or dialog box. An outline of the window or dialog box moves as you press the arrow keys. For smaller movements, press the [Ctrl] key in combination with the arrow keys.

5. When the window or dialog box is where you want it, press [Enter]. You can press [Esc] anytime before you press [Enter] to cancel the move.

As you can see, it is much easier to use a mouse than the keyboard when moving a window or dialog box.

Changing the Size of a Window

There will be times when you want to change the size and shape of the windows that are opened on your desktop. You can make a window occupy the entire screen or a portion of the screen, or even reduce it to the size of an icon. Changes can be made with either the mouse or the keyboard.

GUIDED ACTIVITY 2.7

Sizing a Window

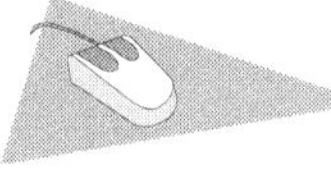

1. Select the window you want to change. For this activity, select Clock.

2. Point to a border or corner that you want to move. (The pointer changes to a two-headed arrow.)

3. Press and hold the mouse button to drag the corner or border until the window is the size you want.

4. Release the mouse button.

Windows can be changed both horizontally and vertically by choosing the Size command, by pressing two arrow keys alternately (for example, [↑] then [→]), and finally by pressing [Enter] to complete the action. You may cancel the resizing when using the mouse by pressing [Esc] before you release the mouse button.

Sizing a Window

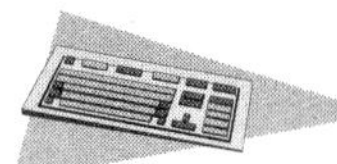

1. Determine the window you want to resize. Press [Alt][Tab] to cycle to the application window you want—for this application select Clock.

2. Open the Control menu. For an application window, press [Alt][Spacebar]. (For a document window, press [Alt][-] [hyphen].)

3. Choose the Size command. (The pointer changes to a four-headed arrow.)

4. Press one of the arrow keys to move the pointer to the border you want to move.

5. Press an arrow key to move the border.

6. Press [Enter] to complete the process.

Windows can be changed both horizontally and vertically by choosing the Size command, by pressing two arrow keys alternately (for example, [↑] then [→]), and finally by pressing [Enter] to complete the action. You may cancel the resizing when using the keyboard by pressing [Esc] before you press [Enter].

Minimizing a Window to an Icon

Open windows on your desktop may become crowded because, as you progress through a number of windows, your workspace becomes limited. To make room for other applications, you can shrink a window to an icon without actually closing the application. To shrink a window, use the minimize button—the down-pointing triangle located in the top-right corner of the window. Placing the pointer on the minimize button and using a single click will reduce the window to an icon. When you shrink an application window to an icon, the application still runs in memory, but its window is not taking up space on your desktop. Application windows reduced to an icon can be instantly restored for use at a later time.

A window can be shrunk using the keyboard commands: Call the Control menu using [Alt][Spacebar], then select Minimize or press [N].

Minimizing a Window

1. Select the Clock Window

2. Minimize the window to an icon:

   Move the mouse pointer to the minimize button in the upper-right corner of the clock window and click.

GUIDED ACTIVITY 2.10

Minimizing a Window

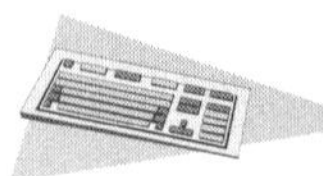

1. Select the Clock Window

2. Minimize the window to an icon:

Press [Alt] [Spacebar] to call the Control menu, then select Mi*n*imize (note that you press [N], not [M]).

GUIDED ACTIVITY 2.11

Restoring a Window from an Icon

Using a mouse, double-click on the Clock to restore the window. Using the keyboard, press [Alt] [Tab] until the icon title is highlighted. Release the [Alt] key and the window will be restored.

Maximizing a Window

A window can be expanded to fill the entire desktop. For example, if you are working with Paintbrush, you will want as much workspace as possible. To enlarge a window, place the pointer on the maximize button—the up-pointing triangle located in the top-right corner of the window. Click the mouse button to complete the action. The window enlarges to its maximum size, and the maximize button is replaced by the restore button—the up- and down-pointing triangles. With the keyboard, call the Control menu and select Ma*x*imize. When one window is maximized, you cannot see the other windows and icons, although they are still available through the Task List or [Alt] [Tab] methods.

GUIDED ACTIVITY 2.12

Maximizing a Window

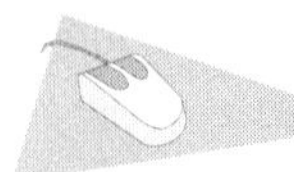

1. Select the Clock window.

2. Maximize the window to full-screen size:

Move the mouse pointer to the maximize box in the upper-right corner of the clock window and click.

Maximizing a Window

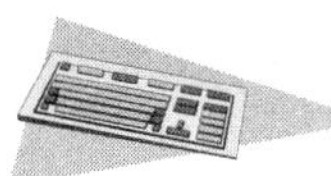

1. Select the Clock window.

2. Maximize the window to full-screen size:

Press [Alt] [Spacebar] to call the Control menu, then select Maximize by pressing [X] (not [M]).

Restoring a Window from Maximum Size

A window or an icon that has been maximized can be restored to its previous size (less than full-screen) by simply clicking the restore button. You usually restore a window to its previous size so that you can view and access other windows. Note that this does not reverse the effect of a window-sizing operation; it merely changes from full-screen to whatever size the window was before maximizing.

Restoring a Window from Maximum Size

1. Using a mouse, click on the restore button to reduce the Clock to its normal size. Using the keyboard, open the Control menu ([Alt] [Spacebar]), then choose Restore.

Closing a Window

When you are finished with a particular application window, it should be closed. Open applications, even those that have been reduced to icons, take up computer memory and processing time, making other operations less efficient, particularly on a slower computer.

There are several ways to close a window. One method is to exit from the application using the *Exit* command, which is *usually* found on the File menu (although some application windows do not have a File menu or Exit command). Another method is to double-click on the Control Menu box at the upper-left corner of the window. Or you can open the Control menu with a single click (or [Alt] [Spacebar]), then choose *Close*.

Most application programs that deal with separate files (such as spreadsheets and word processors) will know whether you have saved your work since the last changes were made, and will ask if you want to save before exiting. Often a simple mouse click or press of the [Enter] key is all that is necessary to save before exiting.

The document window Control menu, [Alt] [-] (hyphen), contains a Close command that is used to close document windows, such as the program groups in Program Manager or documents in Word, but this does not close the application, only the document within the application.

GUIDED ACTIVITY 2.15

Closing an Application

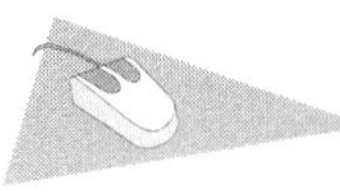

1. Make Clock the active window by clicking on it or pressing [Alt][Tab] as needed.

2. Close the window:

    Double-click on the Control Menu box. If your clicks aren't quick enough, choose Close from the Control menu.

3. The clock should disappear from the screen. If you want it back, you must restart the program as discussed earlier in this unit.

GUIDED ACTIVITY 2.16

Closing an Application

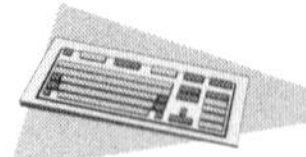

1. Make Clock the active window by clicking on it or pressing [Alt][Tab] as needed.

2. Close the window:

    Press [Alt][Spacebar], then choose Close.

3. The clock should disappear from the screen. If you want it back, you must restart the program as discussed earlier in this unit.

Getting Help

Windows 3.1 provides excellent on-line help. For example, if you are in Program Manager and have a question, help is readily available through the drop-down menu shown in Figure 2.9.

Using Help

Help answers questions about the keyboard, basic skills, commands, and procedures, and it also provides a glossary. "Using Help" is a quick tutorial on how Windows Help works. Help menus for Program Manager are similar to the Help menus of most other Windows applications. Figure 2.10 shows the first portion of the Help contents.

FIGURE 2.9
Program Manager Help topics

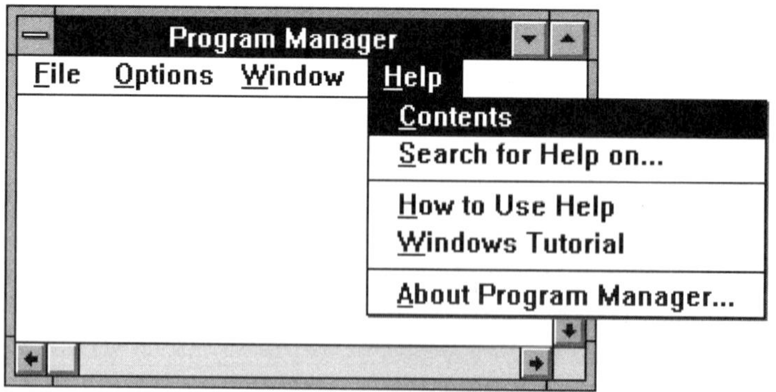

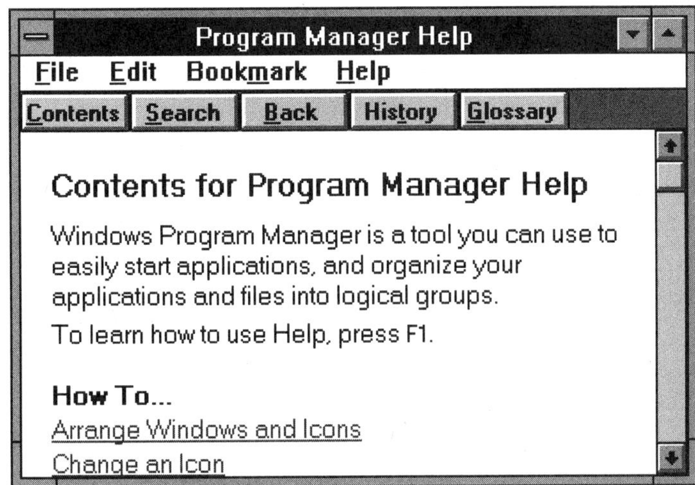

GUIDED ACTIVITY 2.17

Starting Help

1. Open Program Manager (if it is not already active).

2. Place the mouse pointer on Help and click, or, if using the keyboard, press 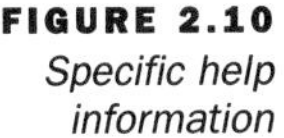.

GUIDED ACTIVITY 2.18

Using the Help Index

1. Select Contents using the mouse or the keyboard. This will produce a listing of nine topics.

2. Place the mouse pointer on the line that reads `Start an Application` listed in green (on color monitors) under the title `How to....` The mouse pointer will appear in the shape of a hand with the index finger extended, indicating that additional information is available. If you are using the keyboard, press `Tab` until the line is highlighted; use `Shift Tab` to move up the list if you tab too far.

3. Click or press `Enter` to summon information about how to start an application.

4. Select `Starting an Application from a Group`. The solid underscores for topics indicate that these lead to additional topics. Some words, such as `group` on the current screen (after you have selected `Starting an Application from a Group`), have a broken underscore.

5. Click on, or press `Enter` after you tab to, the word `group`. A definition will appear until you again press the mouse button or `Enter`.

GUIDED ACTIVITY 2.19

Using the Back Button

1. Place the mouse pointer on the Back button and click to go to the previous topic, the portion of the index from which you selected "Starting an Application." Or, using the keyboard, press B.

2. Choose Back once again to arrive back at the original Index window.

GUIDED ACTIVITY 2.20

Using the Search Button

1. Choose the Search button from Help with the mouse, or press S.

2. Use the scroll bar to find the term Quitting in the list box. With the keyboard, Tab to the list, ↓ to Quitting, then press Enter.

3. Choose Quitting Windows.

4. Since the phrase Quitting Windows is already highlighted, click on the Go To button or press Enter.

5. When you are finished viewing Help, give the File Exit command, which closes the Help window (but not Program Manager itself).

Review Questions

The answers to questions marked with an asterisk are contained in Appendix C.

1. Briefly describe the mouse control functions (a) pointing and (b) selecting or clicking.

*2. What is a principal advantage in using the keyboard for input as opposed to using the mouse? Discuss the purpose of the Alt key or the F10 (function key) in keyboard commands.

3. Which mouse command(s) would be used to open a file? Which keyboard command(s) would be used?

*4. When a menu command has an ellipsis (…) after the name, what does this indicate? Command in gray? Check mark? Key combination?

*5. What is a dialog box, and when does it appear?

Key Terms

The following terms are introduced in this unit. Be sure you know what each of them means.

Active window	Command button	Nonactive window
Application window	Dialog box	Option button
Cascading menu	Document window	Switch To
Check box	Drop-down list box	Task List
Close	Exit	Text box

Documentation Research

Using the book *Getting Started in Windows* and the *User's Guide, determine the answers for the following questions. You may wish to write the number of this page next to the discussion of each question. In addition, some of the discussion questions will require you to use the on-line Help menu contained within Windows. Appendix B to this book may also be used.*

1. On which page do you find information on installing Windows? How do you install it?

2. If you cannot complete a command, how does Windows let you know of the consequences?

3. List the two most important kinds of windows.

4. Explain the different kinds of windows.

5. Using the on-line Help in Program Manager, open the Help menu. How many help topics are available?

6. Using the on-line Help in Program Manager, how do you choose an item from a selected menu using (a) the mouse and (b) the keyboard?

Program Manager

Program Manager is the default shell within Windows 3.1. This means that every time you start a Windows 3.1 session, Program Manager is automatically loaded. When you quit Windows at the end of a day, you do so by quitting Program Manager. Therefore, Program Manager is central to the operation of Windows.

Program Manager also serves two additional purposes: it gives you a simple way to start applications, and it makes it easy for you to organize your programs and documents into logical working groups.

Learning Objectives

At the completion of this unit, you should know

1.   the elements of Program Manager,

2.   the procedures for starting applications.

At the completion of this unit, you should be able to

1.   start applications from Program Manager,

2.   use program groups in Program Manager,

3.   quit Windows from Program Manager.

Program Manager

Program Manager is the starting point for all work in Windows.[1] Program Manager automatically starts whenever you enter Windows and remains active until you quit (exit). Program Manager allows you to select Windows or non-Windows applications, as well as Windows "housekeeping" operations such as rearranging the appearance of the desktop. When Windows starts, Program Manager will either be in a window or be minimized to an icon. If it is minimized, restore it by double-clicking the mouse on the Program Manager icon. The result will be similar to the window illustrated in Figure 3.1.

In Figure 3.1, Program Manager is open on the desktop with the Main program group window also open.[2] Other applications groups might be open; if not, they are represented by program group icons on the lower edge of the Program Manager window. Non-Windows applications installed on your hard disk will also be represented by an icon. For example, if you have Lotus 1-2-3 for DOS or dBASE IV on your hard disk, your system manager places an icon in your Non-Windows Applications program group. Some applications programs create their own program groups, so you will see icons or windows for these as well. All applications that you can use in the Windows environment are contained in program groups.

FIGURE 3.1
Typical Program Manager window

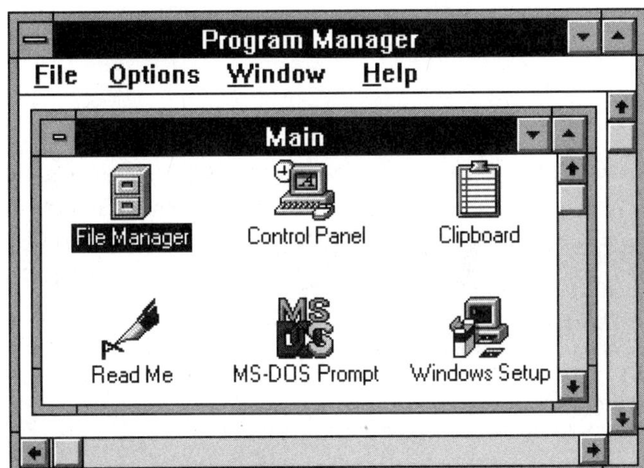

GUIDED ACTIVITY 3.1

Minimizing, Restoring, and Maximizing Program Manager

1. Start Windows. If the Program Manager window does not appear, start it using the technique discussed in Unit 1.

2. Minimize Program Manager by clicking the appropriate button in the upper-right corner of the desktop.

3. Restore Program Manager by double-clicking its icon, which is in the lower portion of the desktop.

---

1 Some organizations have configured their Windows environment to use an application other than Program Manager as the basis of operations. Your instructor or lab manager will inform you if that is the case, and will tell you how closely the application in your organization mimics the instructions given in this unit for Program Manager.

2 Your organization may have customized the Windows desktop. If so, then the arrangement of the program item groups may differ from the example in Figure 3.1.

4. Maximize Program Manager by clicking the appropriate button in the upper-right corner of the desktop.

GUIDED ACTIVITY 3.2

Minimizing, Restoring, and Maximizing Program Manager

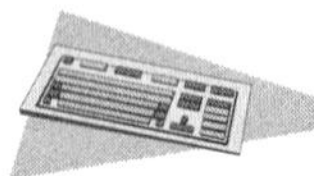

1. Start Windows 3.1. If the Program Manager window does not appear, start it using the technique discussed in Unit 1.

2. Call the Control menu by typing [Alt][Spacebar]. Press [N] to Minimize Program Manager.

3. Restore Program Manager by pressing [Alt][Tab] until the icon title in the lower portion of the desktop is highlighted, then release [Alt].

4. Call the Control Menu by typing [Alt][Spacebar]. Press [X] to Maximize Program Manager.

Program Groups

Program Manager's application window contains a collection of ***program groups***. Each program group contains icons, called ***program items***, representing an application that you can run. In Figure 3.1 you see the Main program group open within the Program Manager window. "File Manager," "Control Panel," and the others are program item icons.

Your system or lab supervisor has probably configured your system to the particular needs of your organization. Program Manager will display several standard program group windows, each with its own program item icons; the names of these are listed in the Window drop-down menu in Figure 3.2.

FIGURE 3.2
The Program Manager Window menu

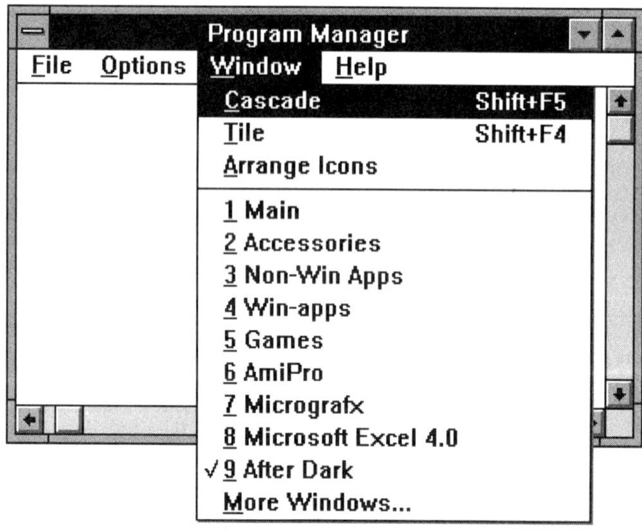

Arranging Program Group Windows

When you open several program groups at one time, their windows will overlap other windows. The Cascade and Tile commands on the Window menu are used to rearrange all of the program groups so that some part of each window is visible.

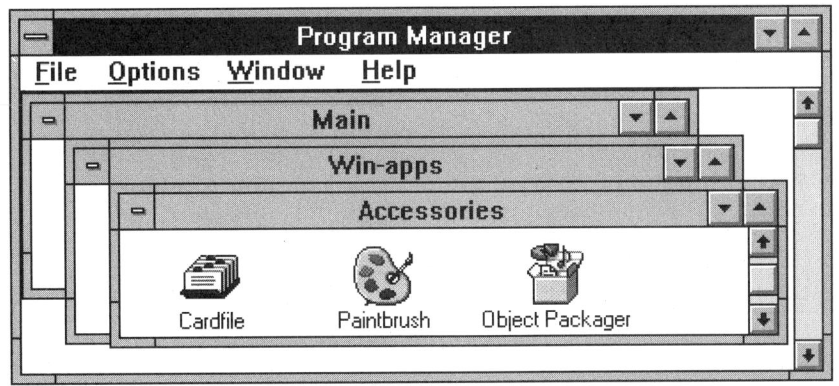

FIGURE 3.3
Cascaded Program Group windows

The Cascade command *cascades* windows like a series of waterfalls, layering the open program group window within Program Manager with each title bar appearing as shown in Figure 3.3.

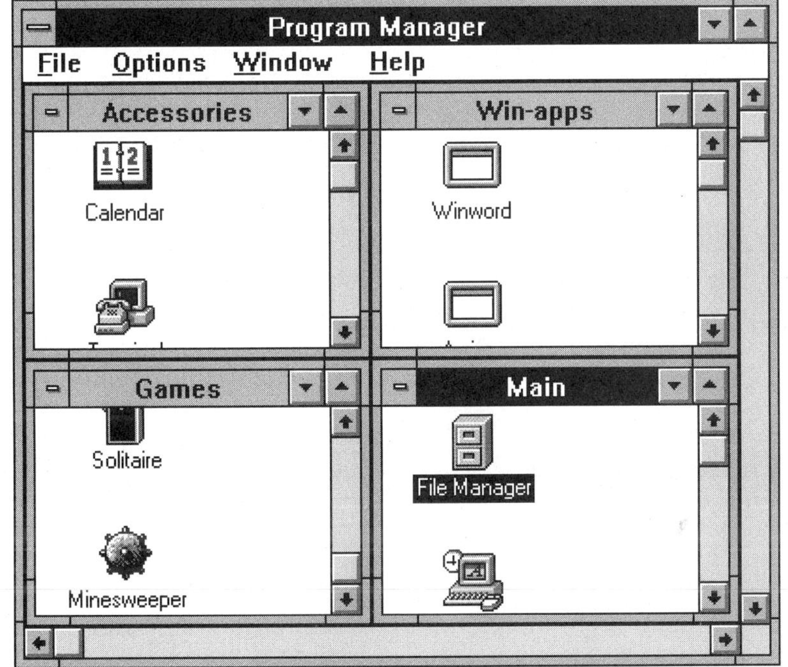

FIGURE 3.4
Tiled Program Group windows

The Tile command *tiles* windows like floor tiles, dividing the Program Manager workspace into smaller windows of similar sizes for each program group window that is open. Program item icons will be placed in each window, space permitting, as illustrated in Figure 3.4.

Opening a Program Group Window

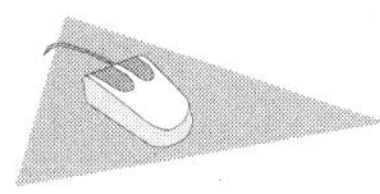

1. The Program Manager window should be open and maximized from Guided Activities 3.1 or 3.2.

2. Look for the Main group window or Main group icon.

   If the window is not open, double-click on the icon to open the Main group window.

GUIDED ACTIVITY 3.4

Opening a Program Group Window

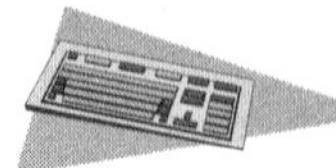

1. The Program Manager window should be open and maximized from Guided Activities 3.1 or 3.2.

2. Look for the Main group window or Main group icon.

   If the window is not open, press [Ctrl][Tab] until the icon title is highlighted, then press [Enter].

The DOS Prompt Application

One of the applications available in the Main program group is called "MS-DOS Prompt." This aids users who are familiar with DOS and want to execute a DOS procedure (such as checking the directories of several floppy disks or formatting a floppy disk) without using the appropriate Windows programs. *It is not a good idea to use the DOS Prompt to execute a non-Windows program such as dBASE IV; in fact, memory restrictions often prevent your doing so.* Do not use the CHKDSK command—it will report errors that do not exist because Windows stores temporary data on the disk in such a way that CHKDSK will interpret it to be in error. Once the DOS procedure is accomplished, type EXIT and press [Enter] to return to Windows.

GUIDED ACTIVITY 3.5

Executing the MS-DOS Prompt Application

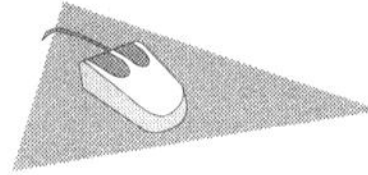

1. Program Manager and the Main program group window should be open from the previous Guided Activity.

2. Start the MS-DOS Prompt application:

   Double-click on the MS-DOS Prompt icon in the Main group window.

3. (*Optional:*) Put a floppy disk in drive A:, type the command DIR A:, and press [Enter]. Perform other DOS commands if you wish.

4. Return to Windows by typing EXIT and pressing [Enter] at the DOS prompt.

GUIDED ACTIVITY 3.6

Executing the MS-DOS Prompt Application

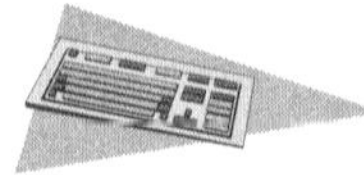

1. Program Manager and the Main program group window should be open from the previous Guided Activity.

2. Start the MS-DOS Prompt application:

    Use the arrow keys to highlight the title of the MS-DOS Prompt application, then press **Enter**.

3. (*Optional:*) Put a floppy disk in drive A:, type the command `DIR A:`, and press **Enter**. Perform other DOS commands if you wish.

4. Return to Windows by typing `EXIT` and pressing **Enter** at the DOS prompt.

GUIDED ACTIVITY 3.7

Closing a Program Group Window

1. Place the mouse pointer on the Main program group Control Menu box in the top-left corner of the Main program group window, then click. Using the keyboard, press **Alt**-**-** (hyphen).

2. Select the Close command.

GUIDED ACTIVITY 3.8

Opening Other Program Group Windows

1. Activate the Main program group.

2. Activate the following program group windows (if they are not already active). On your system some of these might not be present, or the names might vary slightly:

    - Accessories

    - Windows Applications

    - Games

    - Non-Windows Applications

GUIDED ACTIVITY 3.9

Arranging Open Windows

1. Select the Window command.

2. Choose Tile from the list. The screen should be evenly divided by the windows so that you can see them simultaneously.

3. Select the Window command again.

4. Choose Cascade from the list. The screen should have the open windows overlapping each other.

5. As you read the following section, click on the title bar of each program group window and compare the program groups on your system with those illustrated here.

Arranging Open Windows

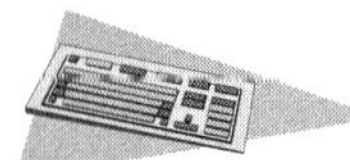

1. Press [Alt][W].

2. Press [T] to tile the windows. The screen should be evenly divided by the windows so that you can see them simultaneously.

3. Press [Alt][W] to select the Window command again.

4. Press [C] to cascade the windows. The screen should have the open windows overlapping each other.

5. As you read the following section, press [Ctrl][Tab] until the desired window is on top. Compare the program groups on your system with those illustrated here.

Typical Windows Program Groups

One of the selling points of Windows 3.1 is the ease with which a system manager can configure it to meet the needs of a particular organization. We cannot in this short book begin to cover all the possible arrangements of program groups and programs within Windows, although in this section we review some fairly typical groups. As you read this section, compare what we describe with what is available on your system. You might have more, or fewer, or different programs.

MAIN GROUP (partially illustrated in Figure 3.5) consists of the File Manager, Control Panel, MS-DOS Prompt, Print Manager, Windows Setup, and Clipboard. Read Me is a file with information about Windows that does not appear in the manuals.

FIGURE 3.5
Main program group

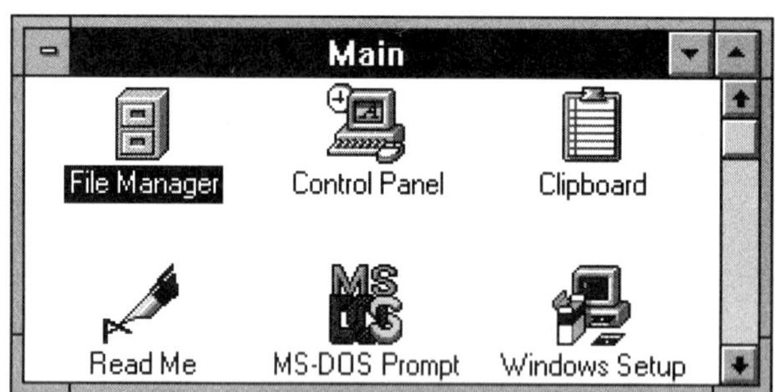

ACCESSORIES GROUP (some of which is shown in Figure 3.6) includes Write, Paintbrush, Terminal, Notepad, Recorder, Cardfile, Calendar, Calculator, Clock, PIF Editor, Character Map, Media Player, and Sound Recorder. To see or select other items in the window, use the scroll bar.

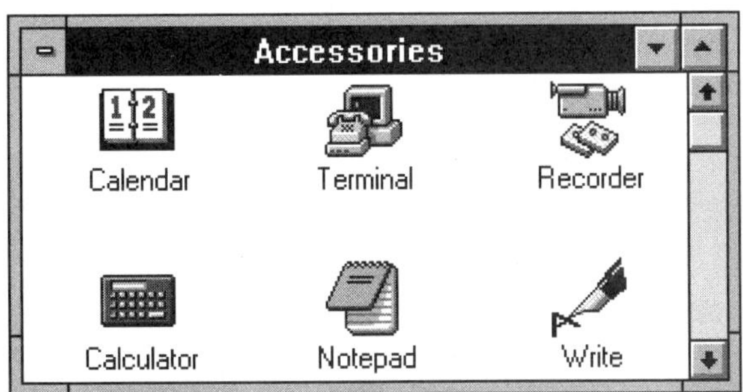

FIGURE 3.6
Accessories program group

WINDOWS APPLICATIONS GROUP (Figure 3.7) contains programs such as Microsoft Word for Windows (word processing) and Microsoft Excel (spreadsheet). The programs in this group vary from one organization or system to another, depending on what has been purchased; these programs are not included in the basic Windows package. You might also find some of the programs from the Main or Accessories program groups duplicated in this group. In Figure 3.7, note that File Manager appears in this group.

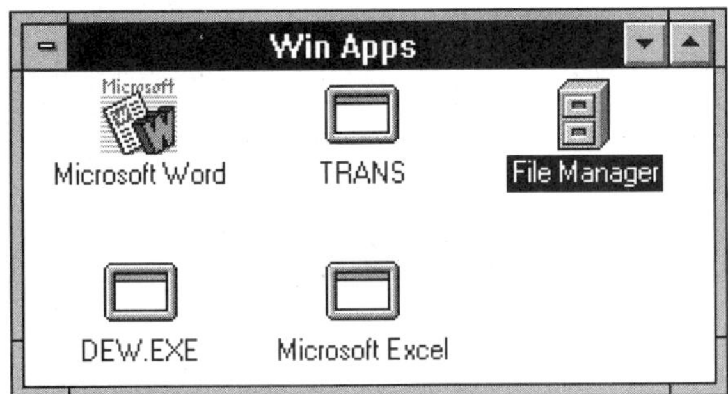

FIGURE 3.7
Typical Windows Applications program group

NON-WINDOWS APPLICATIONS GROUP (Figure 3.8) contains programs such as WordPerfect for DOS, Quattro Pro for DOS, and Norton Utilities. Your laboratory configuration may vary depending on the specific non-Windows applications your system manager has decided to install.

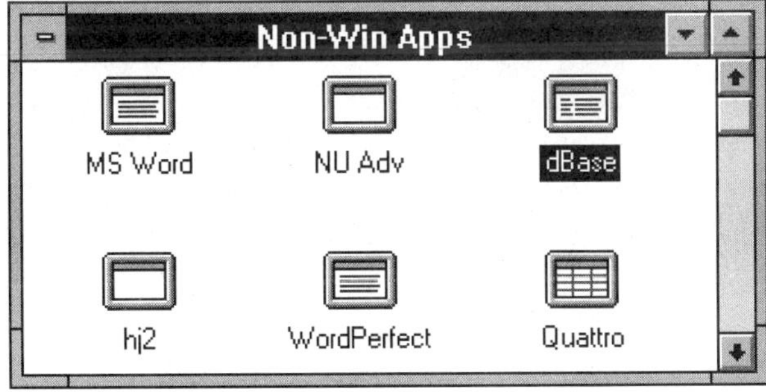

FIGURE 3.8
Typical Non-Windows Applications program group

GAMES GROUP (Figure 3.9) displays three games, Solitaire, Minesweeper, and Reversi. Your organization might have added additional games—or might have removed this group entirely so that you won't be distracted!

FIGURE 3.9
Games program group

GUIDED ACTIVITY 3.11

Minimizing Program Groups

1. Minimize each program group in turn by pressing the Minimize button in the upper-right corner of the program group window.

2. Minimize each successive window by repeating step 1.

GUIDED ACTIVITY 3.12

Minimizing Program Groups

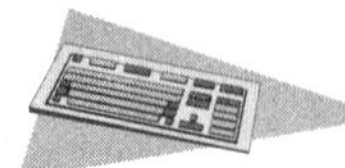

1. Minimize the current window by pressing [Alt][-] (hyphen) to call the Control menu, then pressing [N] (Mi_nimize).

2. Minimize each successive window by repeating step 1.

Exiting Windows from Program Manager

To end your Windows session, you must return to Program Manager and click on the Control Menu box twice. An information window appears to let you know that you are about to terminate your Windows session. If you called the Quit command by mistake, you can avoid quitting by clicking on the Cancel button or pressing [Esc] to stay in Windows. To confirm that you *do* want to exit Windows, click the OK button, or press [Enter]. As mentioned in the discussion of the Options menu in Unit 2, the Save Changes option choice is used to instruct Windows to remember changes you have made to the Program Manager window, or not to save the changes. To save the changes you have made to the arrangement of items in the Program Manager Window, you must choose that menu item before exiting Windows. If you have opened group windows or rearranged those windows, saving changes will preserve the current arrangement for future Windows sessions. In many lab situations, your lab supervisor would prefer that you *do not* save changes, so that the Windows environment for the next user will be the organization's standard.

GUIDED ACTIVITY 3.13

Exiting Windows

1. Double-click on Program Manager's Control Menu box.

2. When the Exit Windows dialog box appears, select OK.

GUIDED ACTIVITY 3.14

Exiting Windows

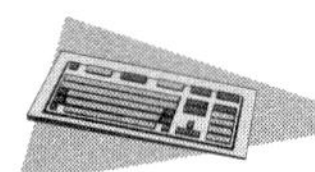

1. Call Program Manager's Control Menu box by pressing [Alt] [Spacebar].

2. Choose Close.

3. When the Exit Windows dialog box appears, press [Enter] to select OK.

Review Questions

1. What are the functions of the Program Manager? How are applications started from Program Manager?

*2. If you accidentally try to exit Windows, what command must you select to avoid exiting?

*3. What is a program group? What do program items represent?

*4. Program group windows can be arranged in two ways. What are they, and how are they different?

*5. Name the five typical program groups, and briefly describe the contents of each.

Key Terms

Cascade	Program item
Program group	Tile

Documentation Research

Use Chapter 3, "Program Manager," of the *User's Guide* to answer the following questions. Check the guide's index to find pages with the needed information. We recommend that you also write the relevant page number next to each question.

1. How do you add new program items from your hard disk to existing groups?

2. Can group icons be moved to a new location? If so, how?

3. Using the on-line Help in Program Manager, list the steps in creating groups.

4. Using the on-line Help in Program Manager, how do you change group properties?

File Manager

File Manager, like Program Manager, is a Windows shell program. It is not the default shell, however, unless you set up your Windows as such. File Manager enables you to view and manipulate the work that you save on a hard or floppy disk. It allows you to view all files and directories and then to build a structure of those files and directories that makes sense to you. File Manager's fundamental purpose is to help you work effectively to organize your files.

Learning Objectives

At the completion of this unit, you should know

1. the purpose of File Manager,

2. the features of File Manager.

At the completion of this unit, you should be able to

1. start and quit File Manager,

2. work with Directory Tree,

3. create directories,

4. search files and directories,

5. move and copy files,

6. delete files and directories,

7. rename files,

8. use Directory Window,

9. format and copy disks.

Introduction to File Manager

File Manager is a powerful tool that helps you organize your files and directories. A *directory* is a collection of files stored under the same directory name. You use File Manager to view your files and then build a structure for those files and directories in a fashion that suits your needs. Directories allow for the overall organization of files, similar to a file cabinet in your office where you dedicate a drawer for certain subjects and then further divide the drawer into sections.

File Manager, like Program Manager, is a Windows *shell program*. A shell program is defined as an alternate interface intended to facilitate your use of the computer. The shell program in Windows is used as a starting point for all Windows applications. If you designate File Manager as the *default shell*, Windows sessions will start and end with File Manager instead of Program Manager.

File Manager is much more than a program starter, however. It is designed to help you organize the files on your hard disk or floppy disks. If you work with many applications and store a large number of files, you will find it easier to keep track of these files if you maintain a logical and orderly filing system.

By organizing related files in their own directories, you develop your own filing system. For example, you may organize memos and letters in one directory and spreadsheets in another. Most of your application programs will be set up with their own individual directories (for example, Microsoft Word, WordPerfect, Lotus 1-2-3). Directories will enable you to operate more efficiently by identifying where related files and programs are located.

Starting File Manager

File Manager is started from Program Manager. The program icon for File Manager appears in the Main group window shown in Figure 4.1.

Double-click on the File Manager program icon, or, if using the keyboard, press the  or ▶ arrow key to move the highlight to the File Manager program icon. Then press Enter or choose Open from the File menu. File Manager displays the Directory window for your current disk drive, as shown in Figure 4.2.

FIGURE 4.1
Locating the File Manager icon

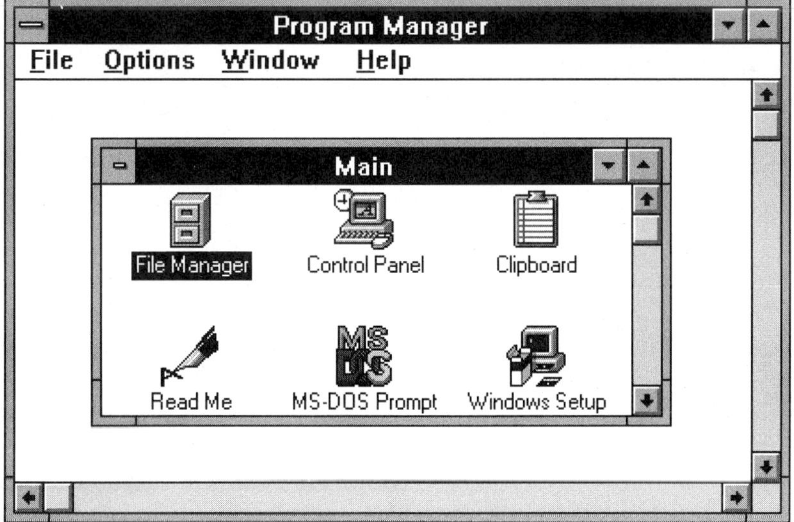

If File Manager is Not in the Main Program Group . . .

The Windows Setup program puts an icon for File Manager in the Main program group, but system managers can move it elsewhere. If you cannot find the icon, you can start File Manager in the following manner:

1. Pull down the File menu, then choose Run.

2. Type WINFILE.EXE in the dialog box, then press [Enter].

FIGURE 4.2
Directory Tree for drive C:

Selecting the Disk Drive

File Manager usually starts with drive C: as its default, as illustrated in Figure 4.2. Often, you will want to deal with your data disk, which will (usually) be in drive A: (make sure you have a disk in the A: drive before you do this). To change disk drives with a mouse, click on the drive A: icon. To change drives from the keyboard, press [Ctrl] and the drive letter—for example, [Ctrl][A]. After you have changed drives, the directory tree for the new drive will appear as illustrated in Figure 4.3.

Quitting File Manager

To quit File Manager, select (click or choose) the Exit command from the File menu. To save the positions and views of your open directory window, make sure the Save Settings on Exit command on the Options menu has a check mark next to it.

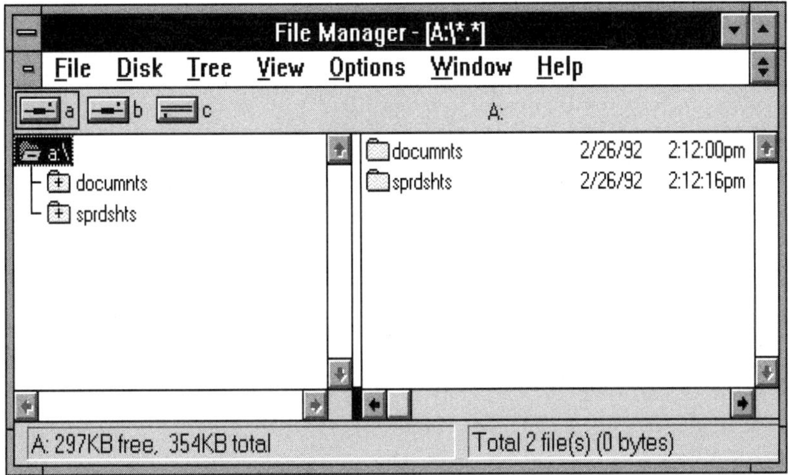

GUIDED ACTIVITY 4.1

Opening and Closing File Manager

The Guided Activities in this unit assume that you have obtained a copy of the *Student Data Disk to Accompany Understanding and Using Microsoft Windows 3.1*, which is used to illustrate File Manager operations. Your instructor or lab manager will tell you how to obtain a copy. Guided Activities 4.3 (mouse) and 4.4 (keyboard) instruct you how to make a copy of the disk for your own use.

1. Open File Manager from the Main program group in Program Manager by double-clicking on its icon. After starting File Manager you will see both a directory tree and a list of subdirectories and files. If the item Save Settings on Exit on the File Manager Options directory has been checked, then File Manager will attempt to display the same disks and directories as were displayed the last time File Manager was used.

2. Insert the Student Data Disk in drive A:.

3. Point to the drive A: icon and click the mouse. You will see the directory structure of the Student Data Disk.

4. Close File Manager by clicking on File, then on Exit. Confirm your choice in the dialog box by clicking on OK.

GUIDED ACTIVITY 4.2

Opening and Closing File Manager

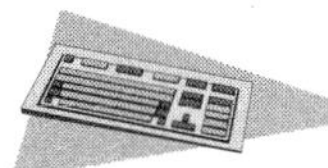

1. Open File Manager from the Main program group in Program Manager by highlighting its icon and pressing [Enter].

2. Insert the Student Data Disk in drive A:.

3. Press [Ctrl][A] to call the directory tree for drive A:. You will see the directory structure of the Student Data Disk.

4. Close File Manager by pressing [Alt][Spacebar] to call the Control menu. Select Close from the menu.

Preparation of Disks

With File Manager you can format new floppy disks, copy from one disk to another, and label a disk. You will *not* be able to inadvertently format a hard disk, which can lead to a disastrous result—the loss of all data.

Formatting Disks

The purpose of formatting a disk is to prepare it for storing data. If you format an old disk, any data or information contained on that disk will be erased. To format a disk, select Disk from File Manager, as shown in Figure 4.4.

Insert the disk you want to format in the appropriate drive; then choose Format Disk from the Disk menu.

Selecting Format Disk from the menu will cause a Format Disk dialog box to appear, prompting you to select certain options, as shown in Figure 4.5. For example, if the disk that you want formatted is a high-capacity disk, select the Capacity box. You will then see the choices for disk capacity (1.2MB or 360KB). Click or choose OK.

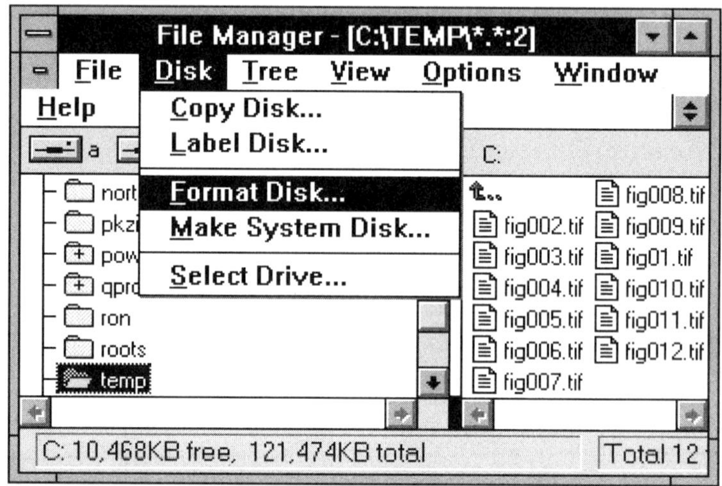

FIGURE 4.4
The Disk menu of File Manager

After this is done, a Confirm Format Disk dialog box will appear with a confirmation message regarding the drive that was selected, as shown in Figure 4.6. Click or choose OK to start the formatting process. A status message will appear to let you know that the formatting process has begun, as well as when formatting has been completed.

FIGURE 4.5
Selecting the disk to format

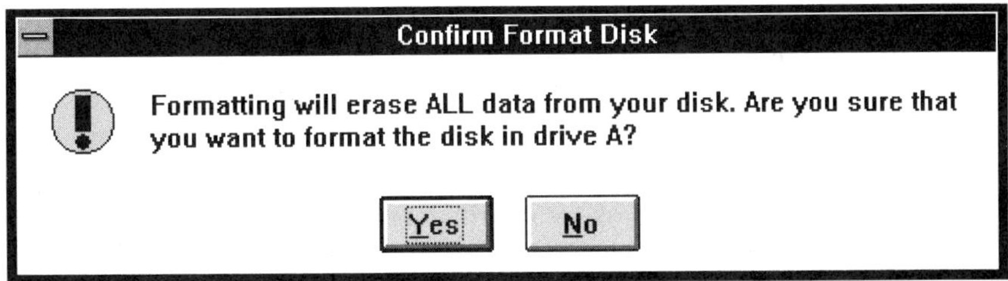

Copying Disks

The entire contents of one disk can be copied to another disk. You use this capability when you want to make an exact backup copy of a disk. Using this procedure, you can copy only disks that have the same disk capacity. For example, if the original disk (the disk you want to copy from) holds 720KB, the destination disk must also be a 720KB disk (in a disk drive that writes 720KB disks). You can copy from and to the same disk drive; you will be told when to insert the original and the destination disks.

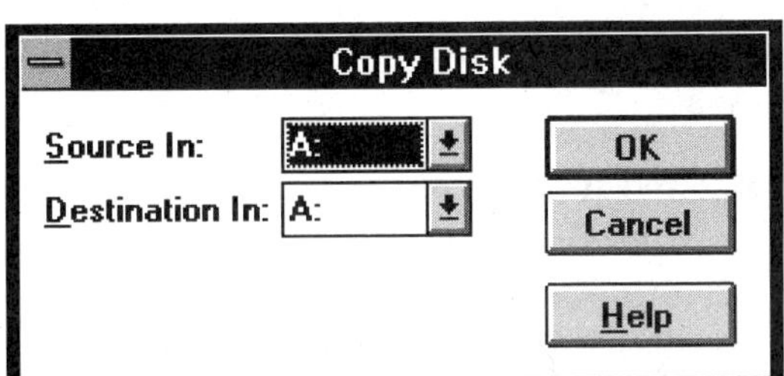

To start, place the source disk in drive A: and click on the disk drive icon for that drive. Select the Copy Disk command from the Disk menu; the dialog box illustrated in Figure 4.7 will appear, asking you to indicate the drive of the disk to which to copy.[1] Select the drive, then choose OK to continue the process. A Confirm Copy Disk dialog box will appear. Selecting OK will begin the copying. A status message will let you know that the copying process has begun, as well as when copying has been completed. If you are using a single drive for the copy, messages will appear instructing you when to change the disks in the drive.

Making a Copy of the Student Data Disk Using the Mouse

A Student Data Disk has been furnished to your instructor with the *Instructor's Manual* for this book. This disk contains a few directories and files to allow you to explore the features of File Manager. In this Guided Activity you make a copy of the Student Data Disk for your own experimentation. You can use the disk you make for other purposes after you finish this unit.

Before starting on this activity, you must have a floppy disk that is the proper size and format for your computer. Your instructor will tell you which of the following you should obtain: either 5.25-inch double-sided, double- or high-density, or 3.5-inch double-sided, double- or high-density. These are often referred to by their

---

1 If your computer has only one floppy disk drive, this dialog box does not appear.

formatted capacity: the 5.25-inch disks are 360KB or 1.2MB, while the 3.5-inch disks are 720KB or 1.44MB, respectively. You can work with a "used" disk from another class, but ensure that the disk does not contain any files you want to keep because they will be erased in the following activity.

In this activity, we assume that your system has only one disk drive—or, if it has two drives, that they are different sizes. Therefore, we give you the instructions for a single-drive copy. If you have two disk drives of the same size and capacity in your computer, your instructor will give you slightly modified instructions for the following.

1. Start Windows and enter the File Manager program using the techniques described in Guided Activity 4.1.

2. Put *your* disk in the disk drive (normally drive A:, although your instructor might tell you otherwise).

3. Format your disk:

    a. Click on the Disk menu, then select Format Disk… from the menu that appears, shown in Figure 4.4.

    b. If the proper drive is not listed in the dialog box shown in Figure 4.5, click on the arrow and select the proper drive. If you are formatting a high-capacity disk in drive A:, ensure that the Capacity box reads 1.2MB (or 1.44MB if using a 3.5-inch disk). If you are *not* formatting a high-capacity disk, ensure that the Capacity choice reads 360KB (or 720KB for a 3.5-inch disk). Also, ensure that the Make System Disk box is *not* X'd. Once the proper drive and capacity are indicated, click on OK to proceed.

    c. The confirmation dialog box will appear as in Figure 4.6; click on Yes to proceed.

    d. Click on OK to proceed. A status message will appear, telling you that formatting has begun, as well as when it is finished. You will be asked if you want to format another disk; answer Yes if you do or No if you don't.

    e. Remove your newly formatted disk from the disk drive.

4. Copy the Student Data Disk:

    a. Put the original Student Data Disk in the disk drive (normally drive A:, although your instructor might tell you otherwise).

    b. Click on the icon for the drive in which you have put the Student Data Disk.

    c. From the Disk menu, choose Copy Disk.

    d. A dialog box will appear, asking for the destination disk (see Figure 4.7). If the proper drive is not listed in the dialog box, click on the arrow and select the proper drive. Once the proper drive is indicated, click on OK to proceed.

    e. A dialog box will appear, warning you that all data will be erased from the destination disk. Select Yes to proceed.

f. Windows will ask for the source disk (that is, the Student Data Disk), which you inserted in step 4a; click OK to proceed. As it progresses through the operation, Windows will copy data from the source disk into the computer's memory, then will ask you to insert the destination disk (that is, your disk) and to click OK when you have done so. Depending on the size of the disk, you might have to swap source and destination disks one or more times.

g. When the copy is complete, Windows returns to the File Manager screen—there is no message telling you that the copy has been successful (but there will be a message if it has failed).

5. Remove your disk and label it with your name and "Copy of Student Data Disk for Windows." Return the original Student Data Disk to your instructor or lab supervisor.

Making a Copy of the Student Data Disk Using the Keyboard

A Student Data Disk has been furnished to your instructor with the *Instructor's Manual* for this book. This disk contains a few directories and files to allow you to explore the features of File Manager. In this Guided Activity you make a copy of the Student Data Disk for your own experimentation. You can use the disk you make for other purposes after you finish this unit.

Before starting on this activity, you must have a floppy disk that is the proper size and format for your computer. Your instructor will tell you which of the following you should obtain: either 5.25-inch double-sided, double- or high-density, or 3.5-inch double-sided, double- or high-density. These are often referred to by their formatted capacity: the 5.25-inch disks are 360KB or 1.2MB, while the 3.5-inch disks are 720KB or 1.44MB, respectively. You can work with a "used" disk from another class, but ensure that the disk does not contain any files you want to keep because they will be erased in the following activity.

In this activity, we assume that your system has only one disk drive—or, if it has two drives, that they are different sizes. Therefore, we give you the instructions for a single-drive copy. If you have two disk drives of the same size and capacity in your computer, your instructor will give you slightly modified instructions for the following.

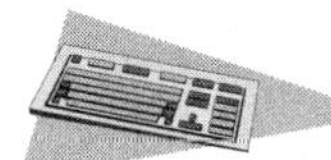

1. Start Windows and enter the File Manager program using the techniques described in Guided Activity 4.2.

2. Put *your* disk in the disk drive (normally drive A:, although your instructor might tell you otherwise).

3. Format your disk:

a. Press [Alt][D] for the Disk menu, then press [F] to select Format Disk... from the menu that appears, shown in Figure 4.4.

   b. If the proper drive is not listed in the dialog box shown in Figure 4.5, press `Alt`+`D` and move the highlight to the proper drive. If you are formatting a high-capacity disk in drive A:, ensure that the Capacity box is set to 1.2MB (or 1.44MB for a 3.5-inch disk). If you are *not* formatting a high-capacity disk, ensure that the Capacity box is set to 360KB (720KB for a 3.5-inch disk). Also, ensure that the Make System Disk box is *not* X'd (press `Alt`+`M` to change). Once the proper drive and capacity are indicated, press `Enter` to proceed.

   c. The Confirm Format Disk box will appear as in Figure 4.6; press `Y`, to proceed.

   d. A status message will appear, telling you that formatting has begun, as well as when it is finished. You will be asked if you want to format another disk; press `Y` if you do or `N` if you don't.

   e. Remove your newly formatted disk from the disk drive.

4. Copy the Student Data Disk:

   a. Put the original Student Data Disk in the disk drive (normally drive A:, although your instructor might tell you otherwise).

   b. Choose the Disk menu, then select Copy Disk by pressing `Alt`+`D`, then `C`.

   c. Press `Ctrl`+`A` to indicate the drive in which you have put the Student Data Disk.

   d. A dialog box will appear, asking for the destination disk. If the proper drive is not listed in the dialog box, press `Alt`+`D` and move the highlight to the proper disk. Once the proper drive is indicated, press `Enter` to proceed.

   e. A Confirm Copy Disk box will appear, warning you that all data will be erased from the destination disk. Press `Y` to proceed.

   f. Windows will ask for the source disk (that is, the Student Data Disk), which you inserted in step 4a; press `Enter` to proceed. As it progresses through the operation, Windows will copy data from the source disk into the computer's memory, then will ask you to insert the destination disk (that is, your disk) and to press `Enter` when you have done so. Depending on the size of the disk, you might have to swap source and destination disks one or more times.

   g. When the copy is complete, Windows returns to the File Manager screen—there is no message telling you that the copy has been successful (but there will be a message if it has failed).

5. Remove your disk and label it with your name and "Copy of Student Data Disk for Windows." Return the original Student Data Disk to your instructor or lab supervisor.

The Directory Window

The Directory Window usually lists the structure of your directories and subdirectories[2] (if any) on the left and a list of files on the right.

The Directory Tree

The directory structure, called the Directory Tree, resembles the branches of a tree. The tree begins with the ***root directory***, which is the first or top-level directory on the disk. The root directory is created when you format a disk. It is represented by the backslash (\). Your workstation will probably designate the C:\ as its root directory. Any subdirectories created will be organized within the root directory.

NOTE *You may wish to consult with your instructor or system manager to learn about your specific system.*

From the Directory Tree, you can change the Directory List displayed on the right to list files as well as subdirectories of any individual directories. You can also select different disk drives to view their directory structures. For example, you may wish to list the files in a particular directory on drive A: or drive B:. To do so, click on the appropriate directory icon. If you are using the keyboard, hold down the `Ctrl` key and press the letter associated with the disk drive you want to display. For example, to see the directory in disk drive B:, press `Ctrl` `B`.

The Directory Tree window contains the following parts, as shown in Figure 4.8:

- The ***disk drive icon*** represents the disk drives on your computer. A drive letter follows each icon.

- The ***directory path*** for the Directory Tree appears in the status line beside the drive icons.

- The ***current directory*** is the directory that is highlighted in the Directory Tree window.

- The ***directory icons*** represent each directory on the current drive.

- A scroll bar appears if there are more directories and subdirectories than will fit in the Directory Tree window.

SUBDIRECTORIES IN DIRECTORY TREE

The Directory Tree in File Manager can also display any subdirectories. The directory icons might contain a plus (+) or minus (–) sign indicating expanded or collapsed directories. The default configuration of File Manager does not indicate expandable directories, but many persons change the default. If you want this indication, check Indicate Expandable Branches on the Tree menu. Regardless, the current directory is indicated by an open file folder icon and the subdirectories to the current

---

2 The term "subdirectory" is sometimes used instead of "directory." In DOS, all directories but one are actually subordinate to another directory and the terms are interchangeable.

directory are listed on the right side of the screen in conjunction with files in the current directory. Notice that the directory in Figure 4.8 contains a plus sign (+) in the icon for DOCUMNTS. The plus sign means that one or more subdirectories exist beneath that directory.

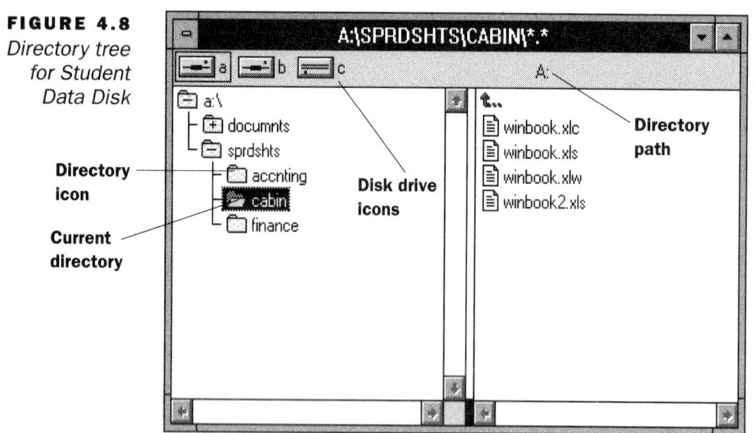

FIGURE 4.8
Directory tree for Student Data Disk

You can click on any directory icon with a plus sign to reveal the subdirectories associated with its parent directory. This is called *expanding* the directory. The directory icon for an expanded directory contains a minus sign (–) as shown in the directory SPRDSHTS in Figure 4.8.

To select a new current directory, click once on its file folder icon. If there are subdirectories to the current directory, they will be listed. To display the subdirectories of a directory on the left side of the window, double-click on its icon. To remove the display of subdirectories on the left side, double-click on the icon a second time. Figure 4.8 shows the structure of the Student Data Disk on the left; the right side of the window shows the contents of the A:\SPRDSHTS\CABIN directory.

TO EXPAND A DIRECTORY

1. Click the directory icon next to the name of the directory you want to expand. Or, use the arrow keys to select the directory you want to expand.

2. Choose Expand One Level from the Tree menu.

CHANGING DIRECTORIES

The highlighted directory is the *active* (current) *directory*. If you want to change to another directory, simply position the selection cursor (mouse pointer) on the directory desired. Click on the directory name that you want to select.

Use the following keys to select a directory:

To Move To	*Press*
A directory in the list above or below the active directory	↑ ↓
The root directory, which is always the first directory in the list	Home
The last directory in the list	End
The first subdirectory of an expanded directory	→
The directory level above the current directory	←

The directory one window up from the current directory   `PgUp`

The directory one window down from the current directory   `PgDn`

A specific directory   The first letter of the directory name, then ↓ if necessary

Directory List

The Directory Tree shows the overall structure of your directories. To see the individual files, you must look at the *Directory List*. On the list, File Manager displays the files and subdirectories. You can change the information you see, or rearrange the listed files.

The icon to the left of the file name shows whether the file is a directory, a program file, a document file, or another type of file. The interpretation of these icons is as follows:

Kind of Icon	*Kind of File*
Directory icons	Directories are listed first, in alphabetical order
Program file icons	Program files and batch files, with extensions .EXE, .COM, .PIF, and .BAT; these are executable files used to start applications
Document item icons	Document files, created by specific applications and recognized as such by Windows
Open file folder icons	Indicates the current open directory
Data file icons	Other files

CHANGING INFORMATION DISPLAYED IN DIRECTORY LIST

File names in a directory window are usually listed alphabetically, but you can change the way that they are listed. The View and Option menus in File Manager are used to rearrange files and to specify the information to be displayed.

From the View menu select Partial Details..., then select the information you want to see from among the following: Size, Last Modification Date, Last Modification Time, and File Attributes. To complete the selection, choose OK.

You can also change the order that the files are to be displayed. Use the View menu shown in Figure 4.9 to obtain the dialog box that lists Name, All File Details,

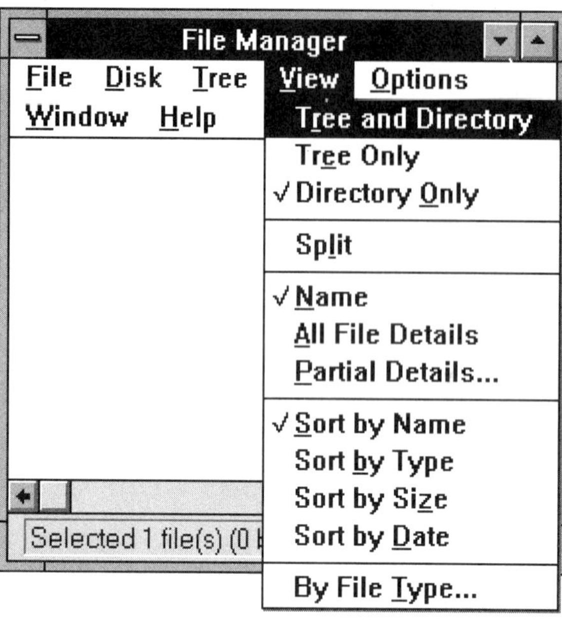

FIGURE 4.9
The View menu

Partial Details…. A check mark indicates the current selection. Choosing Namc or All File Details will immediately make the change.

By default, the contents of a directory are listed alphabetically, with directories listed first, followed by file names. You can sort the files and directories by Name, Type, Size, or Date the file was last modified. The Sort commands do not affect the directory tree. If you select Sort by Name, the current directory will be sorted (alphabetically) first by directories, then files. To sort files and directories by type, select View, then choose Sort by Type. Directories and then files will be listed alphabetically by extension in the active directory window. In addition, you can sort files by size. Select View, then choose Sort by Size. Files are listed by size, with the largest file listed first. You can also sort by last modification date. From the View menu, choose Sort by Date. Directories are listed first, sorted by date. Then files are listed by date, with the most recently modified file listed first.

Finally, you can select the type of file to display. You may wish to have File Manager display certain types of files, or files with similar file names or extensions. Choose By File Type from the View menu; the By File Type dialog box will appear as in Figure 4.10. Select the options that indicate the files you want to display (directories, programs, documents, other files, or hidden/system files). To complete the selection, click or choose OK.

FIGURE 4.10
The By File Type dialog box

Close Directory Window

To close an active directory window, double-click on the Control Menu box, located in the upper-left corner of the screen. The Control menu shown in Figure 4.11 will appear. If you are not using a mouse, press [Alt][-] (hyphen), and choose Close from the Control menu.

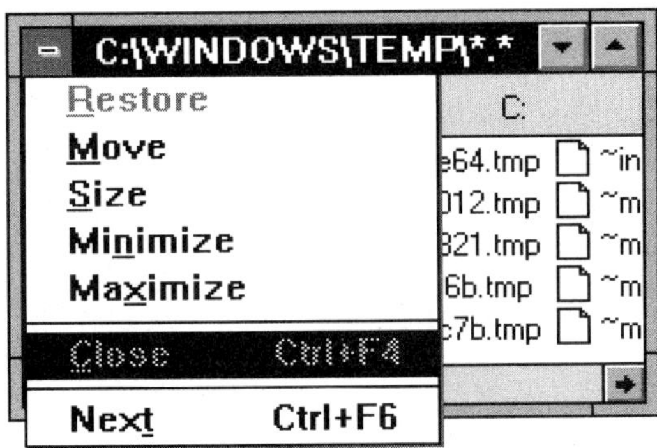

FIGURE 4.11
The Control menu

GUIDED ACTIVITY 4.5

Exploring the Directory Tree on Drive A:

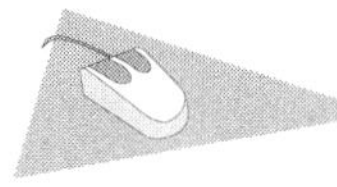

1. Open File Manager in the Main program group in the Program Manager.

2. Make sure you have your copy of the Student Data Disk in drive A:. Click on the drive A: icon.

3. Click on Tree from the menu bar in File Manager.

4. Click on Expand All. Note the tree structure of this disk.

5. When finished, close the Directory Tree window by clicking on the Control Menu box, and then click on Close.

GUIDED ACTIVITY 4.6

Exploring the Directory Tree on Drive A:

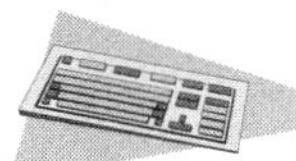

1. Open File Manager in the Main program group in the Program Manager.

2. Make sure you have your copy of the Student Data Disk in drive A:. Press [Ctrl][A] to activate drive A:.

3. Press [Alt][T] for the Tree menu.

4. Select Expand All. Note the tree structure of this disk.

5. Press [Alt][Spacebar] for the Control Menu box, then choose Close to close the Directory Tree window.

Files and Directories

File Manager allows you to perform such operations as naming, creating, searching for, copying, renaming, moving, and deleting both files and directories. These tasks follow the rules of MS-DOS for naming files. For instance, a file name or directory consists of two parts: the name and an extension (optional). The two parts are separated by a period (.), also called a "dot." File names can consist of a maximum of eight alphanumeric characters, with an extension of up to three characters. File names must start with either a letter or a number. For example, FILENAME.EXT is a valid file name. The following symbols *cannot* be used in a file name:

Period	.	Quotation marks	"
Comma	,	Brackets	[ ]
Colon	:	Vertical Bar	|
Semicolon	;	Slash	/
Backslash	\	Equal sign	=

Other symbol characters can be used within the name, but we suggest that you do not use any symbol other than the _ (underscore) character because some software programs restrict the set of acceptable file names more than DOS does. In addition, you cannot use as file names the following reserved words, which address hardware devices: CON, AUX, COM1, COM2, COM3, COM4, COM5, LPT1, LPT2, LPT3, LPT4, NUL, or PRN.

Creating Directories

Directories can be created on the hard disk or on a floppy disk. A directory is created from the File menu shown in Figure 4.12.

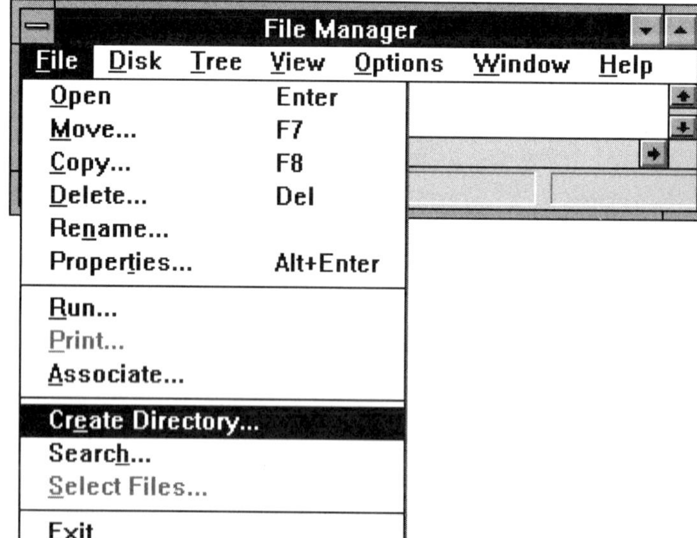

When you select Create Directory from the File menu, a dialog box will appear as shown in Figure 4.13.

This dialog box displays the name of the current directory and prompts you to furnish a name for the subdirectory you wish to create. The name of the directory must conform to the rules of file names (maximum of eight characters—or one to eight characters, a period, then

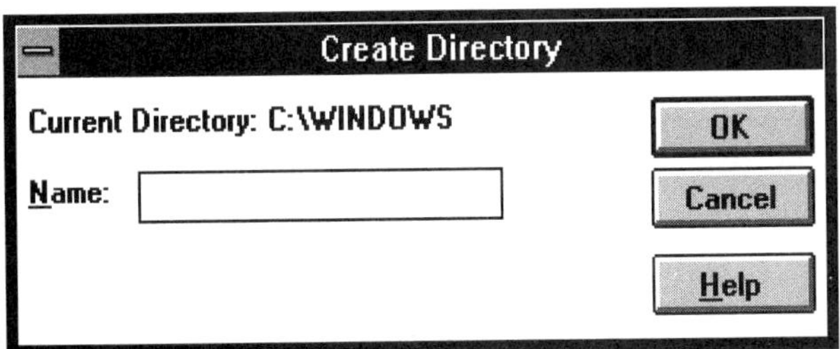

FIGURE 4.13
The Create Directory dialog box

one to three additional characters). To complete the creation of a directory, click or choose OK. File Manager will then proceed to create the directory within its parent directory.

GUIDED ACTIVITY 4.7

Creating a Subdirectory

1. Open File Manager from the Main program group in the Program Manager. Make sure your data disk is in drive A:, and click on the drive A: icon.

2. Click on File from the menu bar.

3. Click on Create Directory from the File menu.

4. In the Name text box, type WPDOC (directory to contain your word processing files).

5. Click on OK to confirm the creation of the directory.

6. Close File Manager by clicking on its Control Menu box and then Close.

GUIDED ACTIVITY 4.8

Creating a Subdirectory

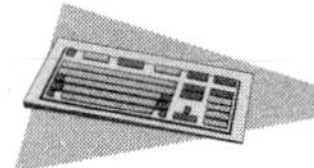

1. Open File Manager from the Main program group in the Program Manager. Press Ctrl A to activate drive A:.

2. Press Alt F for the File menu.

3. Select Create Directory.

4. In the Name text box, type WPDOC (directory to contain your word processing files).

5. Press Enter to confirm the creation of the directory.

6. Press Alt Spacebar for the Control Menu box. Then, select Close to close File Manager.

Searching for Files and Directories

As you spend time on your computer, you will most likely create many files and many directories. It may become difficult to remember where a particular file is located. You can use the Search command from the File menu to locate files or directories. The Search dialog box will appear, as shown in Figure 4.14. It contains a Start From: text box. This displays the current directory when you first execute the command. To change, so that the entire disk is searched, erase everything after the leftmost backslash—as has been done in Figure 4.14.

Type the name of the file or directory in the Search For: text box. Use *wild cards* if you want to search for a group of files or directories with similar names or extensions. For example, if you want to search for all files with a .DOC extension, you would type ∗.DOC (the ∗ is a MS-DOS wild card that is a "global match" character). To complete the action, click or choose OK. File Manager will search for all such files on the entire disk and then provide a Search Results window like the one shown in Figure 4.15.

FIGURE 4.14
The Search dialog box

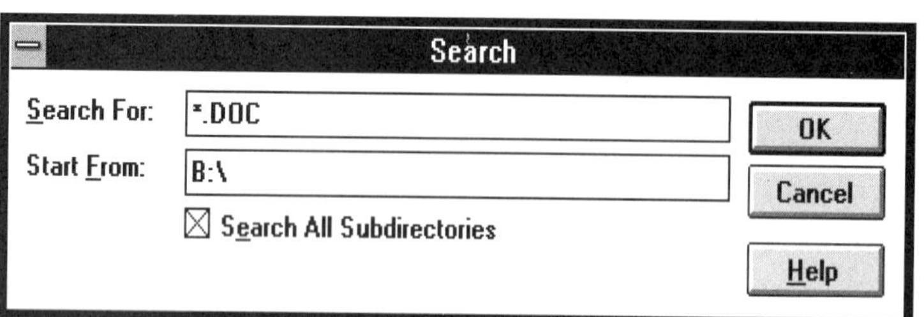

FIGURE 4.15
The Search Results window

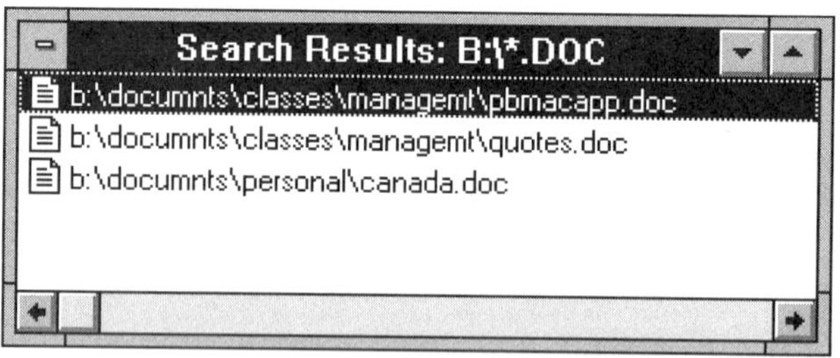

The Search Results window appears as a directory window, except that the full path name (for example, B:\DOCUMNTS\CLASSES\MANAGEMT\QUOTES.DOC) is portrayed. You can use the scroll bar on the right border to move through the window if there are more "hits" (finds) than fit in the window. You will be able to copy or move files to other disks or directories using the techniques discussed later in this unit.

Searching for a Specific Program File

1. Open File Manager from the Main program group. Select drive C:.

2. Click on Search from the File menu.

3. Type the file name WRITE.EXE.

4. Ensure that the Start From: box reads C:\ and the Search All Subdirectories box is checked.

5. Click on OK to start the search.

6. The search will probably find one file named WRITE.EXE in the C:\WINDOWS directory, unless your system has been configured differently by the system manager.

7. Close the Search Results window by clicking on the Control Menu box and selecting Close.

Searching for a Specific Program File

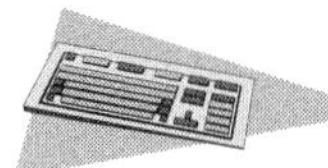

1. Open File Manager from the Main Program Group. Select drive C: if it is not already selected.

2. Press [Alt][F] for the File menu. Select Search from the menu.

3. Type the file name WRITE.EXE.

4. Ensure that the Start From: box reads C:\ and the Search All Subdirectories box is checked.

5. Press [Enter] to start the search.

6. The search will probably find one file named WRITE.EXE in the C:\WINDOWS directory, unless your system has been configured differently by the system manager.

7. Close the Search Results window by pressing [Alt][Spacebar] and selecting Close.

Copying and Moving Files and Directories

As you work with files, you will often want to have a second copy of a file, perhaps as a backup copy on a separate disk or as a record of the file at a point in time, prior to changing the file. To *copy* a file means to create an exact duplicate of the file. The duplicate can be on a different disk or directory with the same file name as the original file, or it can be on the same disk or directory with a different name than the original, or it can be on a different disk/directory with a different name.

There are also occasions when you have a file on one disk or directory and you want it on another. To *move* a file means to copy it to another disk or directory and to erase it from its original disk or directory. Moving a file from one disk to another frees space on the original disk and occupies space on the destination disk. Copying a file from one disk to another has no effect on the space available on the original disk but occupies space on the destination disk.

Moving Files

Files or directories can be moved from one location (source) to another (destination) by dragging the source file or directory with the mouse or by using the Move command. If you are using the mouse, the file being moved and the destination (disk

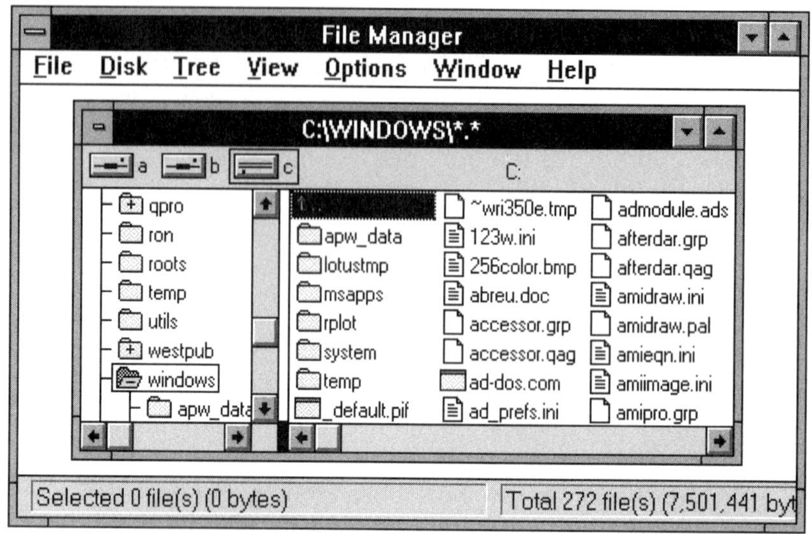

drive icon) must both be visible, as shown in Figure 4.16. You simply select the source (file or directory) and drag it to its destination (drive A:, drive B:, or another directory that you select). Make certain that there is a disk inserted in the disk drive you are designating, or you will receive an error message.

To move a file to a disk in a different disk drive:

1. Using the techniques discussed earlier in this unit, open File Manager.

2. Press and hold down the [Alt] key, point to the icon for the file, then hold down the mouse button and drag the icon to the destination disk drive icon.

3. Release the mouse button, and then release [Alt]. A confirmation message will appear.

4. Complete the move by clicking Yes.

1. Choose Move from the File menu.

2. A Move dialog box will appear, prompting you for a file name in the From: box shown in Figure 4.17. If you have already highlighted a file name in a directory window, that name will appear in the box.

3. Type a drive or directory in the To: box.

4. Press [Enter] to choose OK. A confirmation message will appear.

5. To complete the move, choose OK by pressing [Enter].

GUIDED ACTIVITY 4.11

Moving a File to a Subdirectory

1. Open File Manager. Make sure the Student Data Disk is in drive A:. Click on the drive A: icon.

2. Click (once) on each directory icon in turn to expand the A:\, DOCUMNTS, and CLASSES directories. Double-click on MANAGEMT to open a directory window.

3. Press and hold the [Alt] key, then drag the icon for PBMACAPP.DOC to the folder for WPDOC in the directory tree window. Respond Yes to the confirmation message that will appear.

4. Open a directory window for WPDOC to verify that the move has been successful.

GUIDED ACTIVITY 4.12

Moving a File to a Subdirectory

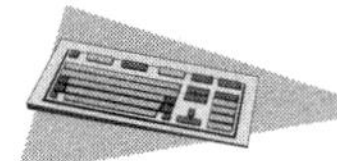

1. Open File Manager. Make sure the Student Data Disk is in drive A:. Press [Ctrl][A] to select drive A:.

2. Using the arrow keys and [Enter] key, expand each directory in turn through the sequence A:\, DOCUMNTS, and CLASSES. Press [Enter] on MANAGEMT to open a directory window.

3. Move the highlight in the directory window so it covers the file PBMACAPP.DOC.

4. Press [Alt][F], and then select Move. The file just highlighted (PBMACAPP.DOC) should appear in the From: box. If not, type `A:\DOCUMNTS\CLASSES\ MANAGEMT\PBMACAPP.DOC` in the box.

5. Press [Alt][T] and type `A:\WPDOC` in the To: box. Press [Enter].

6. Press [Enter] to confirm the operation.

7. Open a directory window for WPDOC to verify that the move has been successful.

Copying Files

Copying files is very similar to the move procedure, with the following exceptions. To copy using the mouse, you need to hold down the [Ctrl] key while you drag the file or directory to the destination window, icon, or disk drive. If you are using the keyboard, choose Copy from the File menu; the Copy dialog box will appear as shown in Figure 4.18. Enter the source (From:) and destination (To:), completing the action by selecting the OK button at the right of the dialog box. File Manager will display a warning message if the file that you are copying happens to have the same file name as a file that already exists in the destination directory. If you are certain that

FIGURE 4.18
The Copy dialog box

you want to replace the existing file, choose OK. To copy a file, changing the name of the file in the process, you use the File menu, selecting the Copy command. When prompted for a destination (To:), enter the drive and directory name and the file name; for example, C:\MEMO\NUPOLICY.DOC (C: is the drive, \MEMO is the directory name, NUPOLICY.DOC is the file name).

GUIDED ACTIVITY 4.13

Copying a File to a Directory

1. Open File Manager. Make sure the Student Data Disk is in drive A:. Click on the drive A: icon.

2. Click (twice) on the directory icons to expand the A:\, DOCUMNTS, and CLASSES directories.

3. Press and hold the [Ctrl] key, then drag the icon for PBMACAPP.DOC to the folder for MANAGEMT in the directory tree window.

4. Click on Yes to verify the copy.

5. Click once on MANAGEMT to verify that the copy has been successful.

GUIDED ACTIVITY 4.14

Copying a File to a Directory

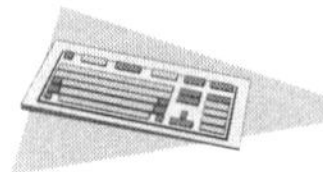

1. Open File Manager. Make sure the Student Data Disk is in drive A:. Press [Ctrl][A] to select drive A:.

2. Using the arrow keys and the [Enter] key, expand each directory in turn through the sequence A:\, DOCUMNTS, and CLASSES. Press [Enter] on WPDOC to open a directory window.

3. Move the highlight in the directory window so it covers the file PBMACAPP.DOC.

4. Press [Alt][F], and then select Copy. The file that was just highlighted (PBMACAPP.DOC) should appear in the From: box. If not, type `A:\WPDOC\ PBMACAPP.DOC` in the box.

5. Press [Alt][T] and type `A:\DOCUMNTS\CLASSES\MANAGEMT` in the To: box. Press [Enter].

6. Press [Enter] to confirm the operation.

7. Open a directory window for MANAGEMT to verify that the copy has been successful.

Deleting Files and Directories

Files and directories can be deleted from any disk drive. Before you can *delete* a file or directory, however, you must first select it from the Directory Tree or directory window. File Manager is much more efficient for deleting directories than deleting in DOS. If you delete a directory, all files and all subdirectories within the directory will be deleted.

WARNING *You need to be extremely careful when deleting files and directories, because the Delete command removes them instantly from your disk, making them unrecoverable without special software.*

FIGURE 4.19
The File Delete menu

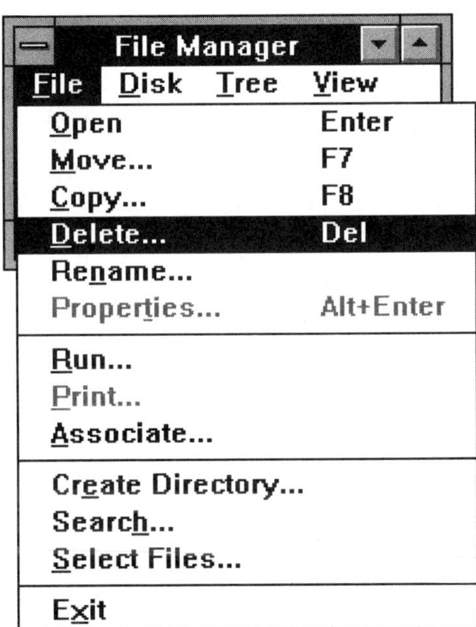

To start, select Delete from the File menu as illustrated in Figure 4.19. The Delete dialog box will appear as shown in Figure 4.20. You will be prompted for the file or directory name. To complete the choice, click or choose OK. You can also cancel the deletion if you happen to change your mind.

FIGURE 4.20
The File Delete dialog box

GUIDED ACTIVITY 4.15

Deleting a File in a Subdirectory

1. Open File Manager. Make sure the Student Data Disk is in drive A:. Click on the drive A: icon.

2. Select the file PBMACAPP.DOC in the WPDOC directory.

3. Click on File and then on Delete. Click on the OK button to confirm that the file is to be deleted.

4. Click on Yes to begin the deletion.

GUIDED ACTIVITY 4.16

Deleting a File in a Subdirectory

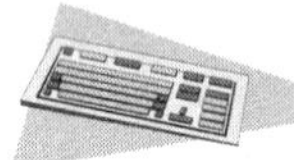

1. Open File Manager. Make sure the Student Data Disk is in drive A:. Press [Ctrl][A] to select drive A:.

2. Using the arrow keys, highlight the WPDOC directory. Press [Enter].

3. Highlight the file PBMACAPP.DOC. Press [Alt][F] and then select Delete. Press [Enter]. To confirm that the file is to be deleted, press [Enter] or [Alt][Y].

GUIDED ACTIVITY 4.17

Deleting a Subdirectory

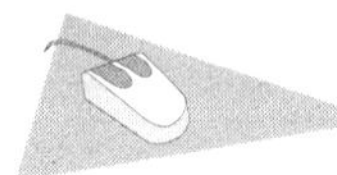

1. Open File Manager. Make sure the Student Data Disk is in drive A:. Click on the drive A: icon.

2. Click on the directory WPDOC.

3. Click on Delete from the File menu.

4. Click on the OK box to verify your desire to delete the directory listed.

5. If there are any files in the directory that you want to delete, they will have to be deleted before the directory itself can be deleted. File Manager will ask you whether to delete those particular files one at a time. Click on Yes each time you are asked to do so.

6. Close File Manager by clicking on the Control Menu box and then on Close.

GUIDED ACTIVITY 4.18

Deleting a Subdirectory

1. Open File Manager. Make sure the Student Data Disk is in drive A:. Press [Ctrl][A] to select drive A:.

2. Using the arrow keys, highlight the directory WPDOC.

3. Press [Alt][F] for the File menu. Select Delete. Press [Enter] or [Alt][D] to confirm your desire to delete the directory that is listed.

4. If there are any files in the directory that you want to delete, they will have to be deleted before the directory itself can be deleted. File Manager will ask you whether to delete those particular files one at a time. Press [Enter] or [Alt][Y] each time you are asked to do so.

5. Press [Alt][Spacebar] for the Control Menu box. Select Close to close File Manager.

Renaming Files and Directories

If you want to change the name of a directory or file, use the **Rename** command from the File menu. As you learned earlier, while deleting files or directories you must select a file or directory from the Directory Tree or directory window in order to be able to rename it. Use the File menu, and select the Rename command, as shown in Figure 4.21.

The Rename dialog box will appear as in Figure 4.22. Type the new name in the To: text box and click on or choose OK. If a duplicate name is used, File Manager will ask if you want to write over the existing file. Click on or choose OK to complete the action, or Cancel if you want a different name.

FIGURE 4.21
The File Rename menu

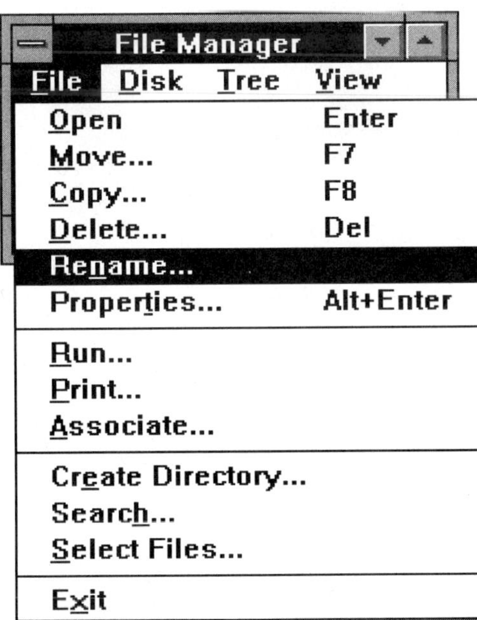

FIGURE 4.22
*The Rename
dialog box*

Rename

Current Directory: C:

From: _______________________

To: _______________________

OK

Cancel

Help

GUIDED ACTIVITY 4.19

Renaming a File

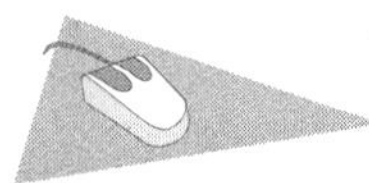

1. Open File Manager. Make sure the Student Data Disk is in drive A:. Click on the drive A: icon.

2. Open a directory window that contains the file A:\DOCUMNTS\PERSONAL\ CANADA.DOC and highlight the file.

3. Click on File and then on Rename.

4. In the To: text box, type a new name for the file: `PERMISSN.DOC`.

5. Click on the OK button.

6. Close File Manager.

GUIDED ACTIVITY 4.20

Renaming a File

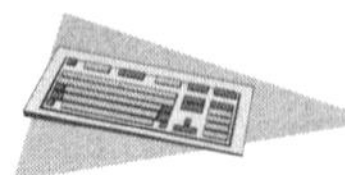

1. Open File Manager. Make sure the Student Data Disk is in drive A:. Press `Ctrl` `A` to select drive A:.

2. Using the direction arrows, highlight the file A:\DOCUMNTS\PERSONAL\ CANADA.DOC.

3. Press `Alt` `F` for the File menu. Select Rename.

4. In the To: text box, type a new name for the file: `PERMISSN.DOC`.

5. Press `Enter` to complete the renaming.

6. Close File Manager.

Review Questions

*1. What is the role of File Manager? How is it started?

2. Draw on paper a Directory Tree showing the individual directories VAR, TEMP, MEMO, with the root directory being A:\. The emphasis is on structure and not

on quality or shape of the drawing. Include the following: disk drive representation, directory path, current directory, and directory representation.

*3. How are directories that have subdirectories represented in the Directory Tree?

4. To change to the root directory, which key has to be pressed? (Review other situations involving changing directories.)

*5. If you wanted to list the individual files in a particular directory, what must you do?

*6. Briefly, list and describe the different icons used to represent files, directories, and programs.

7. Describe the process that involves displaying only certain files (such as programs, documents, or spreadsheets).

8. What are the mouse commands to close an active directory? Keyboard commands?

*9. What is the maximum number of characters that a file name may contain? What type(s) of characters may begin a file name? Identify three reserved words that cannot be used as file names. Explain why they cannot be used.

10. To create a directory within Windows 3.1, would you select File/Create Directory *for* a menu or File/Create Directory *from* the menu? (Select the correct sequence.)

11. Can files be copied from or moved to the Search Results window? What is the purpose of the Search Command?

12. If you are using the mouse to move a file or a directory, is it possible to do so without using the keyboard (other than using the [Alt] or [Ctrl] keys)? What about if you want to copy them? (This may be a difficult question to answer. Review the steps and perform them on your computer to see if your answer is correct.)

*13. Why should you be extremely careful in deleting files?

14. Review the processes to rename files or directories, format and copy disks, and quit File Manager.

Key Terms

Active directory	Directory path	Rename file
Copy file	Directory window	Root directory
Current directory	Disk drive icon	Shell program
Data file icon	Document item icon	Up arrow icon
Default shell	Expand a directory	Wild card
Delete file	Move file	WINFILE.EXE
Directory	Open file folder icon	
Directory icon	Program file icon	

Documentation Research

To answer the following questions, use Chapter 4, "File Manager," of the *User's Guide*. Check the guide's index to find pages with the information needed. We recommend that you also write the relevant page number next to each question. For additional aid, you may need to use File Manager's on-line Help menu.

1. If you are connected to a network, how do you connect to and disconnect from network drives?

2. What words cannot be used in naming files and directories?

3. List and explain the four file attributes.

4. Using File Manager's on-line Help, what command is used to run an application and open a document?

5. Using File Manager's on-line Help, determine when a directory tree is active.

6. Using File Manager's on-line Help, determine the steps to search for the File Details View Menu Commands.

Control Panel

Control Panel allows you to customize Windows' automatic startup settings (the defaults) by changing color schemes, desktop arrangement, printer configuration, mouse or keyboard speed, and monitor type.

Learning Objectives

At the completion of this unit, you should know

1. the features available with Control Panel for customizing Windows.

At the completion of this unit, you should be able to

1. start and exit Control Panel,

2. change a color scheme,

3. change or remove fonts,

4. make desktop changes,

5. adjust keyboard speed,

6. change system date and time,

7. configure the printer.

Introduction to the Control Panel

This unit presents the basic Control Panel features that affect your hardware and connections. Control Panel consists of 12 icons (11 icons in Standard mode), as shown in Figure 5.1. These allow you to change color, fonts, mouse, desktop, keyboard, date/time, printers, and so forth. The remaining icons are for advanced operations, including ports, international, sound, drivers, and 386 Enhanced. You may need to consult the Microsoft Windows *User's Guide* for detailed discussions of these advanced topics.

FIGURE 5.1
The Control Panel window

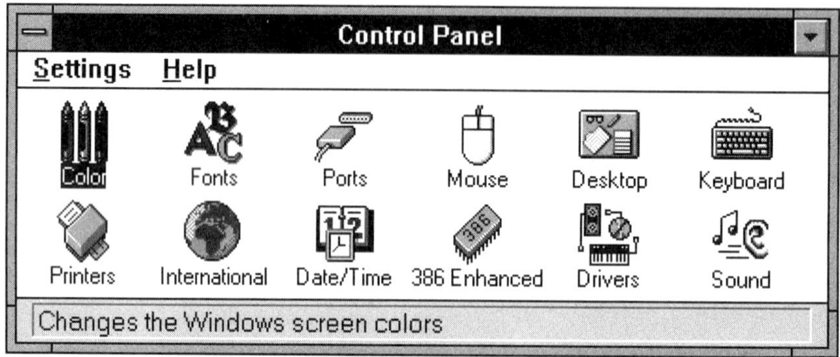

To start Control Panel, you must first open the Main program group window of Program Manager. Double-click on the Control Panel icon or, on the keyboard, use the arrow keys to highlight the Control Panel icon, then press Enter to complete the selection. Windows will then display the Control Panel window illustrated in Figure 5.1. The individual icons are the entry points for all operations. Each icon has its particular purpose and meaning:

Icon	*Purpose*
Color	Set the color scheme of the desktop
Fonts	Add or remove fonts for printer and monitor
Ports	Set communications parameters
Mouse	Set up mouse, including speed
Desktop	Customize patterns for desktop and set cursor blink rate

Specify how applications run (advanced topic)

Install and configure printers

Set international options, such as country and language, number and currency formats, and date and time display formats

Set keyboard speed

Change system date and time

Enable/disable warning beep for error conditions

Install, remove, and configure drivers that control additional devices, such as sound cards and video players, that you add to your system.[1]

Colors

If you want to change the *color scheme*, choose the Color icon from the Control Panel window. A Color dialog box will appear similar to that shown in Figure 5.2, listing the parts of the Color dialog box. The name of the current color scheme is shown, along with a sample screen of colors. The Color Schemes list box is located in the upper-right corner. Clicking the mouse on the arrow will call the drop-down list box that contains the colors. The colors available include Windows Default, Arizona, Bordeaux, Designer, Fluorescent, Monochrome, Ocean, Pastel, Patchwork, Rugby, Wing Tips, and many more. You can scroll through the list and select a scheme that you like. Click or choose OK to complete the choice of scheme. If you are using the keyboard, press [Alt][↓] to open the Color Schemes list box.

Changing an Existing Color Scheme

If you prefer another color scheme, you can change any of the default color schemes. The default color schemes are the predetermined colors provided by Microsoft. To change the scheme, select the color scheme you want from the Color Schemes list box, then click or choose the Color Palette button.

---

1 Windows cannot recognize a device, even though it is physically installed on the system, until the appropriate device driver has been installed in Control Panel; device drivers are usually contained in files with a .DRV extension.

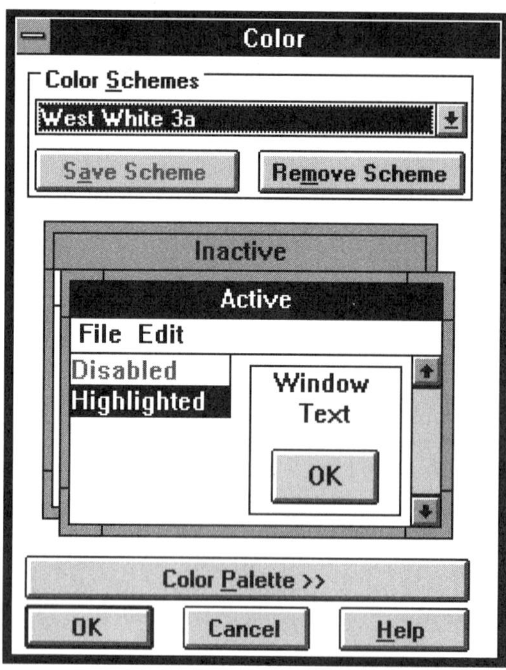

The Control Panel will then bring up an expanded color dialog box like the one shown in Figure 5.3 that shows a list of elements, a palette of basic colors, and, until you select additional colors, an empty *color palette* called Custom Colors. In the color sample screen, click the element whose color you wish to change. If you are using the keyboard, press [Alt][↓] to open the Screen Element list box. Select a color by clicking the mouse button in the Basic Colors palette. (Using the keyboard, you press [Tab] to move to the palette, the arrow keys to move the dotted rectangle to the color you want, and then [Spacebar] to ultimately select the color.) The illustration in this text

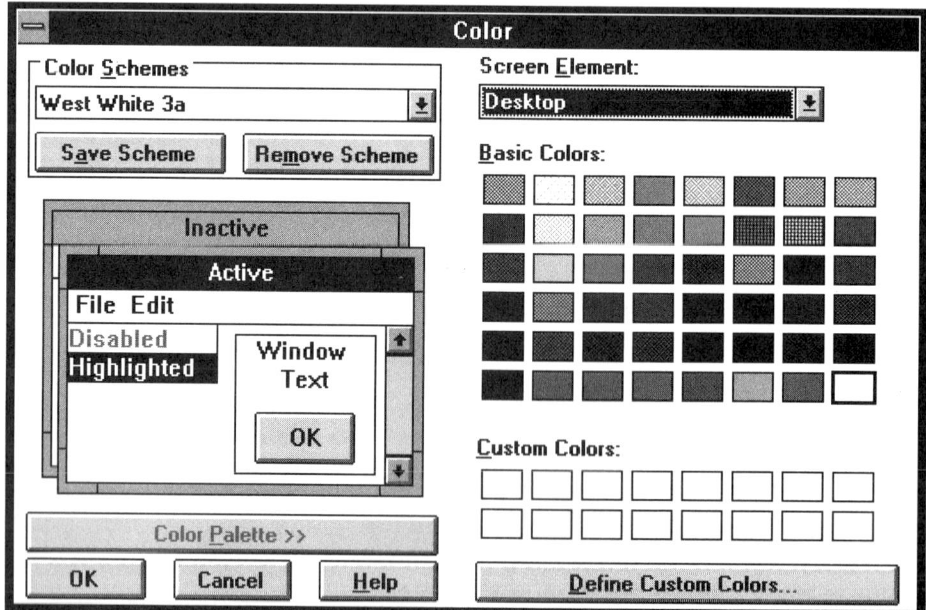

will not be the same as on your monitor. Remember that your monitor is probably a color monitor and accordingly should show the Basic Colors palette in color. When you are finished selecting the color of your choice, click or choose Save Scheme, and type a name for the scheme. We developed the "West White 3a" scheme for this book to provide clearer black-and-white screen images.

GUIDED ACTIVITY 5.1

Changing Color Scheme

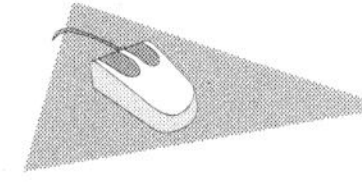

1. Open the Control Panel window from the Main program group in Program Manager. Remember, to open the window, you will have to double-click on the Control Panel icon.

2. Double-click on the Color icon.

3. Click on the Color Palette box.

4. Click on the Application Workspace. This area is on the left side of the scroll bars. In the Screen Element box, the name of the particular area that you clicked on will appear. If a color is changed, only the color in that particular area will change.

5. Look at the Basic Colors palette on the right side of the screen. Check the color of the current Screen Element. The current color is indicated by a black frame around the color. This may be difficult to see; click on the arrow to the right of the Screen Element box and change the current element in order to see the black frame. Change the current color by clicking on a light shade of blue.

6. Experiment with the other screen elements and with different color combinations.

7. If your instructor requests, save the color selections by clicking on Save Scheme and giving it a file name; click on OK to complete the process. If your instructor does not want you to alter the color scheme, click on Cancel.

GUIDED ACTIVITY 5.2

Changing Color Scheme

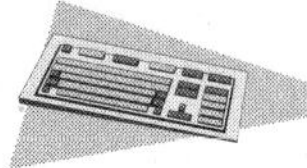

1. Open the Control Panel window from the Main program group in Program Manager. Remember, to open the window, you will have to highlight the Control Panel icon using the arrow keys and press [Enter].

2. Press [Alt][S] for the Settings menu. Select Color. You can highlight the Color icon and press [Enter] to avoid going through a menu.

3. Press [Alt][P] to see the Color Palette.

4. Press [Alt][E] and use the arrow keys to change the current Screen Element. If a color is changed, only the color in that particular area will change.

5. Look at the Basic Color palette on the right side of the screen. Check the color of the current Screen Element. The current color is indicated by a black frame around the color. This may be difficult to see; use the arrow keys to change the current Screen Element in order to see the black frame. Change the current color by pressing [Alt][B] to enter the Basic Colors area. Use the arrow keys to indicate a color, then press [Spacebar] to select the color.

6. Experiment with the other screen elements and with different color combinations.

7. If your instructor requests, save the color selections by pressing [Alt][A] for the Save Scheme command and giving it a file name; press [Enter] to complete the process. If your instructor does not want you to alter the color scheme, press [Esc].

Using Fonts

The manner in which the characters appear on the screen will depend on the type fonts that you choose. If you want to change the font, select (double-click) on the Fonts icon in the Control Panel. A *font* is a graphic design that affects the appearance of numerals, symbols, and characters. Different fonts are available for providing emphasis (bold, italics, or underline). They allow you to give your work a professional or casual appearance. Selecting the right font will take some practice, however, and we strongly recommend that you experiment with fonts.

When you select the Fonts icon in the Control Panel, the Fonts dialog box in Figure 5.4 will appear. The fonts on your system may be different from those in the figure.

Click or choose the Add button, and the Control Panel will prompt you for a file name so that you may install the font set that you want. At this time, select a file name from the text box with the available fonts. To complete the action, click or choose OK.

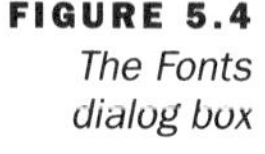

GUIDED ACTIVITY 5.3

Looking at Fonts

1. If Control Panel is still open, close it by double-clicking the Control Menu box.

2. Open Write in the Accessories program group in Program Manager.

3. Compose a couple of paragraphs of text—perhaps a short letter to Dad explaining why you need to buy a new tennis racquet. Type the letter into the Write window.

4. Change the first paragraph to the Courier font by first marking the text. This is done by going to the first letter in the paragraph, pressing and holding the left mouse button, dragging the mouse pointer to the last letter in the paragraph, and releasing the mouse button. The paragraph should be highlighted. Next, click on Character from the menu bar. Then click on Fonts and select Courier from the list of choices. If you do not see Courier, Scroll up or down the list until it appears. Click on OK.

5. Close Write by double-clicking the Control Menu box.

NOTE *Font options are determined by the kind of printer you are using. Therefore, your choices will depend on the printer you have available, and might not correspond with what is illustrated in this book.*

GUIDED ACTIVITY 5.4

Looking at Fonts

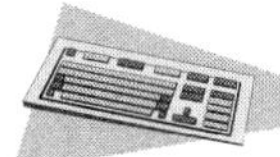

1. If Control Panel is still open, close it by pressing [Alt] [Spacebar], then select Close.

2. Open Write in the Accessories program group in Program Manager.

3. Compose a couple of paragraphs of text—perhaps a short letter to Dad explaining why you need to buy a new tennis racquet. Type the letter into the Write window.

4. Change the first paragraph to the Courier font by first marking the text. This is done by going to the first letter in the paragraph, pressing and holding [Shift], using the arrow keys to mark the text until reaching the last letter in the paragraph, and releasing [Shift]. The paragraph should be highlighted. Press [Alt] [C] for the Character menu, then [F] for fonts. Select Courier. If you do not see Courier, arrow up or down the list until it appears. Press [Enter].

5. Close Write by pressing [Alt] [Spacebar], then selecting Close.

NOTE *Font options are determined by the kind of printer you are using. Therefore, your choices will depend on the printer you have available, and might not correspond with what is illustrated in this book.*

Removing a Font

Fonts that have been added will use memory. If you are not planning to use one or more of the fonts that you added, it is best to remove them. You will soon appreciate the need for memory conservation for your other applications, since any wasted memory will result in storage problems (in RAM) later. To remove a font, click or choose the Fonts icon from the Control Panel window; when the Fonts dialog box appears, select the font you wish to remove. Next, click or choose Remove, and another dialog box will appear, asking you to verify that you wish to remove the selected font. To complete this process, click or choose OK. The font will be removed from your Windows setup, but not deleted from your hard disk.

GUIDED ACTIVITY 5.5   *(OPTIONAL)*

Removing a Font *(TO BE COMPLETED ONLY IF INSTRUCTOR APPROVES!)*

1. Open Control Panel in the Main program group.

2. Double-click on the Fonts icon.

3. Click on the scroll bar to view the Installed Fonts.

   If your instructor approves removing the font:

4. Click on the font you wish to remove.

5. Click on Remove. Verify the removal by clicking on Yes.

6. Close Fonts by clicking on Close.

7. Close Control Panel by clicking on the Control Menu box and then on Close.

GUIDED ACTIVITY 5.6   *(OPTIONAL)*

Removing a Font *(TO BE COMPLETED ONLY IF INSTRUCTOR APPROVES!)*

1. Open Control Panel in the Main program group.

2. Press [Alt][S] for the Settings menu. Select Fonts. You can highlight the Fonts icon by using the arrow keys and pressing [Enter] to avoid going through a menu.

3. Press [Alt][F] and use the arrow keys to view the Installed Fonts.

   If your instructor approves removing the font:

4. Highlight the font you wish to remove.

5. Press [Alt][R] to select the Remove command. Press [Enter] or [Alt][Y] to verify the removal.

6. Close Fonts by pressing [Enter].

7. Close Control Panel by pressing [Alt][Spacebar] for the Control menu. Select Close.

Making Desktop Changes

Desktop patterns can be changed using the Desktop icon in the Control Panel. When you first install Windows 3.1, the default pattern will be installed. Usually it is a pattern referred to as *None*. The available patterns include 50% Gray, Boxes, Critters, Diamonds, Paisley, Quilt, Scottie, Spinner, Thatches, Tulip, Waffle, Weave, and others. As you can see, there are many patterns from which to choose. You may wish to experiment with each pattern until you find one that is pleasing to you. You can change this pattern anytime if you so wish. In addition to the predetermined patterns available in Windows, you can design your own (see "Changing Desktop Options" in Chapter 5 of the *User's Guide* for more information).

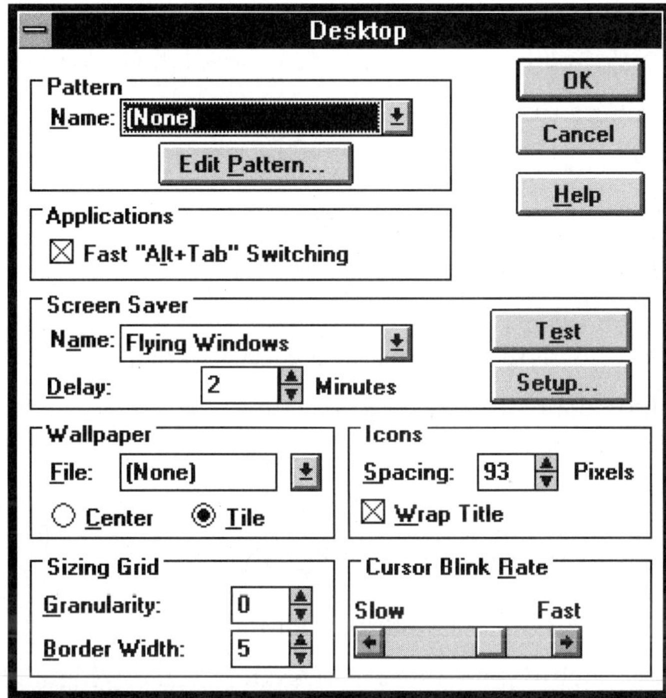

FIGURE 5.5
The Desktop dialog box

To choose a pattern, double-click or choose the Desktop icon in the Control Panel. The Desktop dialog box in Figure 5.5 will appear.

Click or choose the down arrow in the Pattern Name list box; a drop-down list will appear. The default pattern will remain "None" until it is changed. The available patterns will appear once you click or choose the down arrow. If you are using the keyboard, press Alt $↓$. Select a pattern from the list, and press $Enter$ to complete the action. You may want to experiment with several patterns until you find one that appeals to you.

To remove a pattern, choose the Edit Pattern button in the Desktop dialog box; select the pattern you wish to remove, and click on the Remove button. Select Yes to verify the removal and finally OK to complete the action.

When run on a computer with at least 2MB of memory, Windows 3.1 allows you to specify *wallpaper*. This is a picture that is displayed on the desktop behind all windows. Wallpaper must be in the form of a .BMP file and the file must be in the WINDOWS directory. Large pictures are usually displayed *centered*, only once on the screen. Space not covered by a centered picture will be covered by the desktop pattern. Small pictures are often *tiled*, repeated as many times as they will fit, completely covering the desktop pattern. There are many sources of wallpaper patterns, including the Windows software, commercial packages, shareware, and other users of Windows. You can even develop your own wallpaper using the Paint program supplied with Windows.

Changing Desktop Pattern and Wallpaper

1. Open Control Panel from Main in Program Manager.

2. Double-click on the Desktop icon.

3. Click on the down arrow that is to the right of the Pattern Name box. This will cause a drop-down list to appear. The scroll bar to the right of this list can be used to view additional portions of the list.

4. Click on the Paisley pattern. You may have to scroll down to find this pattern.

5. Click on Edit Pattern to see what the Paisley pattern looks like.

6. Click on Cancel to return to the main dialog box.

7. Click on the down arrow to the right of the Wallpaper box.

8. Click on PARTY.BMP from the Wallpaper list. If PARTY.BMP is not on the list, choose a different file.

9. If you are satisfied with the pattern and wallpaper, click on OK.

10. Close the Desktop dialog box by clicking on OK. Close Control Panel.

Changing Desktop Pattern and Wallpaper

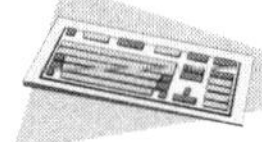

1. Open Control Panel from Main in Program Manager.

2. Press [Alt][S] for the Settings menu. Select Desktop. You can highlight the Desktop icon and press [Enter] to avoid using a menu.

3. Press [Alt][N] for the Name box. Use the arrow keys to select the Paisley pattern.

4. Press [Alt][P] for the Edit Pattern command to see what the Paisley pattern looks like.

5. Press [Enter] to return to the main dialog box.

6. Press [Alt][F] for the Wallpaper box. Use [↑] and [↓] to see a list of the different options.

7. Stop when PARTY.BMP appears in box. If PARTY.BMP is not on the list, choose a different file.

8. If you are satisfied with the pattern and wallpaper, press [Enter].

9. Close the Desktop dialog box by pressing [Enter]. Close Control Panel.

Adjusting Keyboard Speed

The Keyboard icon allows you to control the speed with which a key repeats itself when you hold it down. Your keyboard has *typematic keys*, which are very sensitive if you are not used to the touch-type method. To change the keyboard repeat speed, select the Keyboard icon from the Control Panel, and the Keyboard dialog box in Figure 5.6 will appear.

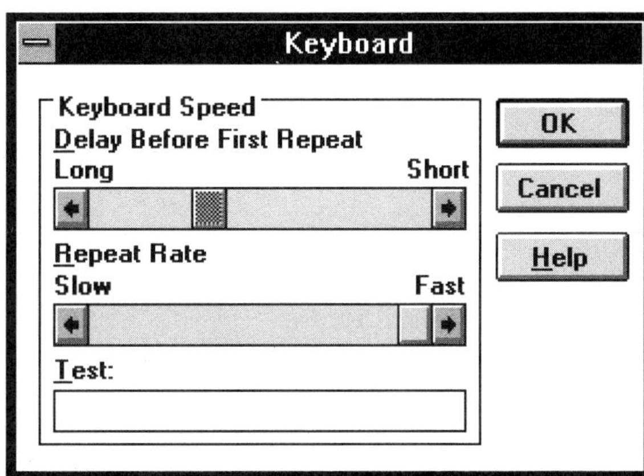

FIGURE 5.6
The Keyboard dialog box

Drag the scroll box toward Fast or Slow. You may use the Fast or Slow arrow. If you are using the keyboard, press ▶ or ◀ to increase or decrease the speed. You can test the speed by moving to the Test box and holding down any key on the keyboard. Complete the process of adjusting the keyboard speed by clicking on or choosing OK.

Changing the System Date and Time

You can change the system date and time by double-clicking on or choosing the Date/Time icon in the Control Panel. The time and date are used in Clock and Calendar. Time and date are also used by File Manager to time- and date-stamp files saved on your disk. If your computer system has a built-in clock, you may not have to worry about changing the date or time. Check with your instructor or laboratory manager if you have any questions regarding system default dates and times.

When you select the Date/Time icon from the Control Panel, a Date & Time dialog box will appear, as shown in Figure 5.7.

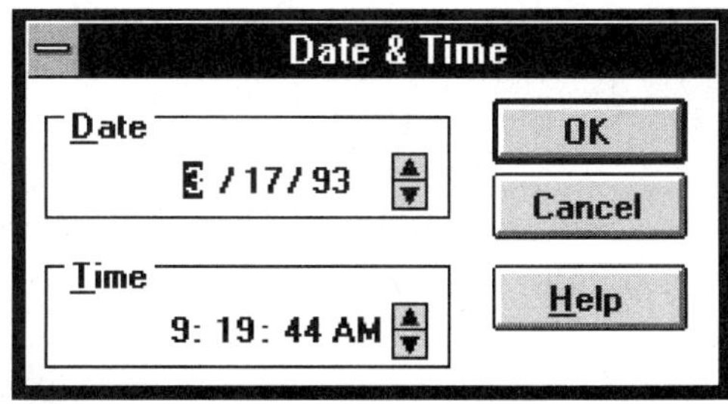

FIGURE 5.7
The Date & Time dialog box

Select the part of the date (day, month, or year) that you want to change. To do this, place the cursor pointer at the location that you want to change. Type in the new number (day, month, or year). If you are using the keyboard, press ⟦Tab⟧ to position the cursor on the number that you wish to change. The time is changed in the same manner that the date is changed. Position the cursor on the time box, selecting the part of the time (hour, minute, second, AM or PM) that you want changed. Type in the new values. To complete the change, click or choose OK. Of course, you can cancel the command if you change your mind.

GUIDED ACTIVITY 5.9

Looking at Date/Time (CHANGE ONLY IF NECESSARY)

1. Open Control Panel from Main in Program Manager.

2. Double-click on the Date/Time icon.

3. If the Date is not correct, click on and highlight the part of the date that is incorrect. You can make the appropriate change by clicking on the up or down arrow to the right of the Date.

4. Repeat step 3 to correct Time.

5. Click on OK to complete the change.

6. Close Control Panel.

GUIDED ACTIVITY 5.10

Looking at Date/Time (CHANGE ONLY IF NECESSARY)

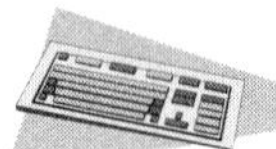

1. Open Control Panel from Main in Program Manager.

2. Press [Alt][S] for the Settings menu. Select Date/Time.

3. If the Date is not correct, press [Alt][D] and use [Tab] to move to the part that is incorrect. Type in the correction.

4. Repeat step 3 to correct Time, except press [Alt][T] instead of [Alt][D].

5. Press [Enter] to complete the change.

6. Close Control Panel.

Configuring the Printer

The Printer icon is a tool that will help you set up your printers and select printer options. Usually, your laboratory manager will install the appropriate printer driver files to support the printer or printers that you will be using. In addition, he or she may determine the port to which the printer is connected. In the event that you need to add printer drivers or change the default drivers, you may want to consult the Windows *User's Guide*.

It is necessary to **configure** your software (Windows 3.1) to the specific hardware (printer). Depending on the type of printer that you will be working with, Windows 3.1 contains a list of supported printers. To choose a printer, double-click on the Printers icon from the Control Panel. The Printers dialog box will appear, as shown in Figure 5.8. Select Connect from the Printers dialog box. From the Connect choice, a dialog box like that in Figure 5.9 will appear, indicating the current options for the selected printer. You may make any changes at this time. To complete the process of changing printers, click or choose OK.

FIGURE 5.8
*The Printers
dialog box*

FIGURE 5.9
*The Connect
dialog box*

If your Windows 3.1 is installed on a ***network***, printing will be placed in the print queue and the job will print in the order that it was received. Your lab supervisor should have installed the appropriate printer drivers for your particular situation and should be consulted if you run into any problems when printing on a network.

GUIDED ACTIVITY 5.11

Looking at the Printer

1. Open Control Panel.

2. Double-click on the Printers icon.

3. A Printers dialog box will appear. Inspect the information *only*. Notice that the box will list the installed printers.

4. Click on the Connect button.

5. Inspect the Ports box. You will see the list of ports available for the printer. *Do not change the current setting!*

6. Click on Cancel to keep the current settings. Click on Cancel again to close Printers.

7. Close Control Panel.

GUIDED ACTIVITY 5.12

Looking at the Printer

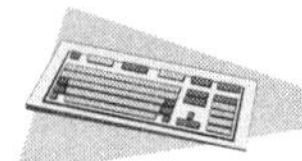

1. Open Control Panel.

2. Press [Alt][S] for the Settings menu. Select Printers.

3. A Printers dialog box will appear. Inspect the information *only*. Notice that the box will list the installed printers.

4. Press [Alt][C] for the Connect command.

5. Inspect the Ports box. You will see the list of ports available for the printer. *Do not change the current setting!*

6. Press [Esc] to keep the current settings. Again press [Esc] to close Printers.

7. Close Control Panel.

Advanced Control Panel Operations

The remaining Control Panel icons, Ports, Drivers, International, Sound, and *386 Enhanced* are considered advanced operations. Since this portion of the text is designed as an introduction to Windows 3.1 basic operations, we will defer further discussion to a later unit.

Review Questions

*1. How many icons are in the Control Panel, and what do they allow you to do?

*2. How can the color scheme be changed using the mouse? Using the keyboard?

*3. What is a font? Why is it recommended that you remove any fonts that will not be used?

4. Review the processes that do the following: change desktop patterns, adjust keyboard speed, change the system date/time, and configure the printer.

Key Terms

386 Enhanced	Connect	Tiled (wallpaper)
Centered (wallpaper)	Font	Typematic key
Color palette	Network	Wallpaper
Color scheme	None (pattern)	

Documentation Research

To answer the following questions, use Chapter 5, "Control Panel," of the *User's Guide*. Check the guide's index to find pages with the information needed. We recommend that you also write the relevant page number next to each question. For additional aid, you may need to use Control Panel's on-line Help menu.

1. How do you remove a desktop pattern that is no longer being used?

2. Give the steps to install a printer driver file by using Control Panel.

3. What can you do if your printer is not listed in the Printers dialog box?

4. If you are using a network, how do you connect to a network printer?

5. Assume that you are a left-handed mouse user. Is it possible to customize the mouse? Explain.

6. Using Control Panel's on-line Help, search for 386 Enhanced Minimum Time Slice Option.

7. Using Control Panel's on-line Help, read the description for 386 Enhanced Multitasking Options for Windows in foreground/background.

Print Manager

Print Manager is the utility in Windows 3.1 that sends information or data that you created through Windows application utilities (such as documents and pictures) to a printer. Print Manager allows you to send several documents to the printer at the same time. When you do this, Print Manager serves as a traffic controller, keeping track of each job in a print queue and sending it to the printer in the order that it was received. Print Manager also shows the status of each print job until it is completed.

This unit assumes that you have properly connected a local printer (or a network printer) to your computer and that the appropriate printer drivers have been installed. If you are running Windows in a network, you may need to consult the *User's Guide* or check with your system's laboratory supervisor for specific questions on printing.

Learning Objectives

At the completion of this unit, you should know

1. the purpose of Print Manager,

2. the various commands and options available in Print Manager.

At the completion of this unit, you should be able to

1. start and exit Print Manager,

2. see the status of the files you are printing,

3. pause and resume printing,

4. delete files waiting to be printed,

5. rearrange the order in which files are to be printed.

Using Print Manager

With Print Manager, printing is done in the *background*, which means that once you send a document to the printer you can continue to work with another application in the *foreground*. You do not have to wait until the printing is completed in order to go on with your work.

If you have more than one printer connected to your system, Print Manager will handle the assignment of a specific printer to a particular application. Print Manager manages a separate *queue* for each printer and sends the data to each printer as it is selected. A queue is a list of items to be printed. For example, you may want to print several documents on a laser printer and others on a dot-matrix printer. If so, Print Manager serves as a "traffic controller," directing the printing in the manner that you select.

Print Manager is extremely efficient if you have large printing jobs from different Windows applications. Print Manager is not recommended for printing of non-Windows applications. As a matter of fact, there may be times when you wish to print non-Windows applications directly, rather than using Print Manager. These applications are normally printed through DOS or through their own print facility. However, keep in mind that you may have to wait until the document is printed before any other work can be done on that document or application, or before you can return to Windows.

Starting Print Manager

Print Manager is normally found in the Main program group in Program Manager. It is started automatically whenever an application program begins to print. In Figure 6.1, the file READM.TXT was opened from Notepad and printing was started. Notice that Print Manager's icon is present in the lower-left corner of the screen.

The icon disappears from the screen as soon as all pending print jobs are sent to the printer. If you restore (open) the icon, you will be able to see the print queues reflecting the status of the job. You can also run Print Manager from Program Manager through the Main program group by double-clicking on its program item icon.

FIGURE 6.1
Print Manager operating in the background while another application is open

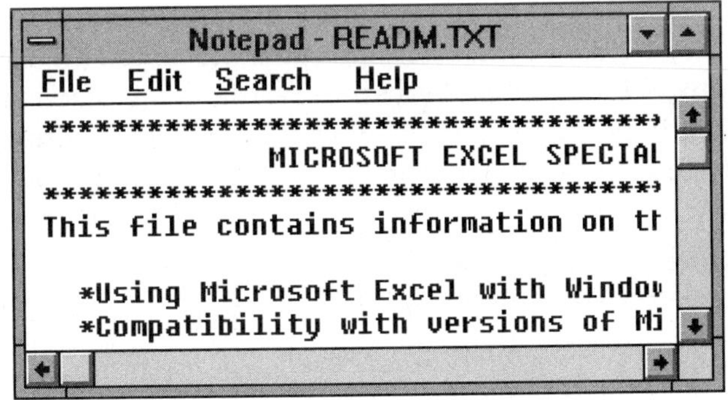

GUIDED ACTIVITY 6.1

Printing a File

1. Open Notepad from the Accessories program group by double-clicking on its icon.

2. Click on File from the menu bar and then on Open.

3. From the File Open dialog box, double-click on the file SETUP.TXT. The file will appear in the Notepad window.

4. Print the file by clicking on File and then on Print. (Make sure the printer is on.)

5. Close Notepad by clicking on the Control Menu box and then on Close.

GUIDED ACTIVITY 6.2

Printing a File

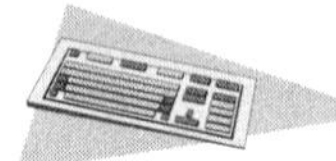

1. Open Notepad from the Accessories program group by highlighting its icon and pressing [Enter].

2. Press [Alt][F] for the File menu. Select Open.

3. From the File Open dialog box, press [Tab]. Using the arrow keys, highlight the file SETUP.TXT, and press [Enter]. The file will appear in the Notepad window.

4. Print the file by pressing [Alt][F]. Select Print. (Make sure the printer is on.)

5. Close Notepad by pressing [Alt][Spacebar] for the Control menu. Then select Close.

The Print Queue

The print queue is where Print Manager maintains the status for any pending print jobs. The dialog box, which appears when Print Manager is activated, will list those files that are currently being printed, as well as those files waiting to be printed, as shown in Figure 6.2. A file's status can be changed anytime prior to the time that the print command is executed. For example, you can Pause the printing, Resume printing after it has been paused, or Delete a job from the print queue.

Print Manager has two types of print queues: local and network. The *local print*

FIGURE 6.2
Print Manager window

Printer queue information line

File information line

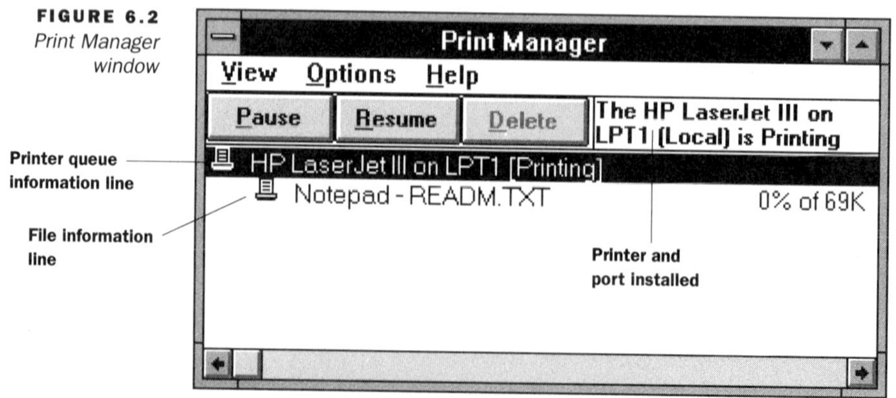

queue means that a printer is connected by a cable directly to your computer. The *network queue* refers to the print queue on the network server. It is managed by a completely separate network print manager, which is different from the one found in Print Manager. Your instructor or laboratory system supervisor should be consulted if you have any questions about using a network.

Quick Printing

Windows 3.1 offers a new "drag-and-drop" printing feature that prints a file if you drag the icon of the file from File Manager to the Print Manager icon. To use this feature, do the following:

1. Open Print Manager by double-clicking on its icon, then click the minimize button.

2. Open File Manager and locate the file to be printed.

3. Drag the file icon from File Manager to the Print Manager icon.

The application that created the file will be opened if is is not already open. This feature allows you to obtain a quick printout of a file without going through the steps of opening its original application.

INSPECTING THE PRINT QUEUE

When you select a file to be printed in an application such as Write, Print Manager is started automatically. Its icon will appear at the bottom of the screen. If you maximize (enlarge) the icon to a window, you will see the print queue for any active printer installed on your computer. If you have more than one printer connected to your computer, you will see multiple printer queue information lines, as well as a print queue for each printer.

GUIDED ACTIVITY 6.3

Inspecting the Print Queue

1. If the SETUP.TXT file is still printing from Guided Activities 6.1 or 6.2, go to step 2. If the file is not printing, open Notepad, open the file, and print it again. Then, immediately proceed with step 2.

2. Double-click on the Print Manager icon (from the keyboard, highlight the icon and press [Enter]) from the Main program group. The *printer queue information line* will tell you (a) the name of the printer, (b) the port where the printer connects to your computer, and (c) the current status of the printer. The *file information line* gives you information specific to the file, including (a) the application and file sent to the printer, (b) the file's position in the queue, (c) the size of the file in kilobytes, and (d) the time and date you sent the file to Print Manager.

Changing the Order of the Queue

You can change the position of a file in a local print queue, as long as that file has not yet started printing. You *cannot* change the order of a file in a network queue. To change the order of a queue, select the file you want to change, drag it to a new position in the print queue, and then release the mouse button. If you are using the keyboard, press Ctrl and ↑ or ↓, simultaneously, to move the file to a new location in the print queue, then release the Ctrl and arrow keys.

Pausing and Resuming Printing

In the event that you wish to temporarily interrupt the printing of a document, Print Manager will allow you to do so. The dialog box shown in Figure 6.3 illustrates the commands for Pause, Resume, and Delete.

FIGURE 6.3
*Print Manager
queue control
buttons*

**Queue control
buttons**

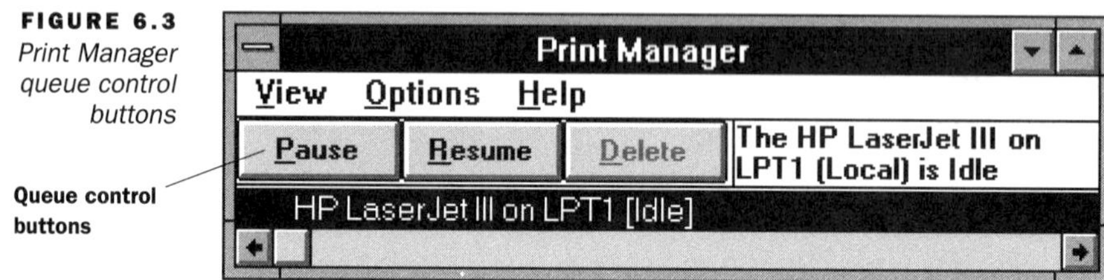

Working with the Print Queue

1. Open Notepad and click on File. Then click on Open. Double-click on a listed file, for instance SETUP.TXT.

2. Click on File and then on Print to print the file.

3. To inspect the queue, immediately double-click on the Print Manager icon, which appears in the lower part of your screen.

4. To interrupt printing, click on the Pause box. The information line will indicate that printing has paused, but the printer might not stop immediately if special hardware or software, called a *buffer*, has been installed. To continue printing after the pause, click on the information line for the printer queue. Then, click on the Resume box. The selected information line changes to indicate that printing has resumed. Your network printer driver may not permit you to pause during printing.

Working with the Print Queue

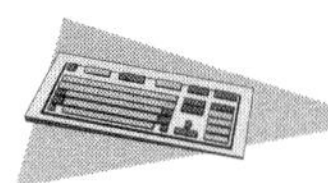

1. Open Notepad and press [Alt][F]. Select Open. Press [Tab], then highlight a listed file, for instance SETUP.TXT, and press [Enter].

2. Press [Alt][F] for the File menu. Select Print to print the file.

3. To inspect the queue, immediately press [Alt][Tab] until the Print Manager icon is highlighted, then release [Alt].

4. To interrupt printing, press [Alt][P] for the Pause box. The information line will indicate that printing has paused, but the printer might not stop immediately if special hardware or software, called a *buffer*, has been installed. To continue printing after the pause, highlight the information line for the printer queue. Then, press [Alt][R] for the Resume box. The selected information line changes to indicate that printing has resumed. Your network printer driver may not permit you to pause during printing.

Deleting a File from a Print Queue

To delete a file from a print queue, use the Delete command in Print Manager. To delete a file, (1) select the information line for the file from the print queue; (2) click or choose the Delete command (or [Alt][D], if using the keyboard), whereupon a dialog box will appear, prompting you to confirm your selection; (3) choose OK to complete the deletion.

If you want to delete *all* files from print queues, (1) select Exit from the View menu, as shown in Figure 6.4, upon which a dialog box will appear; (2) choose or click OK to complete the deletion. Deleting a file from a print queue in a network environment may not be possible. Check with your instructor for any special conditions.

FIGURE 6.4
Print Manager View menu

GUIDED ACTIVITY 6.6

Deleting a Print Job

1. Open Notepad. Click on File and then on Open. Double-click on a file.

2. Click on File and then on Print to print this file. Immediately double-click on the Print Manager icon that will appear at the bottom of the screen.

3. From the Print Manager dialog box, click on the file information line, then click on the Delete box. Click OK to confirm.

4. Close Print Manager by clicking on the Control Menu box (upper-left corner) and then on Close.

5. Close Notepad.

GUIDED ACTIVITY 6.7

Deleting a Print Job

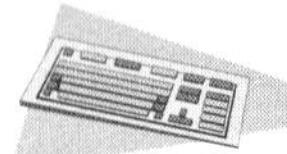

1. Open Notepad. Press [Alt][F] for the File menu. Select Open. Highlight a file and press [Enter].

2. Press [Alt][F], and then select Print to print this file. Immediately press [Alt][Tab] until the Print Manager icon is highlighted, then release [Alt].

3. From the Print Manager dialog box, highlight the file information line, then press [Alt][D] for the Delete command. Press [Enter] to confirm.

4. Close Print Manager by pressing [Alt][Spacebar] for the Control menu. Select Close.

5. Close Notepad.

Exiting from Print Manager

Print Manager (if running from its icon) terminates automatically when it finishes printing the document. You can select the Exit command from the File menu to exit from Print Manager. Be sure that all documents have finished printing before you attempt to exit, since any print jobs remaining may be lost. A warning message (dialog box) will appear if you try to exit with files still in the print queue. At this point, you can cancel the Exit command, which will allow you to finish printing, by selecting the Cancel button on the warning message.

Possible Problems While Printing in Print Manager

Sometimes you may have a problem when printing in Print Manager. Refer to the *User's Guide* for possible solutions. Some problems encountered in printing include:

- Printer does not print.

- Printer advances the paper but does not print.

- Page prints but is formatted incorrectly.

- Printer output is garbled.

- Printer output from two files gets mixed.

- Laser printer does not print your cartridge or soft fonts.

- Printer loses text.

- Only part of a page prints.

- Lines are missing from a Paintbrush drawing.

Your instructor or laboratory system supervisor may be able to help you if you encounter these or other printing problems.

NOTE *Keep in mind that procedures for printing on a network will differ from those for printing on a local printer. If you are using a **Novell network**, you may need to refer to the Novell user's manual for help with any problems you encounter during printing.*

Review Questions

*1. What is meant by printing in the background?

*2. Briefly, identify and describe the types of print queues in Print Manager.

3. List the steps required to change the order of print jobs in a queue.

4. How is the printing of a document temporarily interrupted using Print Manager? How is a file deleted from a print queue?

*5. State at least five problems that may occur while printing in Print Manager.

Key Terms

Background
Buffer
File information line
Foreground

Local print queue
Network queue
Novell network

Printer queue information
line
Queue

Documentation Research

To answer the following questions, use Chapter 6, "Print Manager," of the *User's Guide*. Check the guide's index to find pages with the information needed. We recommend that you also write the relevant page number next to each question. For additional aid, you may need to use Print Manager's on-line Help menu.

1. What happens when information is transferred from Print Manager to the printer using

   a. Low Priority?

   b. Medium Priority?

   c. High Priority?

2. What do the following Print Manager messages mean?

   a. Alert Always

   b. Flash if Inactive

   c. Ignore if Inactive

3. Can you bypass Print Manager when you want to print on a network printer?

4. What are some possible solutions if your printer does not print at all?

5. Using Print Manager's on-line Help, what command is used to delete a file from the print queue?

6. Using Print Manager's on-line Help, how do you print without Print Manager?

Windows Applications

II

■ **PART II** introduces various Windows 3.1 applications. Unit 7 illustrates Windows' built-in word processing capabilities, contained in the program Write. Unit 8 features the program Paintbrush, which is for creating and editing pictures. Unit 9 covers Terminal, used for data communication. Unit 10 presents other Windows 3.1 accessories, such as Calculator, Calendar, Cardfile, Clock, Notepad, Object Packager, Character Map, Media Player, and Sound Recorder. Finally, Unit 11 introduces other members of the Microsoft family of products: Word for Windows, Excel, Project, and PowerPoint.

Write

Microsoft Write is a word processor that allows you to create memos, reports, and letters. It permits you to include pictures as part of your text. It supports most printers using any font that has been installed for your specific printer. Write is another Windows application that incorporates WYSIWYG (what you see is what you get) technology. You can format paragraphs flush left, flush right, centered, or justified and can choose from three line-spacing options. Headers and footers are also an option.

Although Write is not as powerful a word processor as Microsoft Word for Windows, using it offers a good introduction to word processing in a graphical environment. Documents that you create with Write can be transferred through Clipboard to other Windows applications.

Learning Objectives

At the completion of this unit, you should be able to

1.   start and exit Write,

2.   create a document in Write,

3.   save and retrieve a document in Write,

4.   edit a document in Write,

5.   format characters, paragraphs, and pages in Write,

6.   use on-line Help in Write,

7.   print a document in Write.

Starting Write

To start Write, open the Accessories window. Double-click on its icon, shown in the margin. The Write window shown in Figure 7.1 will open.

At the top of the Write window a menu bar lists the commands File, Edit, Find, Character, Paragraph, Document, and Help. In addition, you will see:

- The *insertion point*, which indicates where the text appears (the upper-left corner of the window when you first open Write).

- The *end mark*, which indicates the end of a document. Since Figure 7.1 shows an untitled document that is currently empty, the end mark is next to the insertion point. This adjusts as you enter text.

- The *page status area*, which tells you the page you are on. Until you insert page breaks or create more than one page of text, you will see this as "Page 1."

- The *mouse pointer*, which appears as an *I-beam* (if you have a mouse connected to your computer). It indicates where the mouse is pointing inside the Write window and where the insertion point will move to if you click the button (except that you cannot move the insertion point beyond the end of the document).

The remaining parts of the Write window screen include the familiar scroll bars, mini-mize-maximize buttons, and menus. You can also have a "ruler" at the top of the screen, as discussed later in this unit.

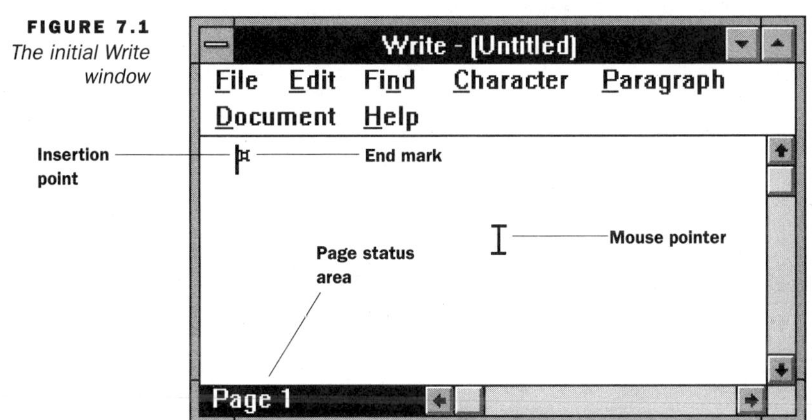

FIGURE 7.1
The initial Write window

Using Help in Write

Write contains an outstanding on-line Help facility. From the menu bar, select Help, and a drop-down dialog box like the one shown in Figure 7.2 will appear. Help is available for Contents, Search for Help on, How to Use Help, and About Write. You should scan these topics to become familiar with the capabilities of Help. Each of the Help topics can be invoked by pressing its appropriate letter or by positioning the mouse pointer on the topic and clicking. Figure 7.3 shows an example of the information available in Help. Help is very thorough and quite informative.

Using Write

Entering text in Write is simplicity itself. When you are ready to begin, just start typing. The text that you enter will appear at the insertion point. As you reach the end of a line, Write uses *word wrap*, which automatically jumps text to the next line. You do not have to press the [Enter] key to start a new line. If a word is too long to fit on the line, Write automatically moves the entire word to the next line. If the Write window is not as wide as the document, you will not see all the text on a line. For instance, in Figure 7.4, the word "as" is off the right side of the screen.

Hard returns (created by pressing [Enter]) are used to create paragraphs. To start a new paragraph, press [Enter] twice, which will leave a blank line between the paragraphs, as shown in Figure 7.4. Or, if you prefer indented paragraphs, press [Enter] once, then [Tab].

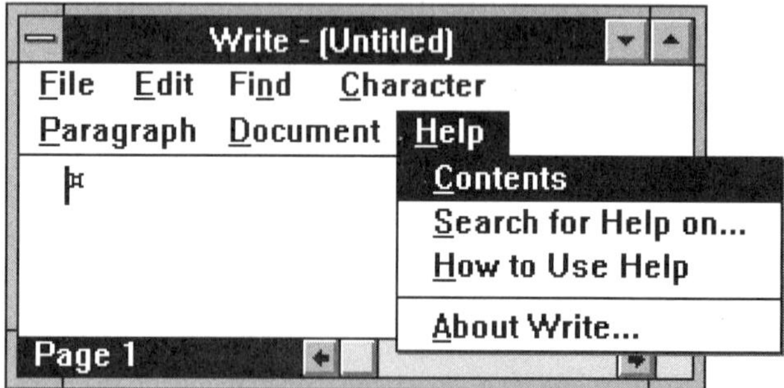

FIGURE 7.2
The Help menu

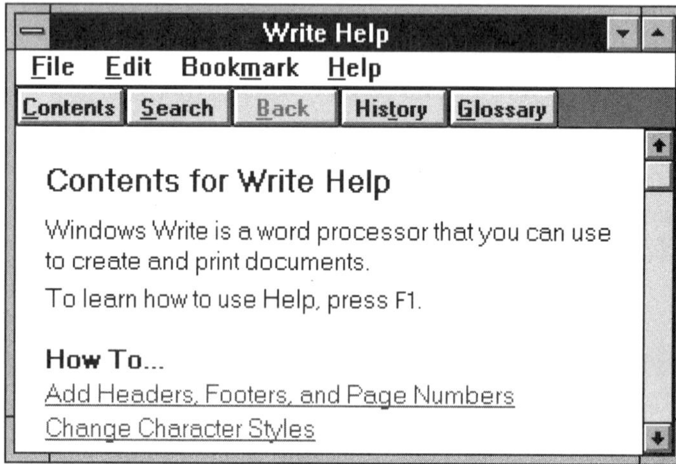

FIGURE 7.3
The Help contents

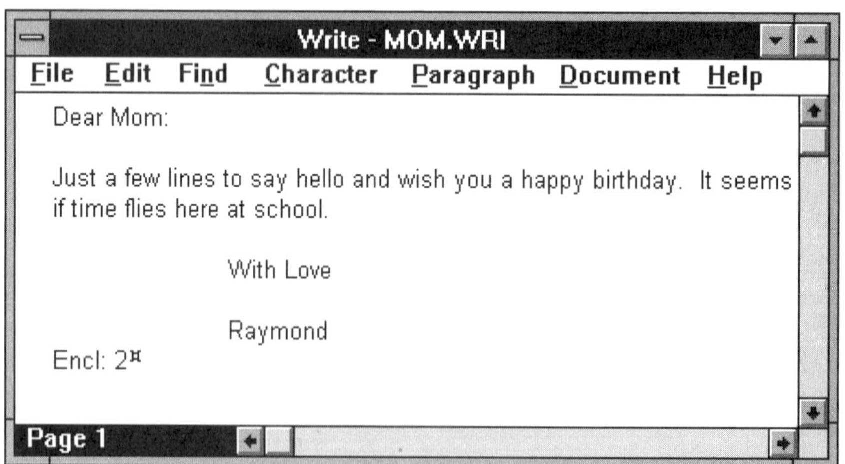

FIGURE 7.4
Creating a letter using Write

Editing Text

Editing in Write is performed very much the same as editing in any other Windows application. You may wish to refer to Unit 2 for a refresher. If you make a mistake while typing, press [Backspace] to erase the mistake. You can also use [Del] and [Ins] when editing.

Pressing the [Ins] key will shift to *overstrike* mode. To replace text, position the cursor with the mouse (or use the arrow keys on the keyboard) on the text you want replaced; then type in the new text. As you do this, notice how the old text disappears as the new text takes its place.

If you want to erase a small portion of text, position the cursor at the insertion point, either before or after the text you want erased. Then, press [Del] or [Backspace]. The [Backspace] key erases text to the left of the insertion point, while [Del] erases text to the right. In the event that you need to erase a large amount of text, you can mark the text that you want erased. To mark text with the mouse, position the cursor on (or to the left of) the first character to be deleted and drag the mouse pointer to highlight all the characters, words, or lines you want to delete. (Using the keyboard, hold down [Shift] and use arrow keys to highlight the text.) You will notice that the block of text will be shaded in black, as shown in Figure 7.5. Press [Del] to erase this block of text. If you delete too much, *immediately* use the Edit Undo command.

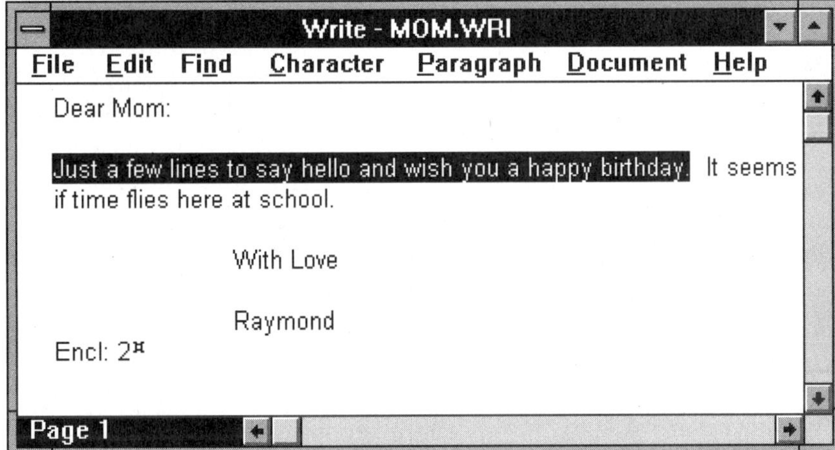

Formatting a Document

After your document has been created, you probably will want to format it. Making your document appear professional entails choosing a suitable type style, ample spacing, legible alignment of lines, and an attractive overall page layout. The WYSIWYG concept applies to formatting since "what you see on the screen is what you get on the printer."

To format with the Character menu, you must first mark the text you want to format, as in Figure 7.5, then select the desired command from the Character menu shown in Figure 7.6.

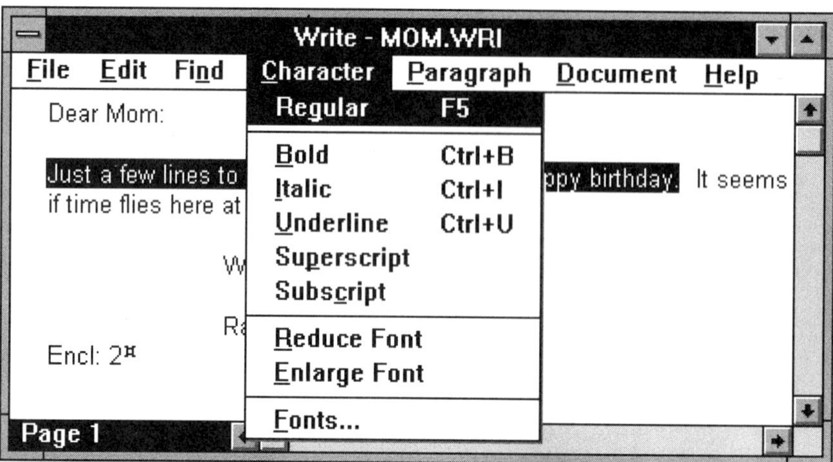

You can use Regular, Bold, Italic, Underline, Superscript, and Subscript. Each of these choices can be invoked with a single letter designation. As a shortcut, press Ctrl with B, I, or U to bypass the menu for bold, italic, or underline style. The six style options are illustrated in Figure 7.7.

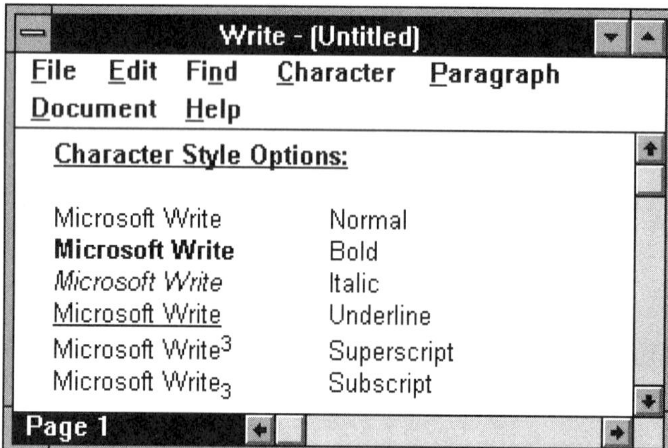

Write saves character formats when you save your document. Also, Write transfers character formats if you copy or move formatted text either to another location in the document or to another Write document.

Using Fonts

Just as you are able to change character styles in Write, you can also change the font. Recall that a font is the design or shape shared by a set of alphanumeric characters. The fonts that are available to you will depend on the type of printer being used. For example, a dot-matrix printer may not contain the same fonts as a laser printer. Figure 7.8 illustrates several different fonts. Normally, printed versions of the fonts look better than the screen versions do.

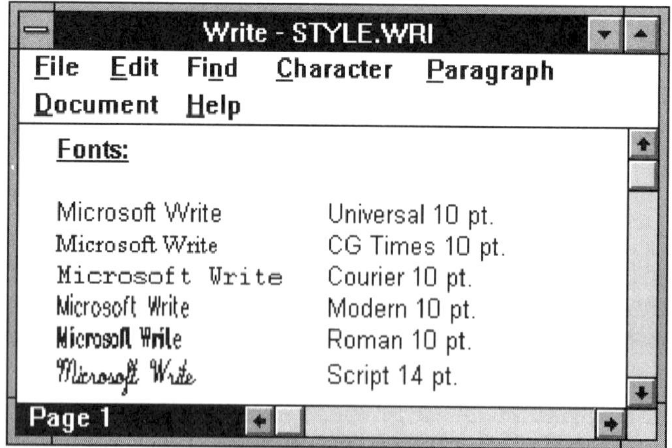

The Font dialog box shown in Figure 7.9 is

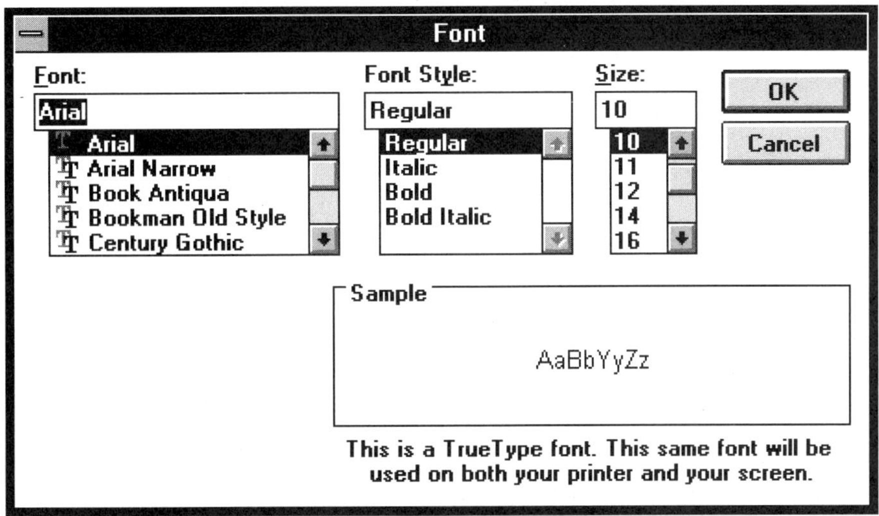

obtained from the Character menu. You can either type the name of the font you want or press [Alt][F] to enter the font list. The list of fonts may be different on your computer, depending on the fonts that have been installed.

Point size can be selected from this dialog box. A point equals ¹⁄₇₂ of an inch and describes the height of a character. The point size is selected with the scroll bar, or you can place the pointer on the list and click the mouse button. You may wish to scroll through the fonts listed to find one that is suitable.

Font and style of text permit you to enlarge or reduce text to add special effects to your document. For instance, if you want to create a memo letterhead, the size of your company name can be set at point size 24. The subject line can be underlined, and the sender's name can be in bold.

Formatting Paragraphs

You can change the format of paragraphs to achieve a more professional look for your document. *Text alignment* can be set to left-aligned, centered, or right-aligned. You may align part or all of your text. Write automatically aligns your text flush with the left margin as you type. A paragraph that is left-aligned will show a straight edge on the left margin, but the right margin will be uneven or jagged. Text can also be centered on the page. Titles are usually centered. Right alignment is the opposite of left alignment, in that the right edge is even and the left margin is jagged. Figure 7.10 shows examples of these formats.

Paragraphs can also be *justified*. The justify command in the Paragraph menu will adjust both margins (left and right) so that they are straight, as well as adjust the text on the line so that spaces between words will appear approximately the same. Text adjustment is a nice feature not offered by all word processors.

Write also allows you to choose the *line spacing* within the paragraph. Your choices are single spaced, double spaced, or one-and-a-half spaced.

You can use commands on the Paragraph menu or the *ruler* to change the format in each paragraph of a document. To display the ruler, choose Ruler On from the

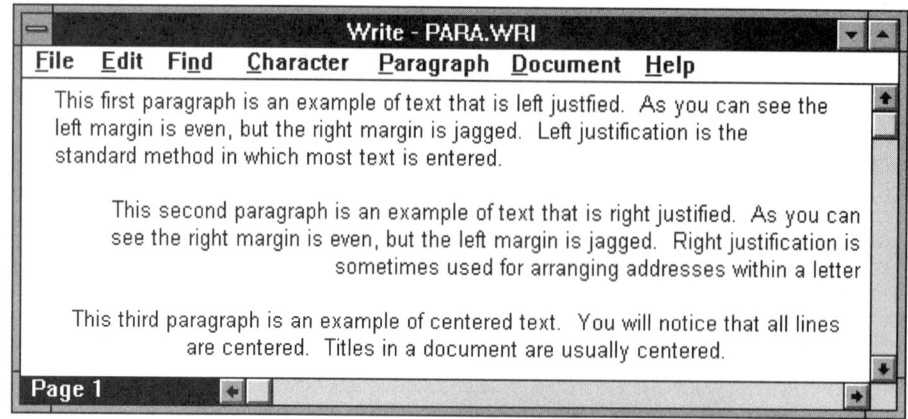

Document menu and the ruler will appear as shown in Figure 7.11. Notice the various icons for justification and line spacing.

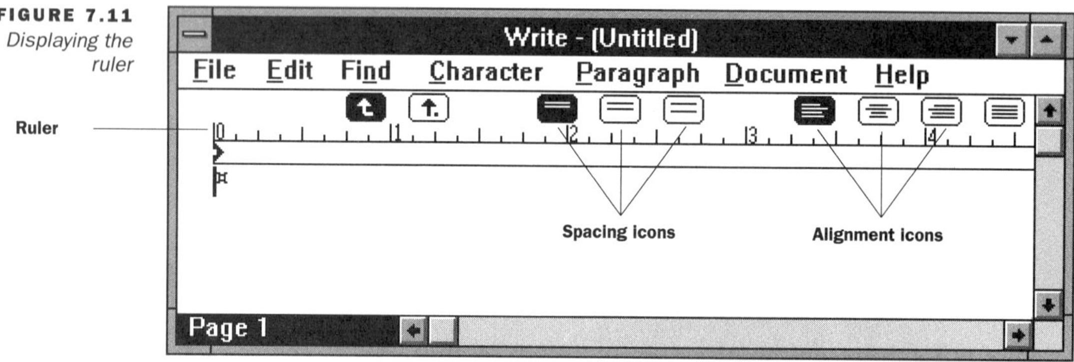

Retrieving, Saving, and Printing a Document

To retrieve or open a Write file, select the Open command from the File menu shown in Figure 7.12, then select the file name from the Open dialog box displayed in Figure 7.13. In most educational settings, you will save your documents on a floppy disk (normally in drive A:). If that is so, double-click on the drop-down list for drives to make the A: drive the default drive.

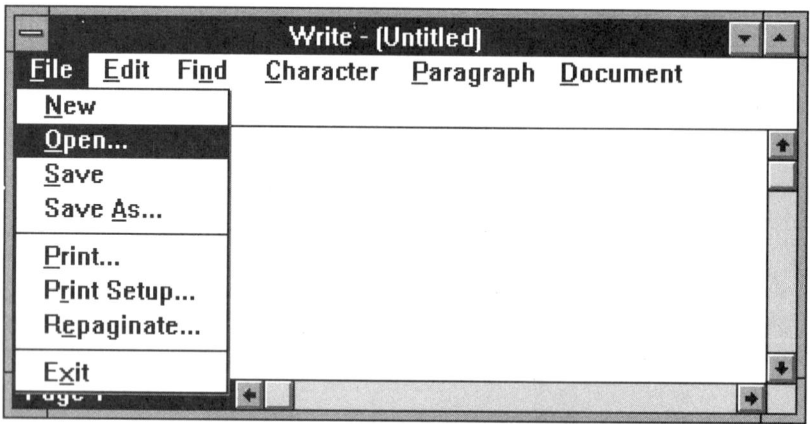

FIGURE 7.13
*The Open
dialog box*

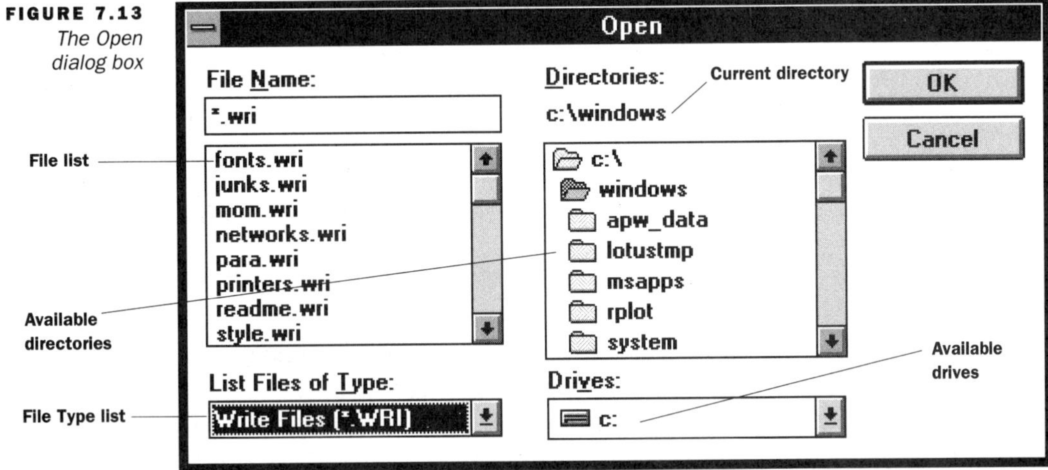

The Open dialog box lists all file names with a .WRI (for Write) extension, as well as directory names. Click on or highlight the name of the file you want to retrieve, then choose or click OK to complete the action.

To save a file, select the Save or Save As command from the File menu. Use Save As the first time you save the file so that it will have a name (other than "Untitled"). Be sure to save to the proper disk (or directory): Usually you will have to designate the proper disk (or directory) by clicking on the drop-down list for drives (your instructor might give you different instructions). Use Save after the first time, unless you want to change the name or file format. When you use Save As, the dialog box illustrated in Figure 7.14 appears, where you can type the file name of the document that you want saved. When you are using Write for a long document, you should save your work often. A good rule of thumb is to save about every 15 minutes or less. Power failures or other unexpected occurrences can result in the loss of your data unless it is saved.

Write allows five formatting options when you save a document. Choose the option you desire from the Save File as Type list box.

FIGURE 7.14
*The Save As
dialog box*

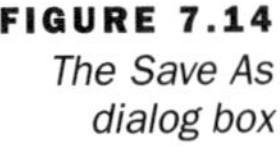

Format	Result
Write Files	A .WRI extension is added to the file name
Word for DOS Files	A .DOC extension is added to the file name
Text Files	A .TXT extension is added to the file name
Word for DOS/Text only	A .DOC file with no text formatting, only the words
All Files	*.* Global wild cards allow you to furnish file name and extension

To print a document, select the Print command from the File menu. Printing in Write is very similar to printing in other Windows applications. Once you select the print command, the Print dialog box appears, as shown in Figure 7.15. Select the print options that you want, then choose or click OK to start printing. Of course, you can Cancel the command if you wish to do so.

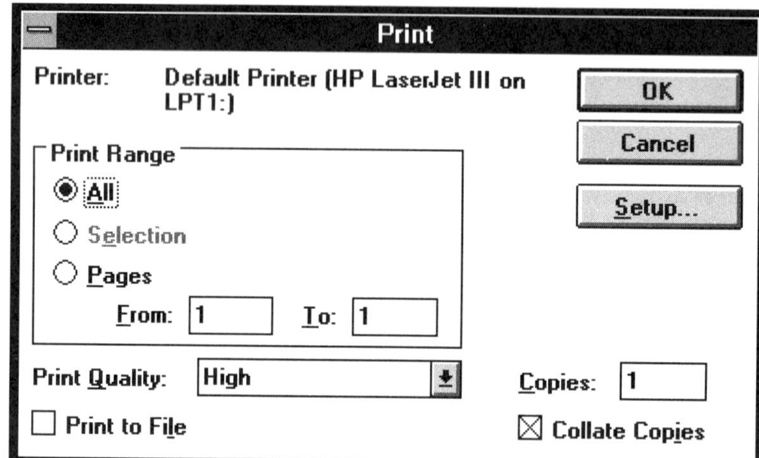

FIGURE 7.15
The Print dialog box

The print options include the number of Copies you want to print, whether you want to print All pages or print From a certain page To a specific page, and a Print Quality option (a quick print of an unformatted copy of the text in your document). Any pictures that you want to print will appear as empty boxes if you select a lower Quality.

NOTE *You may wish to refer to Unit 6 for assistance in printing.*

Exiting Write

When you are finished creating, editing, or printing a document in Write, you will need to save the document and exit. To exit or quit Write, select the Exit command from the File menu. If you have made any changes in your document without saving, a dialog box will appear, asking you to confirm your choice, as in Figure 7.16. You can select Yes, No, or Cancel to complete the process.

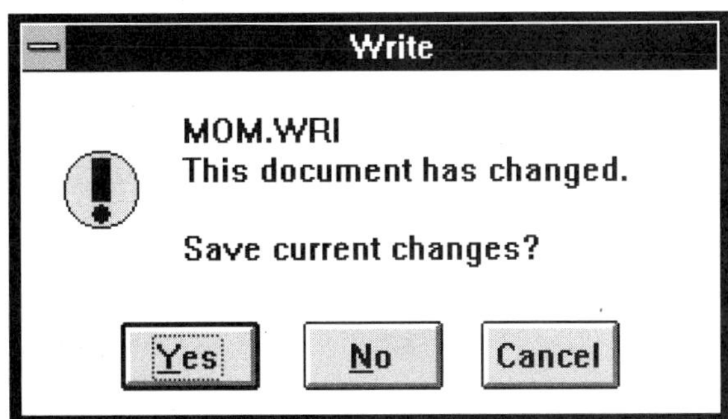

Creating a Document

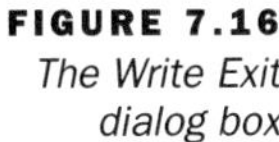

1. Open Write from the Accessories program group.

2. Type a short letter to "Mom" or a friend.

3. Click on File and then on Save As. Click on the drop-down list for drive A: (under "Directories," you might have to scroll up the list to select drive A:. Click File Name, enter MOM, then click on OK.

SHORTCUT *When the File Save As dialog box first appears, type* A : MOM *and press* Enter.

4. Edit the file for these changes (highlight the text using the mouse by going to the first letter of the text, pressing and not releasing the mouse button, moving the mouse to the last letter of text, and releasing the mouse button):

   a. Add or delete phrases.

   b. Using Character, change the salutation to bold.

   c. Using Paragraph, Justify the text.

   d. Using Character, change your name to italic.

   e. Using Fonts in Character, change the font size to 14.

   f. Save the file again (click on File and then on Save).

5. Click on File and then on Print. Click on OK to print the file.

6. Close Write.

Creating a Document

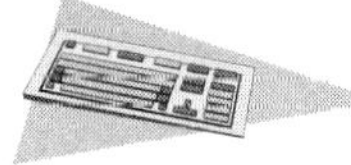

1. Open Write from the Accessories program group.

2. Type a short letter to "Mom" or a friend.

3. Press [Alt][F] for the File menu. Select Save As, then [Tab] to Directories (or press [Alt][D]) and highlight drive A: from the drop-down list and press [Enter], then [Tab] to the File Name box and type the name MOM. Press [Enter] to complete the Save.

SHORTCUT   *When the File Save As box first appears, type* A : MOM *and press* [Enter].

4. Edit the file for the changes that follow (highlight the text using the keyboard by going to the first letter of the text, pressing and holding [Shift], using the arrow keys to highlight the text to be affected, then releasing [Shift]):

   a. Add or delete phrases.

   b. Using Character ([Alt][C]), change the salutation to bold.

   c. Using Paragraph ([Alt][P]), Justify the text.

   d. Using Character ([Alt][C]), change your name to italic.

   e. Using Fonts in Character ([Alt][C]), change the font size to 14.

   f. Save the file again (press [Alt][F], and then select Save).

5. Press [Alt][F] for the File menu. Select Print. Press [Enter] to print the file.

6. Close Write.

Review Questions

1. Briefly explain the following terms: insertion point, end mark, page status area, mouse pointer, and word wrap.

*2. How is a large area of text erased most efficiently?

*3. In Write, do character formats transfer if formatted text is copied or moved to another location and/or Write document?

4. What is a font?

*5. What is meant by text alignment being left-aligned, centered, right-aligned, justi-fied?

6. Review the command(s) to do the following: save, retrieve, and print a document.

7. Briefly, identify and describe the five formatting choices that Write invokes when saving a document.

8. What type(s) of help is (are) available in Write?

Key Terms

End mark	Line spacing	Ruler
Hard return	Mouse pointer	Text alignment
I-beam	Overstrike	Word wrap
Insertion point	Page status area	
Justified	Point size	

Documentation Research

To answer the following questions, use Chapter 9, "Write," of the *User's Guide.* Check the guide's index to find pages with the information needed. We recommend that you also write the page number for each question. For additional aid, you may need to use Write's on-line Help menu.

1. Using the on-line Help in Write, how many help topics are listed for Commands?

2. Using the on-line Help in Write, how do you change paragraph line spacing?

3. Using the on-line Help in Write, how do you change tabs?

4. On what page in the *User's Guide* will you find how to display the ruler?

5. What command is used to hide the ruler?

Paintbrush

Microsoft Windows Paintbrush is a graphics program that allows you to create and edit a variety of drawings. Using Paintbrush, you can prepare greeting cards, newsletters, letterheads, text banners, line diagrams, or sophisticated art. Your imagination is the only limit to Paintbrush!

Learning Objectives

At the completion of this unit, you should know

1. the anatomy of Paintbrush,

2. the differences between raster and vector graphics.

At the completion of this unit, you should be able to

1. start and exit Paintbrush,

2. use the toolbox,

3. create simple drawings.

Introduction

Paintbrush is a computer-aided drawing program. As you progress through this unit, you will understand and be able to use the "tools" that Paintbrush offers. Paintbrush is easy to use because its icons are very descriptive and easily understood. You do not have to be an artist to be able to use and understand Paintbrush. This unit gives a brief introduction to Paintbrush and its capabilities; you will have to experiment, use the on-line Help, and consult the *User's Guide* to become adept at using this creative tool.

Paintbrush makes extensive use of the mouse. As you can well imagine, a mouse is much easier and more efficient to use than the keyboard when creating drawings. However, you can use the keyboard to move around within Paintbrush, using techniques described later in this unit.

Graphics Formats

Paintbrush and many other "paint" programs deal with each "dot" on the screen, affecting its color by altering the amount of red, green, and blue used in its composition. These programs are called *raster graphics* because they are based on the movement of the raster (the electric beam that paints any cathode ray screen). The files are saved in *bitmap* or similar format, using various coding schemes that remember the color of each dot. Depending on your monitor and software setup, you might see these images in 16 or 256 (or up to 16 million!) colors or shades of gray. Bitmap graphics files are easy to create and save, although it is difficult to change the size of a bitmap image.

Other graphics programs deal with objects such as lines, arcs, and polygons. These are described to the computer as vectors, which can be *scaled* (sized) as necessary. Although *vector graphics* files are more complex, it is easier to manipulate discrete objects (such as the image of a chair or table) in this format.

Paint programs like Paintbrush are usually preferred for artistic endeavors, while vector programs are preferred for technical drawing such as in architectural or engineering work. The understanding of raster versus vector graphics is not vital to your use of Paintbrush, but it is useful to know which class of images Paintbrush produces.

Starting Paintbrush

Paintbrush

To start Paintbrush, double-click on its program icon. The icon is usually in the Accessories program group. If you do not have a mouse and are using the keyboard, press [Alt][W]. Program Manager's Window menu will appear. Select Accessories; use the arrow to highlight the Paintbrush icon, and press [Enter]. The opening screen is illustrated in Figure 8.1.

NOTE *The figures in this unit are black and white. On a color monitor, you will see the color palette on the screen instead of the shades of gray boxes as portrayed in the figure.*

Elements of the Paintbrush Window

Paintbrush makes use of the following elements:

- The *workspace* is the area where you will create your drawings.

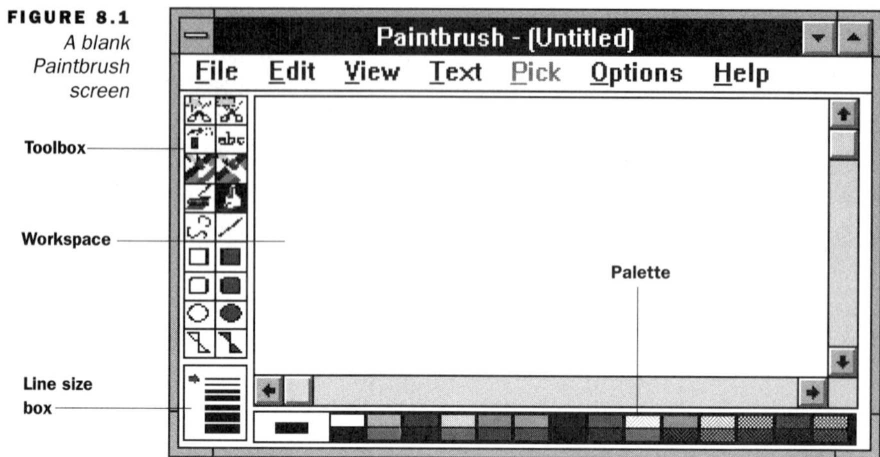

- The *cursor* indicates where a line or other object will be placed when you start your drawings. If you are using the keyboard, press [Tab] or an arrow key. The cursor shape differs, depending on the tool that is being used.

- The *toolbox* contains the tools that you use to create drawings. These tools include fill, airbrush, erase, enter text, cut, and so forth.

- The *palette* contains the colors and patterns available.

- The *line size box* contains the available drawing widths.

Cursor Shapes

Paintbrush uses different cursor shapes, depending on the drawing or editing tool that you are using. Normally, the default tool is the brush. At other times during your drawing, you will see the following cursor shapes:

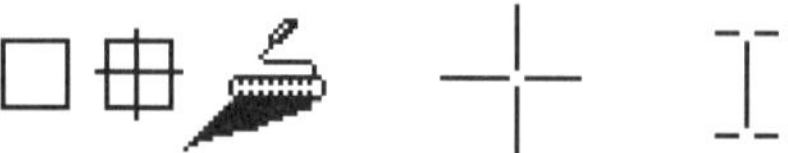

The cursor shapes represent a box, crosshairs in a box, a paint roller, crosshairs, and an I-beam, as well as other shapes depending on the specific drawing tool in use. When you use text, the cursor will appear as an insertion point and an I-beam. You may recall using the I-beam and insertion point in Write. The mouse pointer (also called the "arrow") is used as a cursor as well. When you place the mouse outside the drawing area, the pointer resumes its normal arrow shape and is used to select commands and operations.

The Color Palette

Paintbrush normally offers 16 different colors in the palette at the bottom of the screen. On some systems, you might see as many as 256 colors or shades of gray. In Paintbrush you will use both a *foreground color* and a *background color*. Choose the foreground color by pointing to the desired color and pressing the left mouse button (or [Ins]). Choose the background color by pointing to the desired color and pressing the right mouse button (or [Del]). The foreground color is used for most drawing operations, the background color for backgrounds and some special effects.

Using the Toolbox

Paintbrush uses the toolbox for its drawing *tools*. These tools can be grouped into three categories: graphic, text, and editing. Graphic tools are used for drawing shapes (line, circle, box, brush, and the like). Text tools enable you to add labels to your drawing; text is represented by the ABC icon. The final category, editing tools, permits you to change portions of your drawing. The Scissors, Pick, Color Eraser, and Eraser icons are used to make changes.

The following table lists the name of the tool, its icon, and a short description of each tool.

Name	Icon	Description
Scissors		To select an irregular shaped cutout
Pick		To select a rectangular cutout
Airbrush		To create a "spray paint" effect
Text Tool	abc	To add letters, numbers, and words in various typefaces, sizes, and styles
Color Eraser		To change the foreground color to the background color in a portion of the drawing
Eraser		To remove an object or text from a drawing
Paint Roller		To fill enclosed areas with the foreground color

Name	Icon	Description
Brush		To create freehand lines
Curve		To draw smooth curves
Line		To draw straight lines
Box		To create unfilled rectangles
Filled Box		To create rectangles filled with a color
Rounded Box		To create rectangles with rounded corners: "roundtangles"
Filled Rounded Box		To create "roundtangles" filled with a color
Circle/Ellipse		To create unfilled circles and ellipses
Filled Circle/Ellipse		To create circles and ellipses filled with a color
Polygon		To create irregular closed shapes
Filled Polygon		To create irregular closed shapes filled with a color

The Line Size Box

This box allows you to select the width of the brush and eraser tools, the width of lines, and the size of the border around filled objects. With a mouse, click on the desired width. Using the keyboard, `Tab` to the box and press the arrow keys to select the width.

Simple Drawings

To use a graphic tool, click on the tool that you want and move the pointer first to the workspace and then to the position where you want to begin the drawing. The keyboard equivalents for basic mouse movements are as follows:

For This Mouse Action	*Press This Key or Key Combination*
Click left mouse button	`Ins`
Click right mouse button	`Del`
Double-click left mouse button	`F9` `Ins`
Double-click right mouse button	`F9` `Del`
Drag, hold left button	Hold down `Ins` and use arrow keys
Drag, hold right button	Hold down `Del` and use arrow keys

If you want to do some freehand drawing, your name for example, select the Brush tool from the toolbox, move the cursor to the workspace, and begin drawing, as shown in Figure 8.2. With the mouse, press and hold the left button as you "paint" the screen. With the keyboard, press and hold `Ins` while you use the arrow keys to "paint" the screen. Your initial efforts may be a bit shaky, but with practice you will soon become more skilled at using the various tools.

FIGURE 8.2
Freehand drawing

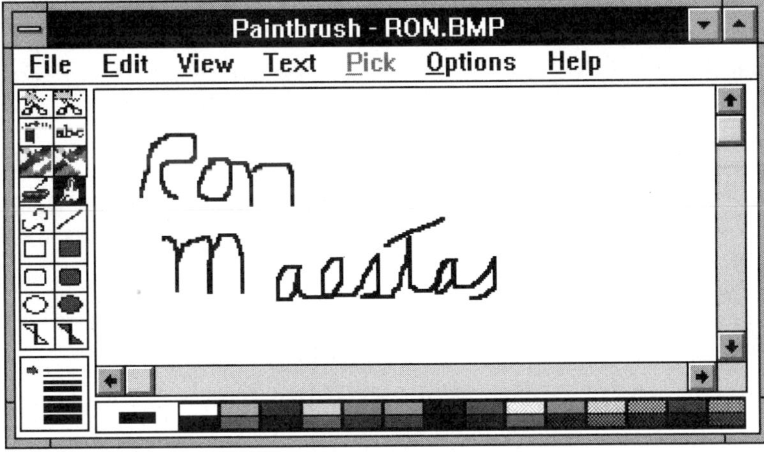

Entering Text

To enter Text, click on its icon, position the cursor in the workspace where you want to begin, and enter the text. Paintbrush allows you to select the Font, the Style,

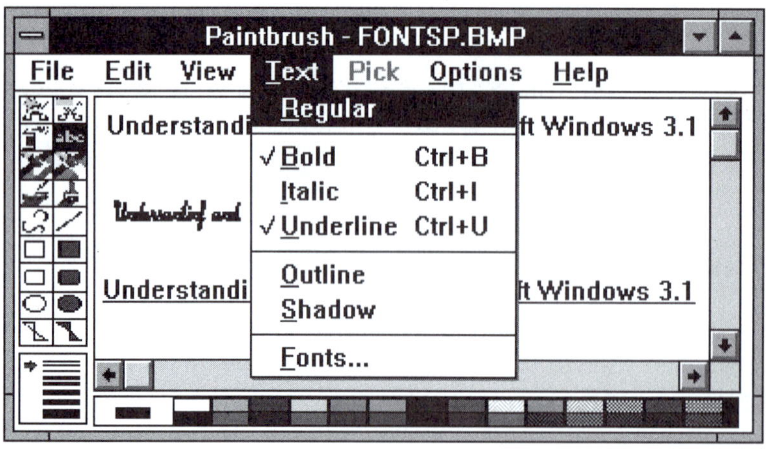

FIGURE 8.3
Paintbrush Text menu

and the Size of the text by selecting the Text command from the menu bar shown in Figure 8.3. Select Fonts from the menu. Another dialog box will appear listing the available styles and fonts installed on your computer. A sample of the chosen typeface is shown in Figure 8.4. Usually, it is a good idea to choose fonts that have the TrueType symbol next to them (such as Times New Roman in Figure 8.4). This symbol indicates a TrueType font. TrueType fonts give the best results on both screen illustrations

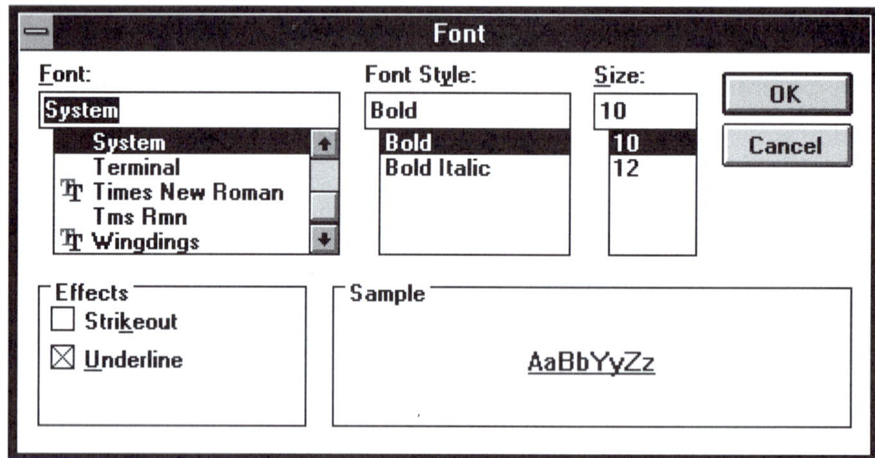

FIGURE 8.4
Font styles and sizes

and printed output. Clicking the top line evokes the regular style (neither bold or italic). Figure 8.5 illustrates various Text effects.

Using Drawing Tools

Before you begin working in the drawing area (workspace), you must select a tool from the toolbox at the left of the Paintbrush window, shown in Figure 8.6.

To select a tool, click the mouse button on it. With the keyboard, use [Tab] to get from the workspace to the toolbox area. When you are in the tools area, use the arrow keys to move the cursor to the tool that you want, then press [Ins] to complete the choice. Paintbrush will highlight the tool that you select.

To draw with the tool you have selected, move the cursor to the drawing area workspace and position it where you want to start drawing. Press the mouse button,

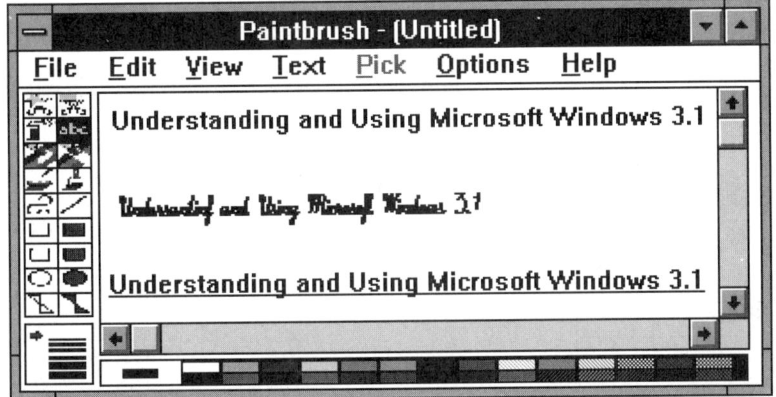

You can edit any mistakes with the Undo command in the Edit menu or with the Eraser tool in the toolbox. If you are using the keyboard, press Alt Backspace. You may want to experiment with drawing and editing. It takes some practice to become familiar with the toolbox, as well as with the drawing area. This experience is much like learning to ride a bicycle. After a few falls, you are able to straighten the wheels and enjoy the ride!

Saving Your Work

Work that has been created with Paintbrush can be saved very easily. Use the Save and Save As commands from the File menu shown in Figure 8.7. Use Save As the first time you save the file, and Save for subsequent saves. Save As also allows you to save the file under a different name or format.

If you select Save As, the File Save As dialog box will appear as in Figure 8.8. You will be prompted to enter a file name or a directory. You will notice a Save File as Type box in the lower-left corner. Save File as Type has a list of available formats for saving your work. Figure 8.9 illustrates some of the options that are available when the Save File as Type command is selected. These formats support compatibility with other graphics software.

Paintbrush will save each completed drawing as a .BMP file (bitmap format is used by many Windows programs). The formats include Monochrome bitmap, 16 Color bitmap, 256 Color bitmap, and 24-bit bitmap. The other available format, .PCX, is compatible with most other drawing programs. Refer to the user's manual of the specific graphics software for the appropriate format, if necessary. Your instructor may also provide you with some additional information regarding the graphic format that you are using. Generally, you will save your work in the .BMP file format.

FIGURE 8.7
The File menu

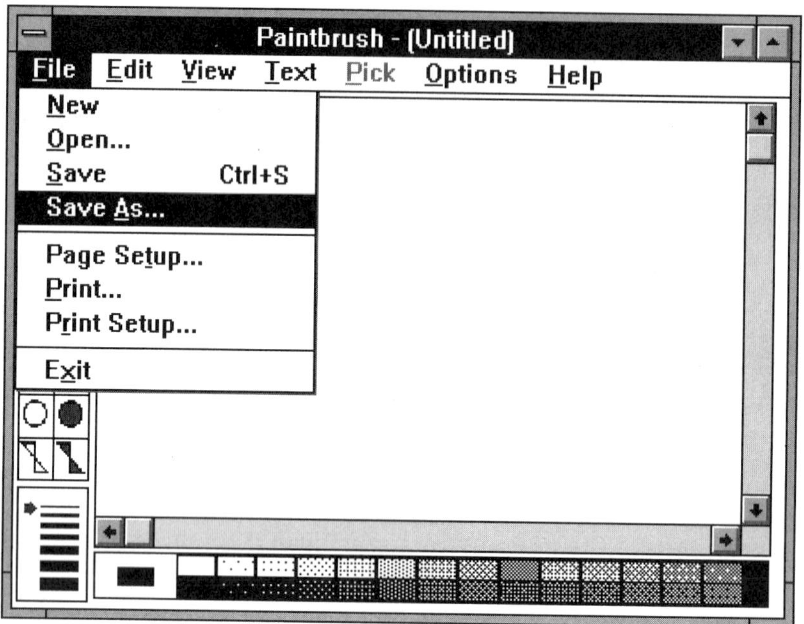

To complete the saving process, click or choose OK. You can, of course, cancel the command prior to your final selection. Remember to select the appropriate drive from the drop-down drive list. A word of caution while saving a drawing to drive A:—since bitmap files are normally quite large, you might not be able to save a file (.BMP) on a 360KB disk. You often need a *high-capacity disk* with 1.2MB or 1.44MB of disk space.

FIGURE 8.8
The File Save As dialog box

Exiting Paintbrush

Exiting Paintbrush is a very simple process, as with most other Windows GUI programs: Select Exit from the File menu as shown in Figure 8.10.

FIGURE 8.9
File Save As options

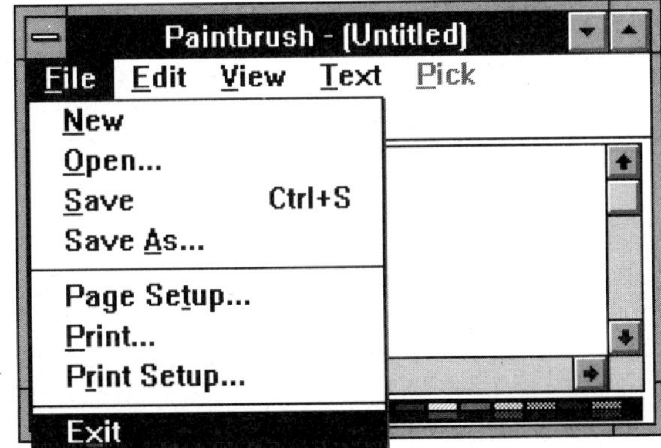

FIGURE 8.10
Exiting Paintbrush

GUIDED ACTIVITY 8.1

Practicing Fundamental Paintbrush Operations

1. Open Paintbrush by double-clicking its icon in the Accessories program group.

2. Click on the color black in the color palette at the bottom of the screen. Click on the Brush tool and move the mouse pointer to the center of the workspace.

3. Draw some circles by clicking and not releasing the left mouse button and moving the mouse in a circular motion. Release the mouse button when you are finished.

4. Click on the Brush tool and "write" your name in the workspace.

5. Clear the workspace by clicking on New from the File menu. You will be asked if you want the image to be saved; click on No.

6. Draw a line from the center of the workspace to the top using the Line tool from the toolbox. Notice that it is difficult to draw a perfectly vertical line. Pressing [Shift] and then dragging the line pointer will give you a vertical line. Draw several other lines.

7. Clear the workspace by clicking on Undo from the Edit menu or on New from the File menu.

8. Click on the Box tool from the toolbox. Draw a rectangular box by placing the mouse pointer near the upper-left corner of the workspace, dragging it near the lower-right corner, and releasing the mouse button. Make several more rectangles.

9. Experiment with the other tools, such as circle/ellipse and filled shapes. Use [Shift] to draw perfect circles.

10. Clear the workspace.

11. Click on the Text tool. Click on a spot in the upper-left part of the workspace; choose a font, size, and style; then enter your name, date, and class.

12. Clear the workspace.

13. Close Paintbrush by clicking on the Control Menu box and then on Close.

Practicing Fundamental Paintbrush Operations

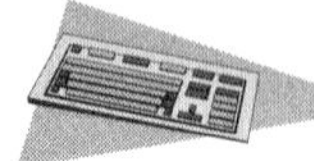

1. Open Paintbrush by highlighting its icon in the Accessories program group and pressing [Enter].

2. Press [Tab] until the pointer is located in the color palette. Using the arrow keys, move the pointer to the color black and press [Ins].

3. Press [Tab] until the pointer is located in the toolbox. Using the arrow keys, move the pointer to the Brush tool and press [Ins]. Press [Tab] until you see the pointer change to a small dot along the bottom border of the workspace. (This may be hard to see.)

4. Draw some designs by pressing and holding down [Ins] while using the arrow keys to move in a particular direction. Release [Ins] when you are finished.

5. Clear the workspace by pressing [Alt][F] for the File menu, and then selecting New. You will be asked if you want the image to be saved; press [N] for No.

6. Press [Tab] until the pointer is in the toolbox. Use the arrow keys to move the pointer to the Box tool. Press [Ins]. Draw a rectangular box by pressing [Tab] until you enter the workspace area. The pointer will change to a large plus sign (+). Using the arrow keys, move the pointer in the workspace to where you would like to begin a box.

7. Press and hold down [Ins]. Press [↑] five times and [→] six times. Release the [Ins] key. Make several more rectangles using the same technique.

8. Experiment with the other tools such as circle and filled shapes.

9. Clear the workspace.

10. Select the Text tool ([Tab] to toolbox, and so on). Move the cursor to a spot in the upper-left part of the workspace; choose a font, size, and style; press [Ins], then enter your name, date, and class.

11. Close Paintbrush by pressing [Alt][Spacebar] for the Control menu and then selecting Close.

Printing a Paintbrush Drawing

Printing a drawing is similar to printing in Write. When Paintbrush prints a drawing, it preserves the proportions of the drawing. It maintains squares and circles as they were originally drawn and does not change them to rectangles and ellipses. To print, select or choose the Print command from the File menu; a drop-down dialog box will appear as in Figure 8.11.

The Print dialog box is used to specify the quality of print (Draft or Proof), window (Whole or Partial), number of copies, and scaling (size) percentage. To complete the print process, select or choose OK. Keep in mind that the quality of the printout will depend on the printers installed on your system and on whether or not you are using a network. You should particularly keep in mind that printing through a Novell network may present some noticeable differences.

The Page Setup command on the File menu is used to change the margins on your drawing or add a header or footer. When Page Setup is selected, the Page Setup dialog box will appear as shown in Figure 8.12.

If you have more than one printer installed on your system, the Print Setup dialog box may need to be invoked. The Print Setup command is con-

FIGURE 8.11
The Print dialog box

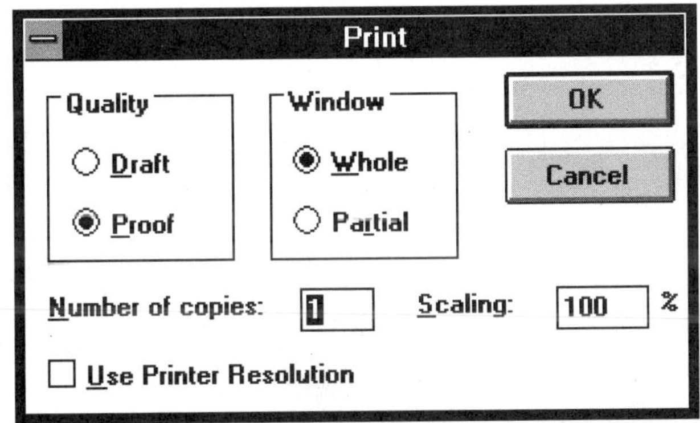

FIGURE 8.12
The Page Setup dialog box

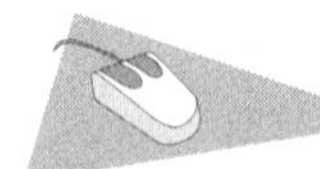

tained in the File menu. As you select this command, a dialog box will appear as shown in Figure 8.13.

This is used to identify the Printer, Paper Source, Paper Size, and Orientation of layout (***Portrait*** [taller than wide] or ***Landscape*** [wider than tall]). Click Options to select Graphics Resolution and Cartridges, if installed on your printer. Choose OK to complete the options and printer setup.

GUIDED ACTIVITY 8.3

Creating, Saving, and Printing a Drawing

1. Open Paintbrush.

2. Maximize the workspace by clicking on the maximize button in the upper-right corner of Paintbrush.

3. Create a sample floor plan for your future "office," using the various tools in the toolbox. Use Figure 8.14 as inspiration. Remember, to use a particular tool, click on that tool, enter the workspace, and begin to "draw."

4. Save the file by clicking on File and then on Save As. Click [- a -] under Directories. The following will appear in the Filename box: A:*.BMP. Highlight the asterisk (*), then type a name for the drawing, for example FLOORPLN. You should see A:FLOORPLN.BMP in the Filename box; click on OK to save the file.

SHORTCUT *When the File Save As dialog box first appears, type* A:FLOORPLN *and press* [Enter].

5. Click on Print from the File menu. Click on Proof from the Quality box in the Print box. Click on Whole from the Window box. Click on OK to print the file.

6. Close Paintbrush.

FIGURE 8.14
Drawing created in Paintbrush

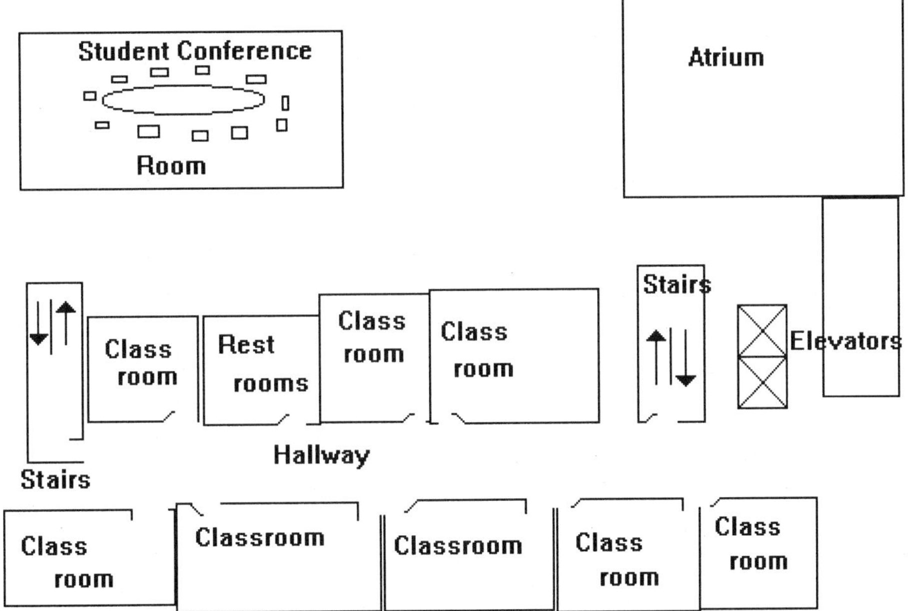

GUIDED ACTIVITY 8.4

Creating, Saving, and Printing a Drawing

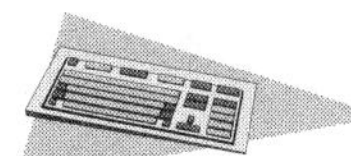

1. Open Paintbrush.

2. Maximize the workspace by pressing [Alt][Spacebar] to display the Control menu and then selecting Maximize.

3. Create a sample floor plan for your future "office," using the various tools in the toolbox. Use Figure 8.14 as inspiration. Remember, to use a particular tool, press [Tab] until the pointer is in the toolbox, use the arrow keys to move the pointer to that tool and press [Ins], then press [Tab] until the pointer is in the color palette. Select a color for the results of the tool, enter the workspace, and begin to "draw."

4. Save the file by selecting File and then Save As ([Alt][F], [A]). When the File Save As dialog box appears, type A:FLOORPLN and press [Enter].

5. Press [Alt][F] for the File menu. Select Print. Press [Alt][P] for Proof from the Quality box in the Print box. Press [Alt][W] for Whole from the Window box. Press [Enter] to print the file.

6. Close Paintbrush.

Transferring Artwork to Write

Artwork or diagrams created with Paintbrush can be transferred to a Write document and even to other word processors, such as Word for Windows, that are compatible with Windows operations. This process is known as ***cut and paste***. While you

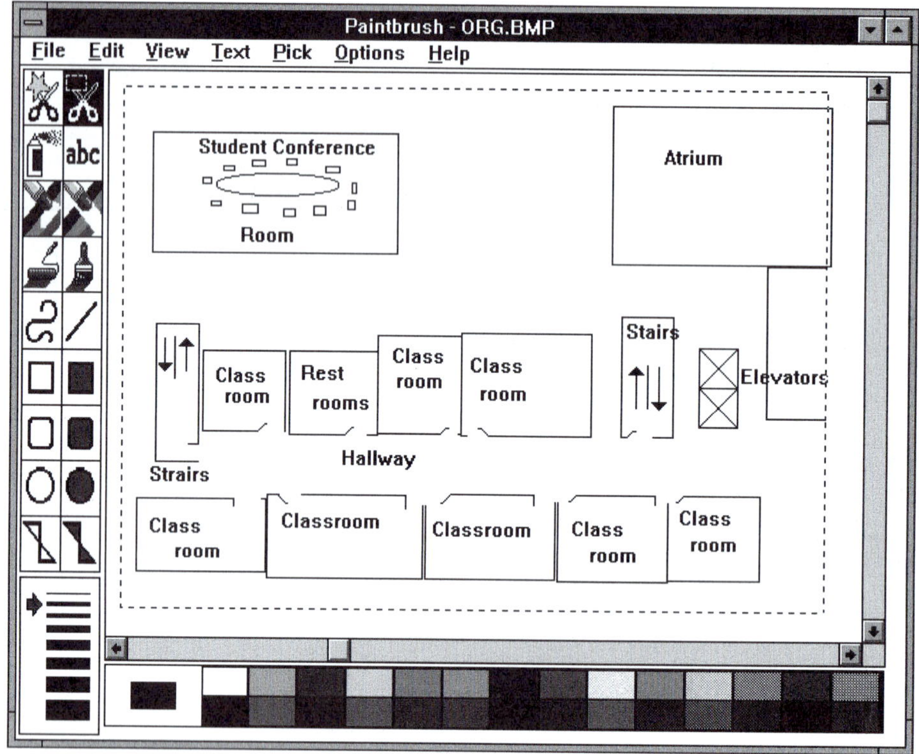

are in Paintbrush, Open the file containing the work that you want to transfer. Using the Pick tool from the toolbox, position the cursor in the upper-left corner of the art-work, drag the mouse pointer to the lower-right corner of the diagram, and release the mouse button. You will see the broken-line outline around the diagram, as shown in Figure 8.15. Select Copy or Cut from the Edit menu shown in Figure 8.16. Nor-

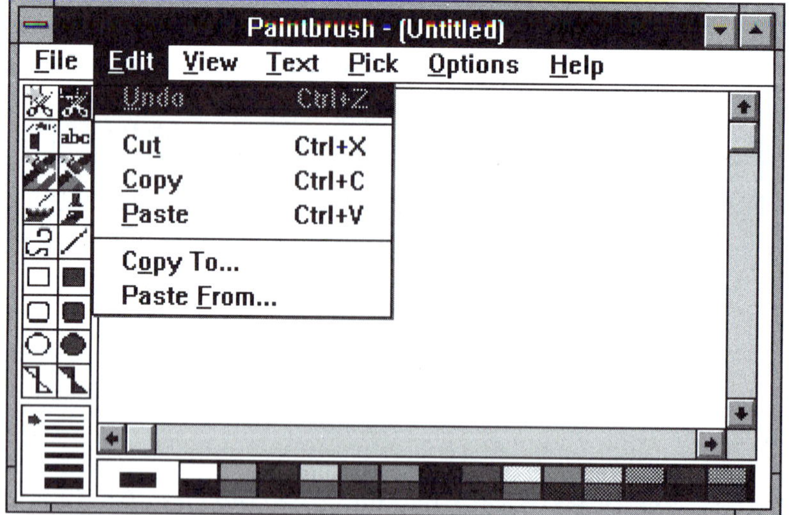

mally you would select Copy because you want to leave the original art intact.

Minimize Paintbrush to its icon. Open Write and select the destination file. Position the mouse pointer at the insertion point (where you want the diagram to appear), and select Paste from the Edit menu.

GUIDED ACTIVITY 8.5

Cutting and Pasting a Diagram to a Write Document

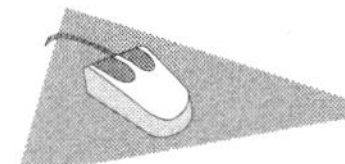

1. Open Write from the Accessories program group.

2. Type a letter to "Dad" telling him about your new position. Minimize Write by clicking on the Minimize button in the upper-right corner of the window.

3. Copy the "office" floor plan that you created in Guided Activity 8.3:

    a. Open Paintbrush by double-clicking on its icon.

    b. Click on File and then on Open. Double-click on the name of the "office" file that you created in Guided Activity 8.3.

    c. Click on the Pick tool from the toolbox. Move to the upper-left corner of the diagram. Click and do not release the mouse button. Drag the pointer to the lower-right corner of the diagram. Release the mouse button. A broken gray box will show the part of the diagram that is marked.

    d. Click on Edit and then on Copy.

    e. Minimize Paintbrush by clicking on the minimize button.

4. Restore Write by double-clicking on its icon. Position the mouse pointer (I-beam) at the point where you want to insert the diagram and click once. Click on Edit and then on Paste.

5. If the diagram that you have just pasted appears too small, you will need to enlarge the picture. Click on the picture. Select Size Picture from the Edit menu. Use the mouse to enlarge the picture. A light gray box will indicate the size of the picture as it is being enlarged. Clicking the mouse button will complete the sizing.

6. Save the file by clicking on File and then on Save. (Remember to choose drive A:.)

7. Click on File and then on Print. Click on OK to print the document with the diagram.

8. Close Write and Paintbrush.

GUIDED ACTIVITY 8.6

Cutting and Pasting a Diagram to a Write Document

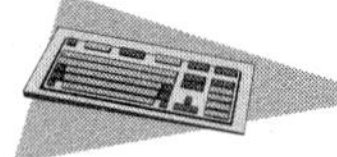

1. Open Write from the Accessories program group.

2. Type a letter to "Dad" telling him about your new position. Minimize Write by pressing [Alt][Spacebar] and then selecting Minimize.

3. Copy the "office" floor plan that you created in Guided Activity 8.4:

    a. Open Paintbrush by highlighting its icon and pressing [Enter].

    b. Press [Alt][F], and then select Open. Highlight the name of the "office" file that you created in Guided Activity 8.4.

    c. Select the Pick tool from the toolbox. Move to the upper-left corner of the diagram in the workspace. Press and hold down the [Ins] key. Using the arrow keys, drag the pointer to the lower-right corner of the diagram. Release [Ins]. A broken gray box will show the part of the diagram that is marked.

    d. Press [Alt][E] for the Edit menu. Select Copy.

    e. Minimize Paintbrush by pressing [Alt][Spacebar] and selecting Minimize.

4. Restore Write by pressing [Alt][Tab] until the Write icon is highlighted, then releasing [Tab]. Position the cursor at the point where you want to insert the diagram. Press [Alt][E] for the Edit menu. Select Paste.

5. If the diagram that you have just pasted appears too small, you will need to enlarge the picture. Move the cursor until the picture is highlighted. Select Size Picture from the Edit menu. Use the arrow keys to enlarge the picture; press [Enter] when done. A light gray box will indicate the size of the picture as it is being enlarged.

6. Save the file by selecting Save from the File menu. (Remember to choose drive A:.)

7. Press [Alt][F], and then select Print. Press [Enter] to print the document with the diagram.

8. Close Write and Paintbrush.

Review Questions

    ***1.** State the six mouse actions mentioned in this unit and their respective keyboard equivalents.

    2. Name the two categories in which images can be grouped. Identify the category of images produced by Paintbrush.

    ***3.** Briefly, identify and describe the elements of the Paintbrush window.

    4. Give an example of each of the following types of tools: graphic, text, and editing.

    ***5.** What is the major difference between the Copy and Cut commands in Paintbrush?

    6. If a mistake is made in Paintbrush, what are the options available to correct the mistake?

    ***7.** Describe the process required to select a tool from the toolbox using the mouse and keyboard.

    8. Review the processes to print and save a drawing and to exit Paintbrush.

    9. What is the name of the process that transfers artwork or diagrams created in Paintbrush to a Write or Word document?

Key Terms

Background color	Landscape	Toolbox
Bitmap	Line size box	Tools
Cursor	Palette	Vector graphics
Cut and paste	Portrait	Workspace
Foreground color	Raster graphics	
High-capacity disk	Scale	

Documentation Research

To answer the following questions, use Chapter 10, "Paintbrush," of the *User's Guide*. Check the guide's index to find pages with the information needed. We recommend that you also write the relevant page number next to each question. For additional aid, you may need to use Paintbrush's on-line Help menu.

1. How do you change the drawing size of Paintbrush?

2. List the advanced Paintbrush features.

3. What is the purpose of the Tilt command?

4. Using the on-line Help in Paintbrush, how do you draw a perfect circle?

Terminal

The Microsoft Windows application Terminal connects your computer to other computers. Its data communication capability enables you to dial remote sites (whether mainframes or other personal computers) so that you can receive or send files via telephone lines. National databases and on-line bulletin boards are readily available to personal computer users. With Terminal, you can use your computer to obtain financial investment data from the Dow Jones News/Retrieval service; shop at home with CompuServe; make reservations for air, lodging, or rental car; or send electronic mail with MCI. Other possible business applications for telecommunications include order entry, credit checking, inventory control, cash management, administrative messages, and resource management.

Before you can use Terminal, however, you must possess certain hardware. You must have a modem installed in or connected to your computer, and you must have a telephone (analog, not digital) line available. You will not be able to talk on the phone line while the computer is using it (a circumstance that causes great distress to our teenage children).

This unit is designed to give you the basics of Terminal's terminology, concepts, and procedures. If the subject of telecommunications is new to you, you might want to obtain additional reference materials. Because communications capabilities vary so much among organizations, we have not included a Guided Activity in this unit. If your school or organization has the appropriate facilities, your instructor or supervisor will provide you with further instruction on the use of Terminal.

Learning Objectives

At the completion of this unit, you should know

1. the anatomy of telecommunications,

2. the purpose and characteristics of a modem,

3. communications protocols.

At the completion of this unit, you should be able to

1. start and exit Terminal,

2. establish Terminal settings,

3. establish communications settings,

4. save and retrieve settings,

5. dial a call,

6. transfer files through a modem using Terminal,

7. send and receive files,

8. copy and paste received text.

Introduction

Telecommunications systems are fast becoming critically important assets to organizations, whether academic or corporate. They can help coordinate the activities of many people in various locations; they can reduce the costs of more traditional methods of communication and routine clerical activities; and they can improve sales through faster and better customer services.

As you probably are aware, we are living in an Information Age. Increasingly, vast amounts of information are readily available through "electronic libraries." In an era when timely information can give a competitive edge, businesses are relying heavily on telecommunications for their day-to-day operations. The wealth of information available to them is easy for you to access as well, but only if you know where and how to ask for and retrieve it. Terminal provides the means to put this vital information at your fingertips.

Telecommunications Concepts

Before you start working with Terminal, you should be aware of some basic telecommunications concepts and terms regarding both your computer and the remote computer with which you will be communicating. These concepts include: modem, baud rate, data bits, stop bits, parity, and data flow control. When you subscribe to an on-line service, you will receive the necessary information for these settings. The settings, which will vary from service to service, are often referred to as the *communications protocol*.

Figure 9.1 illustrates a connection made between two computers. A *modem* (short for *modulator/demodulator*) is a hardware device that converts digital signals (data from the computer) to analog signals (sounds that travel over telephone lines) at the sending end. At the receiving end, analog signals are converted back into digital signals used by terminals and computers. The digital signal must be modulated (converted) into an analog signal so that it can travel over the phone lines. Many

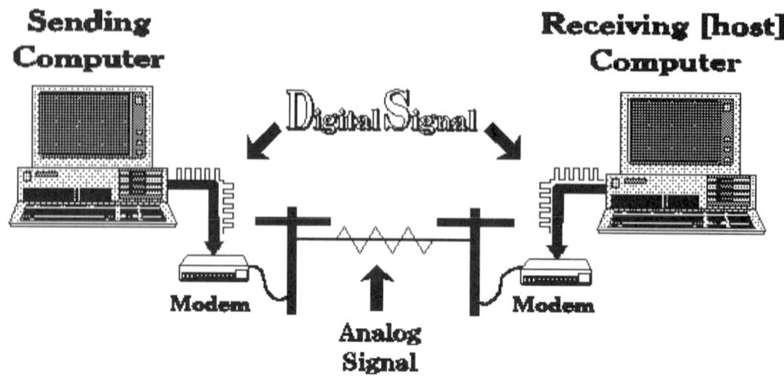

FIGURE 9.1
*Digital and
analog signals*

computers have built-in modems instead of the external modems illustrated in Figure 9.1.

Baud rate is the measure of the speed at which data are sent or received over a telephone line. The higher the rate, the faster the data can be sent. Modems are commonly available in 1200, 2400, and 9600 baud. If you try to connect to a 1200-baud modem from a 2400-baud modem, the 2400-baud modem will automatically switch to the 1200-baud rate. The transmission speed of a modem in characters per second is estimated by dividing the baud rate by 10; thus, a 1200-baud modem sends approximately 120 characters per second.

Data flows through the modem in a series of ones and zeros (digits). The number of ***data bits*** equals the number of ones and zeros in each piece of data, such as a single character. Both computer systems must use the same number of data bits. Two choices are available: 7 bits (which represents all the letters of the alphabet, numbers, punctuation marks, and some special symbols), and 8 bits (which is large enough for the entire IBM-PC character set). Both choices include one start bit and one stop bit. The ***stop bit*** is used as a signal to tell the receiving computer where one character ends and another begins. The most common setting is 8 data bits.

Parity is a method of detecting errors in the data being transmitted. By adding a one or a zero after the data, the telecommunications system alters the total number of ones to an even or odd number. Therefore, the choices for parity checking are Odd, Even, or None. The most common setting, when communicating with mainframes and on-line information services, is 7 E 1 (seven data bits, Even parity, and one stop bit). Public bulletin boards usually operate as 8-N-1 (eight data bits, No parity, and one stop bit).

The ***buffer*** area is a portion of memory used to hold incoming data. ***Data flow control*** is designed to notify the remote computer when Terminal's buffer capacity has been reached. Terminal needs to be able to notify the remote system to pause momentarily before sending any more characters; otherwise, incoming data could be lost while previously-received data are being written to a disk file. When Terminal is ready to receive again, it sends another signal to the sending computer. These "pause" and "resume" signals are known as ***handshaking***. The method of handshaking used is determined by the Flow Control setting. Terminal's default choice (Xon/Xoff) is the method most commonly used.

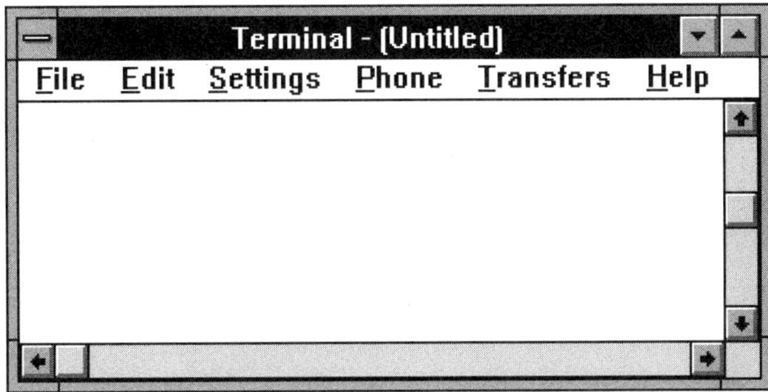

FIGURE 9.2
The initial Terminal screen

Starting Terminal

Terminal

To start Terminal, open the Accessories window. Once the Accessories window is active (opened), double-click on the Terminal icon (shown in the margin). If you are using the keyboard, highlight the Terminal icon and press [Enter]. The Terminal screen will appear as in Figure 9.2.

Terminal Settings

To initiate a Terminal session, you must indicate the settings for the remote computer, as well as any other settings you may want to use. You can use the settings from a previous communications session if you saved them in a ***settings file***. Settings files are saved with a .TRM extension. The choices on the first eight commands in the Settings menu, shown in Figure 9.3, will become Terminal's settings, which can be recorded in a file. Click the File menu and choose Save As; enter a file name for the protocol that you will use (for example, `DJNR` for Dow Jones News/Retrieval, or perhaps `DOW`).

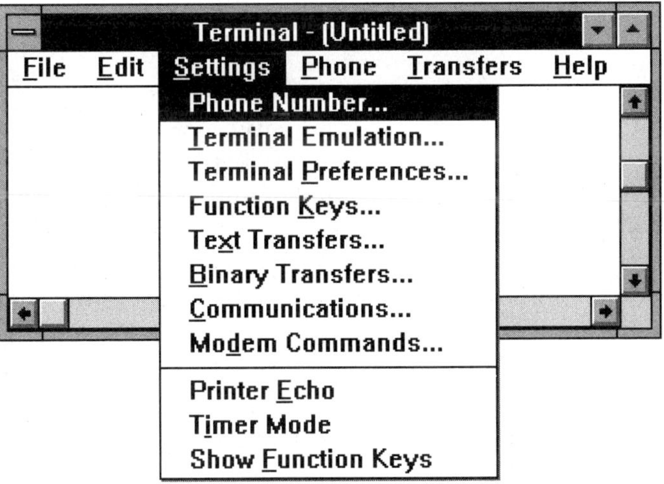

FIGURE 9.3
The Terminal settings file

To use the settings file, choose Open from the File menu. The dialog box will list any .TRM files that exist. Select the file that you want to use for that particular Terminal session.

Phone Number

The first setting is the Phone Number of the computer you want to reach. Its dialog box is used to indicate the telephone number you want to dial. The drop-down dialog box appears as in Figure 9.4.

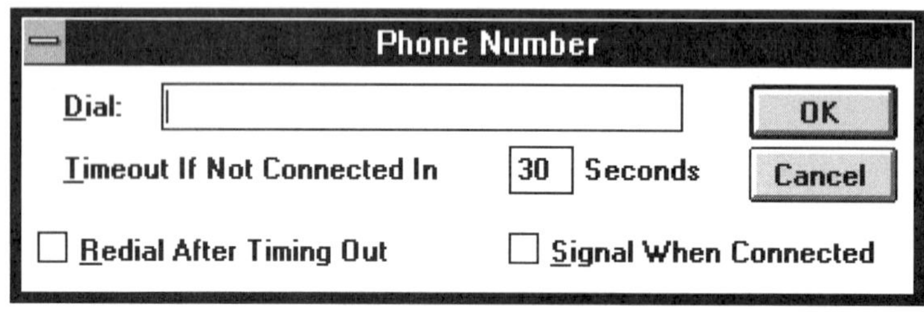

FIGURE 9.4
The Phone Number dialog box

In the Dial box, type the phone number that you want the modem to dial; if appropriate, include a 1 and the area code (for example, 1-505-454-3584). Parentheses or hyphens are *not* required (they are ignored by Terminal), but you can use them to make the number more readable. Use commas to provide any delays needed by your telephone system. A comma represents approximately a two-second delay. If your organization uses an outside line system, you might need to enter a 9, followed by one or more commas before the phone number (for instance, 9,,1-505-454-3584). If you have "Call Waiting" on your phone, you should disable it by adding *70,, to the beginning of the number.

Set the options that appear in the bottom half of the dialog box as necessary. These include: Timeout If Not Connected In (which many users set to 60 seconds), Redial After Timing Out, and Signal When Connected. To complete the Phone Number setting, click or choose OK.

Terminal Emulation

Terminal Emulation is designed to reflect the type of terminal the remote computer expects. Information on terminal type is available from the on-line service to which you are connecting. To select the type of terminal, click or choose Terminal Emulation from the Settings menu. The dialog box illustrated in Figure 9.5 will appear.

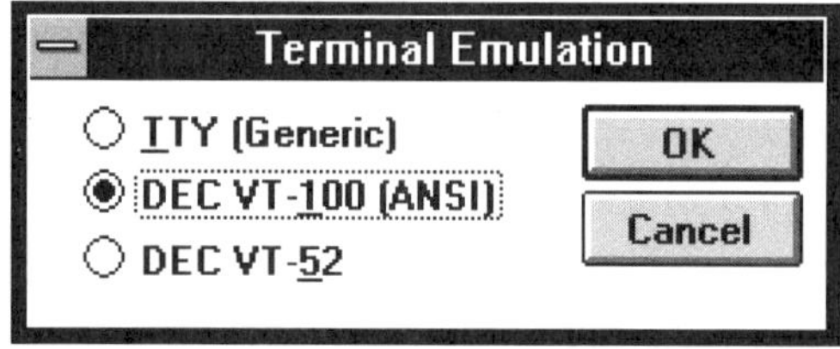

FIGURE 9.5
The Terminal Emulation dialog box

The list of terminal types appears in the dialog box. The choices for terminal type include TTY (Generic), DEC VT-100 (ANSI), and DEC VT-52. The default terminal type is DEC-VT-100 (ANSI). To change the terminal type, place the cursor on the terminal of your choice, and click the mouse button. If you are not sure which terminal type to use, select TTY.

Terminal Preference

Terminal Preference contains several choices that affect how your computer will respond during a communications session. These choices include Terminal Modes, Translation, Columns, Cursor, Terminal Font, CR to CR/LF, Show Scroll Bars, and Buffer Lines. Consult the Windows *User's Guide* for a detailed explanation of each choice. Generally, you should set up the preferences as illustrated in Figure 9.6.

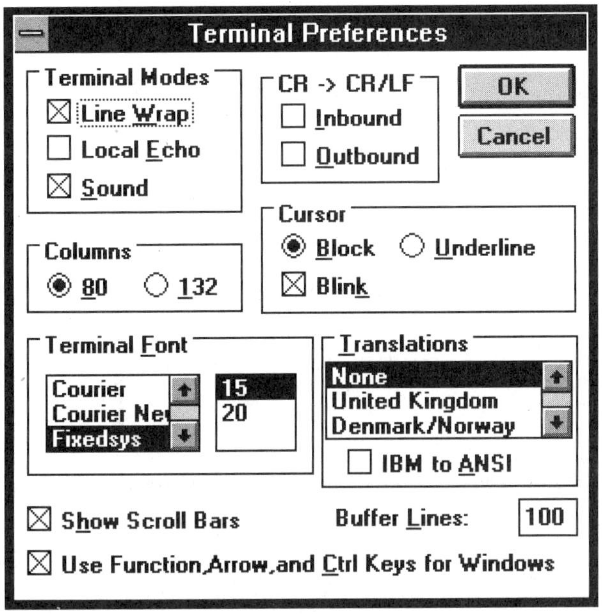

When you are finished selecting the Terminal Preference settings, click or choose OK.

FIGURE 9.6
The Terminal Preferences dialog box

Communications Protocol

Setting the Communications protocol will determine how your data files are packaged and sent over the telephone line. The telephone line must be an analog line.[1] Ask your instructor or laboratory supervisor whether your local telephone system will accommodate telecommunications using Terminal.

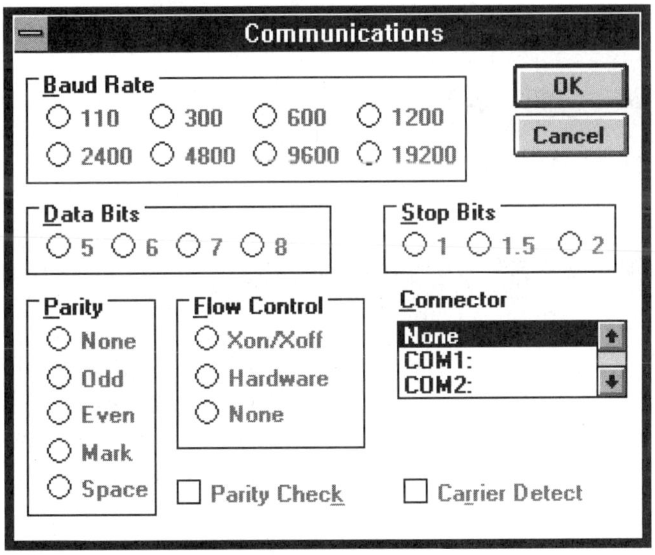

The Communications dialog box contains the choices to set Baud Rate, Data Bits, Stop Bits, Parity, Flow Control, Connector, Parity Check, and Carrier Detect. To select the Communications dialog box, click or choose the command from the Settings menu. The dialog box will appear as in Figure 9.7.

You can make the appropriate communications setting changes for your computer, as well as the remote computer. When you are finished, select or choose OK.

FIGURE 9.7
The Communications dialog box

---

1 Some parts of the country, especially downtown business districts, are being converted to digital phone services. Most personal lines are still analog.

Modem

The Modem Commands dialog box tells Terminal what signals it needs to initiate a call, as well as how to receive a call, dial the telephone, and hang up the telephone. The default settings for the modem are for a Hayes or Hayes-compatible modem, the industry standard. Check with your instructor or laboratory system's supervisor to determine if another type of modem is installed in or onto your computer and what settings it requires. The Modem Commands dialog box is obtained in the Settings menu and appears as in Figure 9.8.

The Modem Commands are used to set or change Dial, Hangup, Binary TX (transmit), Binary RX (receive), and Originate. Predetermined Modem Defaults settings are available for Hayes, MultiTech, and TrailBlazer modems. If your modem is not among those listed, you should select None and set the commands based on your modem documentation.

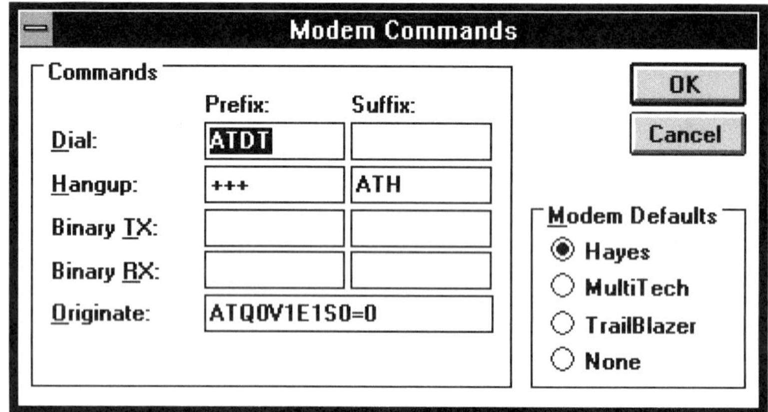

FIGURE 9.8
The Modem Commands dialog box

Saving and Retrieving Terminal Settings Files

After you have entered settings, you can save the file using the File menu shown in Figure 9.9. Saving a file in Terminal is done the same way you save files in other Windows applications.

You can select Save or Save As, and type the file name. Terminal will automatically add the .TRM extension. The selections that you made in the Settings menu are now saved in a file. You are ready to dial a call.

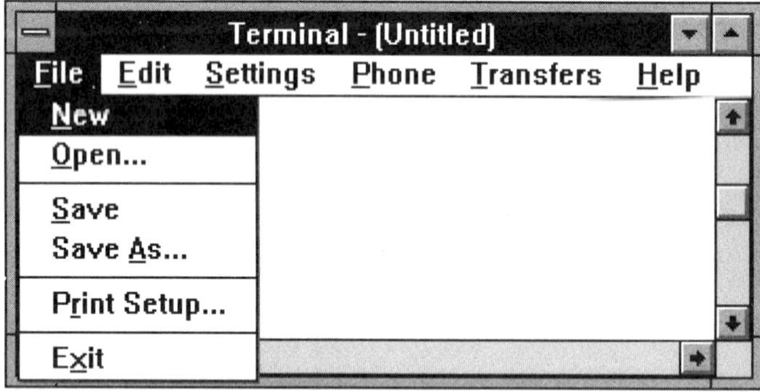

FIGURE 9.9
The File menu

Dialing a Call

Once you have established your communications protocol (settings), you can initiate a call to a remote system. To initiate a call, load the settings file for the service to which you want to connect. Open the Phone menu and choose Dial. If you have not established or retrieved a settings file, you can still initiate a call by choosing Dial from the Phone menu. You will be prompted to enter the telephone number, as shown in Figure 9.10. To proceed with the call, choose OK.

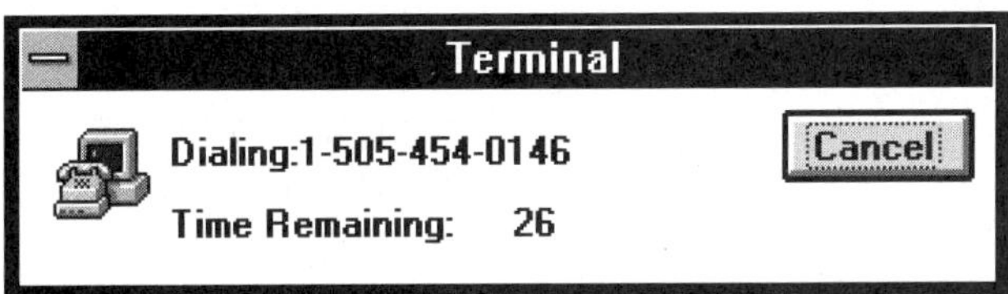

FIGURE 9.10
The Phone Number dialog box

While Terminal is dialing and awaiting an answer, your screen will appear as in Figure 9.11. The phone number that you have dialed and the time remaining in seconds (until Terminal stops waiting for an answer) appear in the Terminal application window.

FIGURE 9.11
Terminal awaiting an answer

When the remote system that you are calling receives your call, the message box will disappear. If the system does not answer, Terminal leaves the line open for the amount of time you specified in the Phone Number dialog box. Once the time has lapsed, the phone hangs up. You can cancel the call at any time before it is answered by choosing Cancel. If for some reason your hardware is not properly installed, you will get an error message in the Terminal dialog box. Check with your instructor or laboratory system supervisor for help. You may also need to refer to the *User's Guide* for equipment setup instructions.

Logging on to a Remote System

Once the call is answered by the remote system, you must perform a ***log-on*** procedure to verify to the system that you are a legitimate user and that you have access to some or all of the system's features. Log-on procedures vary substantially from one system to another. At a college or university, your instructor will tell you how to log on. If you subscribe to a commercial service such as CompuServe, your membership packet will include log-on instructions for various locations. The remainder of this unit deals with procedures performed after you have logged on to the remote system.

Communicating with a Remote System

In some cases, you will log on to a remote system and interact directly with the system to learn about weather, football scores, or stock trading. Most of these systems provide a menu of choices from which to choose, sending the results to you as plain text. The text received from the remote computer and your responses are kept in a buffer in your computer that can be copied to the Clipboard, pasted into Write or another Windows application, or saved as a file.

Transferring Files

When you have connected to the remote computer, you can send or receive *text files* (such as documents) or *binary files* (such as programs). However, before you can send or receive files, you have to indicate the manner in which the transfer will be accomplished.

Text files prepared with a word processor (such as Write or Word) should be saved to disk as unformatted. Unformatted text is saved as an ASCII file and contains both printable ASCII characters and control codes, such as carriage returns and line feeds. Binary files consist of ASCII characters plus the IBM-PC extended-character set.

The two methods of transfer—text and binary—differ in some ways. It is best to send *both* text and binary files in binary, because binary transfers check for errors and loss of data. If you do not need to send formatting codes and are not concerned about loss of data, text transfer is faster. Some systems will not accept binary file transfers, and you can only use text file mode in such cases.

Options for Transferring Files

Options are selected by selecting Text Transfers from the Settings menu in Terminal. The Text Transfers dialog box will appear as in Figure 9.12. These options include Standard Flow Control, Character at a Time, and Line at a Time. In addition, make certain that you indicate the control method with the Communications command (for example, Xon/Xoff). To complete the action, click or choose OK.

To prepare a binary transfer, select Binary Transfers from the Settings menu; its dialog box will appear as shown in Figure 9.13. You must then select the protocol (XModem/CRC or Kermit) by clicking, then

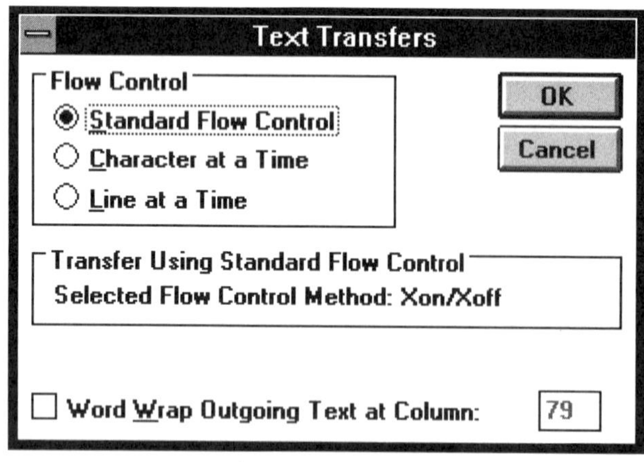

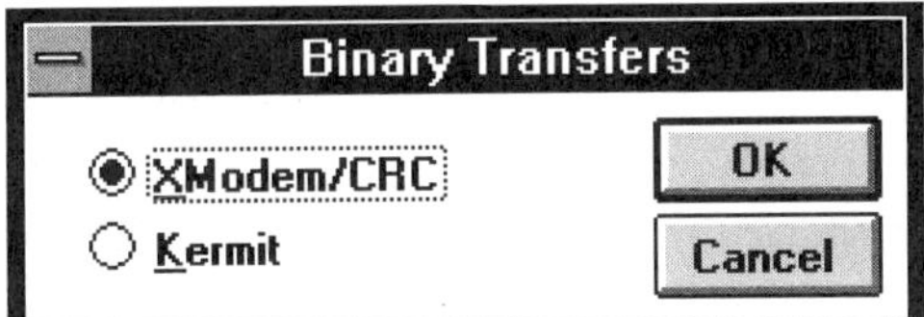

FIGURE 9.13
*The Binary
Transfers
dialog box*

choosing OK to complete the choice. The protocol used is normally determined by the capabilities of the receiving computer.

Sending and Receiving Files

To send a file, select Send Text File (or Send Binary File) from the Transfers menu. The drop-down dialog box will appear as in Figure 9.14.

FIGURE 9.14
*The Send Text
File dialog box*

Select the appropriate file (changing directories if necessary) and then press OK. The transmission window will appear as in Figure 9.15. You can Stop or Pause the transmission if you wish.

FIGURE 9.15
*Transmission
window during
text file transfer*

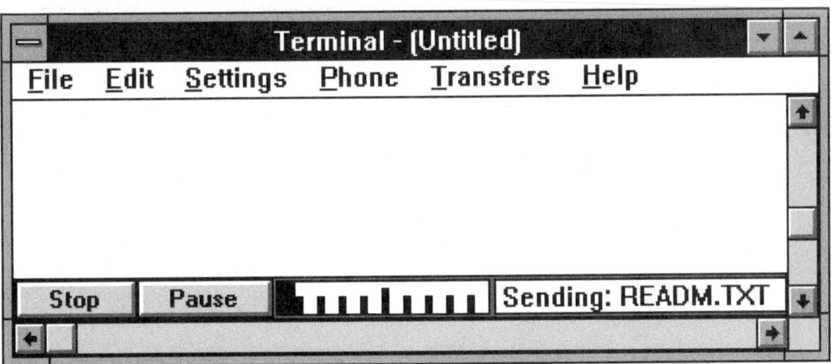

To receive files, choose or click Receive Text File (or Receive Binary File) from the Transfers menu; the dialog box will appear as shown in Figure 9.16. You will be prompted to enter a file name for the file that you are receiving.

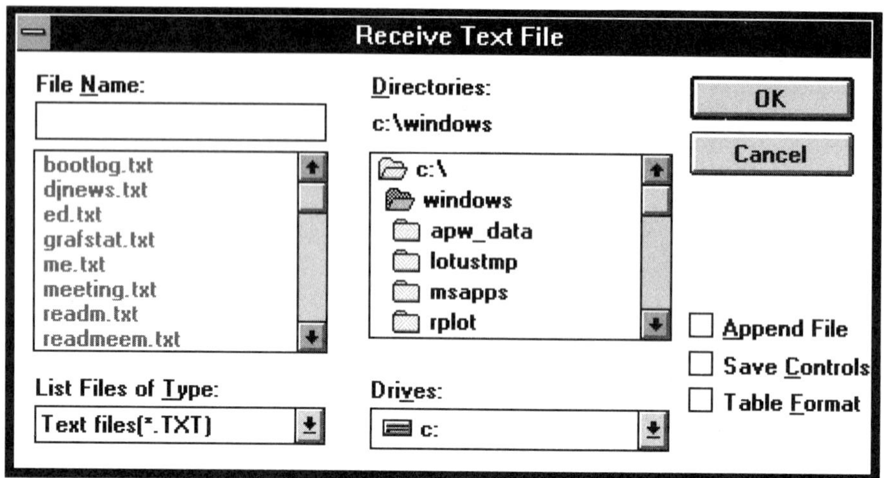

FIGURE 9.16
The Receive Text File dialog box

The options for receiving a file include Append File, Save Controls, and Table Format. Type the desired file name and then the directory where you want this file to be placed. Select any of the options, and choose OK. Then you will see the window in Figure 9.17.

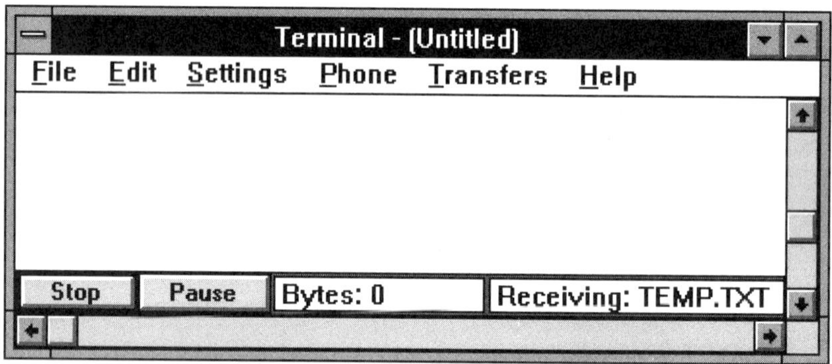

FIGURE 9.17
Transmission window during text file receipt

Copying Text to the Clipboard

You can use the Edit menu, as shown in Figure 9.18, to modify the contents in the Terminal window. You can save or print the contents of a file that has been received. Once you save the text, you can cut and paste any of it into a Write or Word document file. To do this, select (highlight) the text that you want to copy, and select Copy from the Edit menu. The selected copy is placed in Clipboard, from which you can insert it in a new position or file in either Write or Word.

FIGURE 9.18
Edit menu

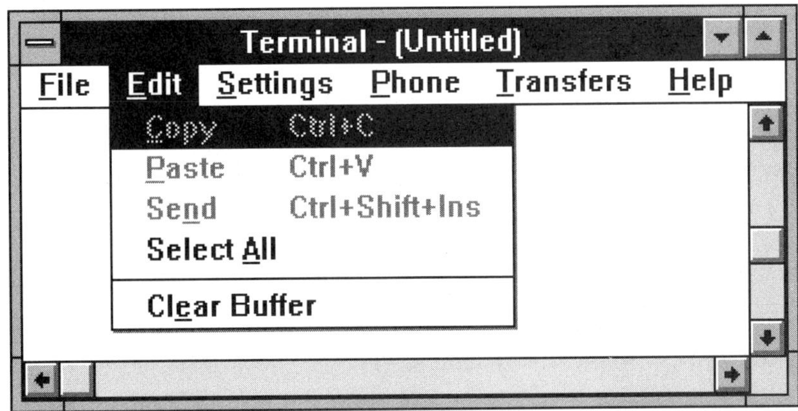

Review Questions

*1. Explain each of the following terms: modem, baud rate, data bits, stop bits, parity, data flow control, and handshaking.

2. Summarize the steps (commands) used to create a new settings file. What is (are) the command(s) required to use an established settings file?

3. Describe the process to enter the phone number 4271234 (in area code 206). Assume that you are calling from an office at work that requires a "9" to gain access to an outside line.

*4. What does the Terminal Emulation setting do? If you are not sure which terminal type to use, which type should you select?

*5. State what communications settings and modem settings accomplish.

6. What must be established before a call can be placed using Terminal? What is (are) the command(s) to place a call? How long does it take Terminal to hang up the phone if the remote system does not answer?

7. What types of files can be sent and received using Terminal? What are the differences between the different types?

Key Terms

Baud rate	Data flow control	Settings file
Binary file	Handshaking	Stop bit
Buffer	Log on	Text file
Communications protocol	Modem	
Data bit	Parity	

Documentation Research

To answer the following questions, use Chapter 11, "Terminal," of the *User's Guide*. Check the guide's index to find pages with the information needed. We recommend that you also write the relevant page number next to each question. For additional aid, you may need to use Terminal's on-line Help menu.

1. What are the hardware requirements to use Terminal?

2. Outline a typical first communication session.

3. How do you change the function keys?

4. List some possible problems and solutions if things go wrong while using Terminal.

5. Using Terminal's on-line Help, explain how to change printers.

6. Using Terminal's on-line Help, how do you disconnect from the remote computer? Give an example of the commands you would use.

Other Windows
Accessory Programs

10

In previous units, you have been working with Windows' primary applications. As you recall, Windows allows you to arrange your electronic "desktop" in very much the same way you organize your desk at work. The items you can use on your windows desktop are Calculator, Calendar, Cardfile, Clock, Notepad, Object Packager, Character Map, Media Player, and Sound Recorder.

In this unit, we will discuss how to use most of these additional Windows accessories.

Learning Objectives

At the completion of this unit, you should know

1. The features available in Windows Accessories applications.

At the completion of this unit, you should be able to

1. start and close Calculator,

2. perform calculations with Calculator,

3. start and close Calendar,

4. enter appointments and alarms in Calendar,

5. start and close Cardfile,

6. add cards to Cardfile,

7. start and close Clock,

8. switch Clock,

9. open and close Notepad,

10. enter text in Notepad,

11. create a time log file,

12. start other accessory programs.

Calculator

Calculator

Windows Calculator is an electronic calculator that includes a standard 10-key calculator as well as a scientific calculator. Calculations derived from Calculator can be transferred into any Windows applications program (Word, Write, Excel, and so on) by using Clipboard. The Calculator icon is shown to the left.

Starting Calculator

Calculator can be started from the Accessories program group window. Remember, to open Accessories, you will need to go through Program Manager, shown in Figure 10.1. From the Accessories window, double-click on the Calculator icon. If you are using the keyboard, highlight the Calculator icon and press [Enter].

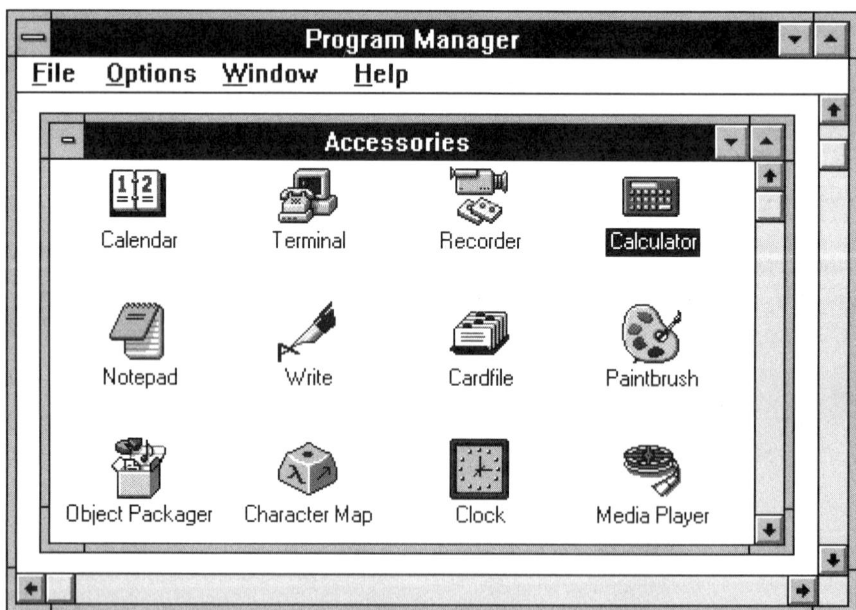

FIGURE 10.1
The Accessories program group

FIGURE 10.2
The Calculator in Standard mode

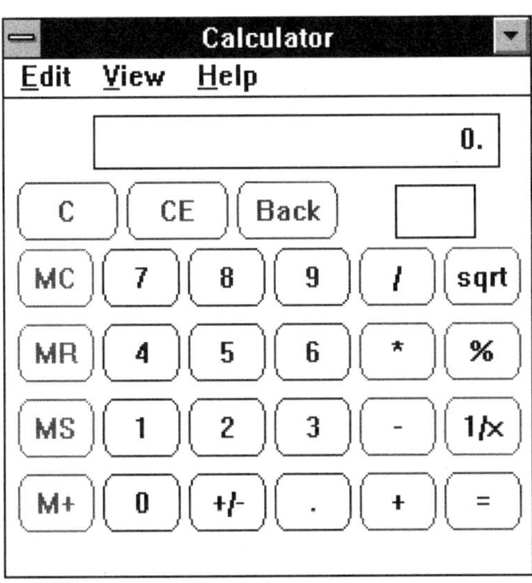

Calculator will appear as in Figure 10.2. By choosing View from the Calculator menu, as shown in Figure 10.3, you can switch from the standard calculator to a scientific calculator, as in Figure 10.4.

The first time Calculator is started on a particular computer, the standard mode will appear. When Calculator is started again, the last calculator mode that was used will appear. Calculator's window cannot be resized, but can be reduced to an icon. The icon will appear at the bottom of the screen and is available to you when you want to perform calculations.

Performing Calculations

Calculator is best operated with a mouse. Using a mouse, point to a Calculator button and click the mouse. If you are using the keyboard, make sure that NumLock is on. You can use the numeric pad as a calculator. The manner in which you make final entries and calculations in Calculator will be based on the type of keyboard you have. On most keyboards, the basic calculator functions of + (addition), – (subtraction), * (multiplication), and / (division) can be found on the numeric keypad. The = (equals) key equivalent is the Enter key.

FIGURE 10.3
The View menu

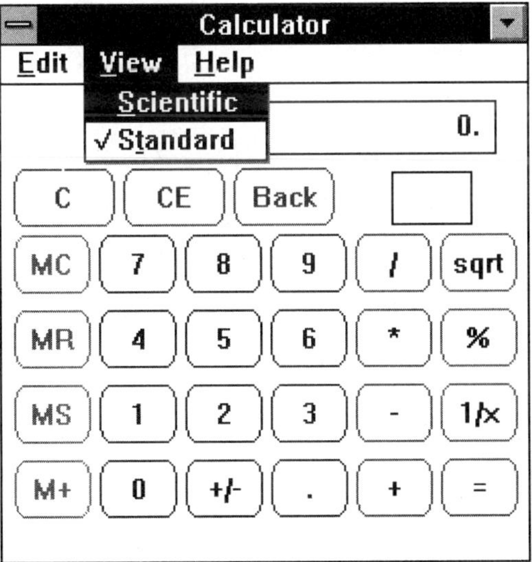

To perform calculations, click on or enter from the keypad the first number in the calculation. The number will appear in the display area of Calculator. Select the operator (addition, subtraction, multiplication, division, and so on) that you want in the calculation. Enter the next number in the calculation. If you make a mistake entering either number, you can click on the Back choice (if using the keyboard, Backspace) or on CE (keyboard Del) to clear the entry. Finally, click on the equals sign (=), or if you are using the keyboard press Enter to complete the calculation.

Calculator uses its own memory to store a value or provide an answer for future use. The MR key displays the value stored in memory; MC clears any value stored in memory. MS stores the displayed value in memory, while M+ adds the displayed value to any value currently stored in Calculator's memory. If you are using

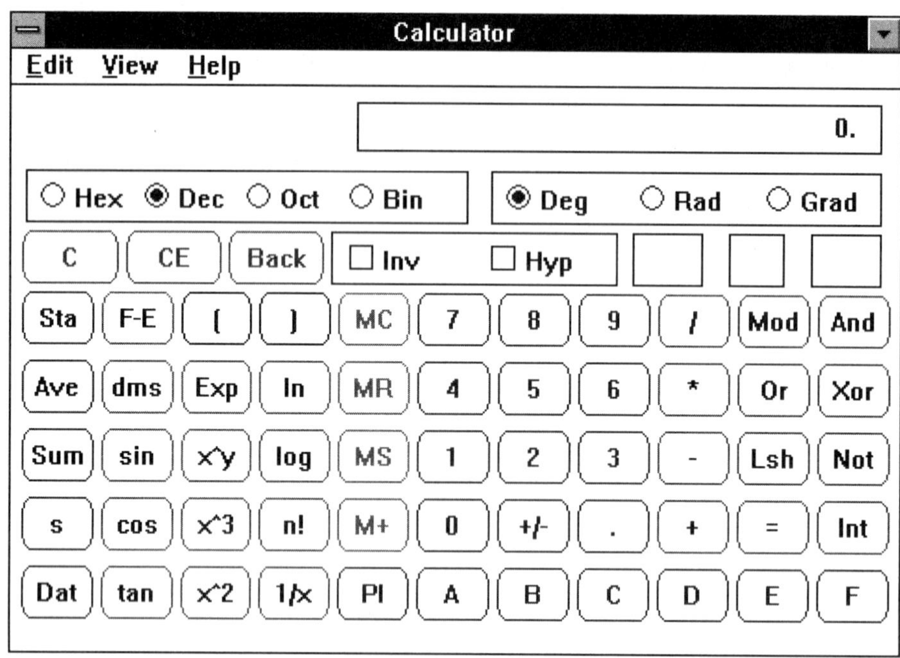

FIGURE 10.4
The Calculator in Scientific mode

Calculator's memory function, an "M" will appear in the box directly above the "/" key. The following table describes each key on the standard calculator, its keyboard equivalent, and its function:

Button	Keystroke	Function
+	+	Addition
−	−	Subtraction
*	*	Multiplication
/	/	Division
sqrt	@	Square root of displayed value
%	%	Percentage
1/x	R	Reciprocal of displayed value
=	= or Enter	Performs the operation between two numbers
+/−	F9	Changes the sign of displayed value
.	. or ,	Inserts a decimal point in displayed value
BACK	Backspace or ←	Deletes the right-most digit of displayed value
CE	Del	Clears the displayed value
C	Esc	Clears the calculation
MC	Ctrl L	Clears the value stored in memory
MR	Ctrl R	Displays the value stored in memory

MS	Ctrl M	Stores the value in memory
M+	Ctrl P	Adds the displayed value to the value stored in memory

The scientific calculator is capable of doing simple programming calculations. In addition, it can be used for exponential and logarithmic operations; calculations in binary, octal, and hexadecimal number systems; and trigonometric calculations. Its statistics window calculates sum, average, and standard deviation as discussed later in this unit. See Appendix B for a list of all keystroke commands for the scientific calculator.

GUIDED ACTIVITY 10.1

Using Calculator

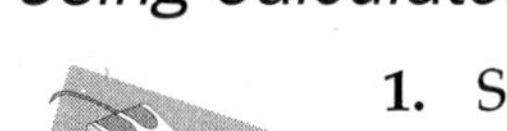

1. Select Accessories from Program Manager.

2. Double-click on the Calculator icon to open it. You should use the standard calculator. If the scientific calculator is present, switch to the standard calculator by clicking on View and then on Standard.

3. Perform the following calculation by clicking on the specific keys. If you make a mistake, choose Back to correct a few digits, or click on CE to clear the entire number.

   2 * 3 + 4

   Press Enter or click on = to get the answer. Your answer should be 10. Click on C to clear the equation.

4. Perform the following calculation:

   3 + 3 * 2

   Your answer should be 12. Press Esc or click on C to clear the equation.

5. Calculate the following percentage:

   400 * 25%

   Your answer should be 100. Clear the equation.

6. Click on View and then on Scientific to switch the standard calculator to scientific. Calculate the sine of 5 by clicking on 5 and then on Sin. Your answer should be .08715574274766.

7. Minimize Calculator to an icon by clicking on its minimize button in the upper-right corner of the calculator. The calculator should now appear as an icon in the lower portion of the screen.

8. Close Calculator by clicking on its icon and then on Close when its Control Menu appears.

GUIDED ACTIVITY 10.2

Using Calculator

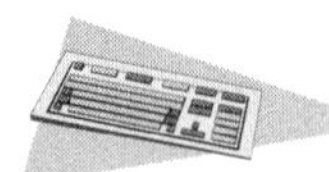

1. Select Accessories from Program Manager by pressing [Alt][W] for the Window menu. Select Accessories.

2. Highlight the Calculator icon and press [Enter] to open it. You should use the standard calculator. To use it, press [Alt][V] for the View menu, and then select Standard.

3. Perform the following calculation by pressing the specific keys. If you make a mistake, press [Backspace] to correct a few digits, or press [Del] to clear the entire number.

      2 * 3 + 4

   Press [Enter] to obtain the result. Your answer should be 10. Press [Esc] to clear the equation.

4. Perform the following calculation:

      3 + 3 * 2

   Your answer should be 12. Press [Esc] to clear the equation.

5. Calculate the following percentage:

      400 * 25%

   Your answer should be 100. Clear the equation.

6. Press [Alt][V] and then select Scientific to switch the standard calculator to scientific. Calculate the sine of 5 by pressing 5 and then S. Your answer should be .08715574274766.

7. Close Calculator by pressing [Alt][Spacebar] and then selecting Close.

Using a Statistics Window

To calculate sums, averages, and standard deviation for groups of numbers, click on the Sta button. The Statistics dialog box will appear, as illustrated in Figure 10.5, superimposed on the scientific calculator. The dialog box is used to record and delete the numbers you have entered. Use the mouse or the Move command from the Control Menu to move the box to the side so you can view both it and the calculator. You can switch from one active area to the other as you enter data and compute results. Do this with the mouse by clicking on the one you want. If you are using the keyboard, press [Alt][R] to move from the statistics box to the calculator. Use [Ctrl][S] to move from the calculator window back to the Statistics box.

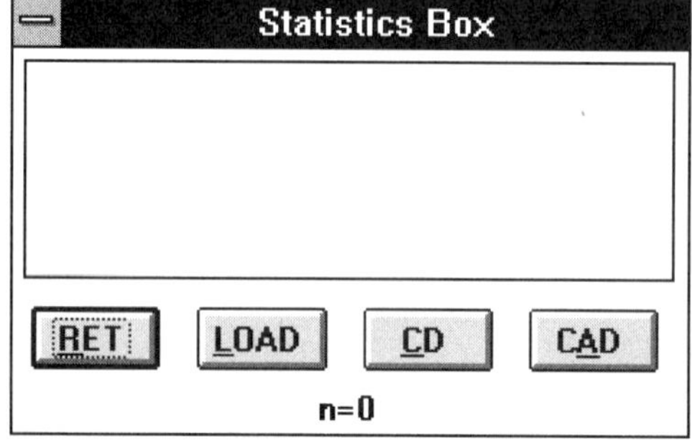

To perform a statistical calculation:

1. Choose Sta or press [Ctrl][S]. The Statistics dialog box will appear, as discussed above.

2. Enter the first value in the set. If you click Calculator buttons with the mouse, the focus returns to Calculator and the value appears in the display area. If you are using the keyboard, press [Alt][R] (for the RET button) before entering the number.

3. Choose Dat or press [Ins] to enter the value in the Statistics box. You will see the value displayed.

4. Enter the remaining numbers in the set, choosing Dat (or pressing [Ins]) each time to enter the number in the Statistics box.

5. Use the Statistics box buttons to edit the data set. Click on the Statistics box or press [Ctrl][S]. The last-entered number will be highlighted. Use the arrow keys to select a different number. The buttons have the following effect:

Button	Keyboard	Function
RET	[Alt][R]	("Return to calculator") Switches to the main calculator and retains the Statistics box entries
LOAD	[Alt][L]	("Load this number into the calculator") Copies the selected number in the Statistics box to the calculator display
CD	[Alt][C]	("Clear datum") Deletes the selected number from the Statistics box
CAD	[Alt][A]	("Clear all data") Deletes all numbers from the Statistics box

6. When all numbers have been entered into the Statistics box, you can perform the following calculations:

Statistic	Mouse Action	Keyboard
Sum	Click the Sum button	[Ctrl][T]
Sum of Squares	Click Inv, Sum	[I], [Ctrl][T]
Mean	Click Ave	[Ctrl][A]
Mean of Squares	Click Inv, Ave	[I], [Ctrl][A]
Standard Deviation (sample)	Click s	[Ctrl][D]
Standard Deviation (population)	Click Inv, s	[I], [Ctrl][D]

GUIDED ACTIVITY 10.3

Statistics

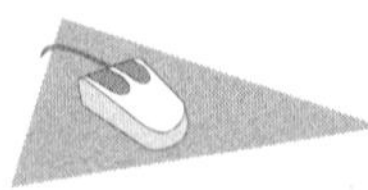

1. Open Calculator and put it into Scientific mode. Open the statistics window by clicking on Sta.

2. Move the Statistics box to another part of the screen so that it does not overlap the Calculator, by placing the mouse pointer in the title box and dragging it to a new location.

3. Activate the calculator by clicking on its window.

4. Enter the following test scores: 55, 87, 99, 100, 75. Use the following procedure:

    a. Enter a number.

    b. Click the Dat button. Notice that the number is displayed in the Statistics box.

    c. Repeat steps a and b for each number.

5. After you have entered all test scores, calculate the following:

    a. Sum: Click the Sum button. (Answer: 416)

    b. Sum of Squares: Click Inv, Sum. (Answer: 36020)

    c. Mean: Click Ave. (Answer: 83.2)

    d. Mean of Squares: Click Inv, Ave. (Answer: 7204)

    e. Sample standard deviation: Click s. (Answer: 18.76699230031)

    f. Population standard deviation: Click Inv, s. (Answer: 16.78570820669)

6. Minimize Calculator to its icon.

GUIDED ACTIVITY 10.4

Statistics

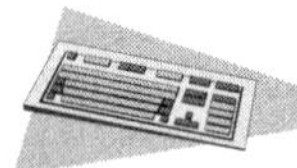

1. Open Calculator and put it into Scientific mode. Open the statistics window by pressing [Ctrl] [S].

2. Move the Statistics box to another part of the screen so that it does not overlap the Calculator. Press [Alt] [Spacebar] and select Move. Using the arrow keys, move the Statistics box to a new location.

3. Activate the main Calculator window by pressing [Alt] [R] (for the RET button).

4. Enter the following test scores: 55, 87, 99, 100, 75. Use the following procedure:

    a. Enter a number.

    b. Press [Ins] (for the Dat button).

    c. Repeat steps a and b for each number in the set.

5. After you have entered all test scores, calculate the following:

   a. Sum: Press [Ctrl][T]. (Answer: 416)

   b. Sum of Squares: Press [I], [Ctrl][T]. (Answer: 36020)

   c. Mean: Press [Ctrl][A]. (Answer: 83.2)

   d. Mean of Squares: Press [I], [Ctrl][A]. (Answer: 7204)

   e. Sample standard deviation: Press [Ctrl][D]. (Answer: 18.76699230031)

   f. Population standard deviation: Press [I], [Ctrl][D]. (Answer: 16.78570820669)

6. Minimize Calculator to its icon.

Copying Calculator Results to the Clipboard

The result of a calculation can be copied to the Clipboard for use in a spreadsheet or word processing document. Simply choose Copy from the Edit menu. The result can then be pasted into another application. (That is how we transferred the precise results of the Guided Activities into the Word for Windows document that became this unit.) Similarly, a number from a spreadsheet or document can be copied to the Clipboard in that application and then pasted into the Calculator display window.

Closing Calculator

When you are finished using Calculator, reduce it to an icon. As mentioned earlier in this unit, you cannot resize a Calculator window; you can only reduce it to an icon. When you have reduced Calculator to its icon, the icon will appear at the bottom of the screen. To close the Calculator, single-click on the icon; Calculator's dialog box will appear. Select Close to finish working with Calculator for this session.

A second method is available to close Calculator. Single-click on Calculator's Control Menu box. From the menu that appears, as shown in Figure 10.6, select Close. The keyboard combination of [Alt][F4] is another fast and easy way to close Calculator.

GUIDED ACTIVITY 10.5

Closing the Calculator

1. If Calculator is not reduced to an icon, click on the Control Menu box (upper-left corner) and then on Close.

2. If Calculator has been minimized to its icon, click on its icon. The Control menu will appear; click on Close.

FIGURE 10.6
*The Calculator
Control menu*

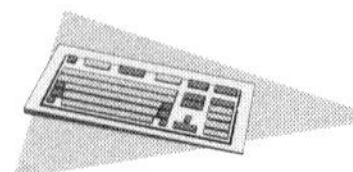

GUIDED ACTIVITY 10.6

Closing the Calculator

1. If Calculator is not reduced to an icon, press ⟦Alt⟧⟦Spacebar⟧ for the Control menu. Select Close.

2. If Calculator has been minimized to its icon, press ⟦Alt⟧⟦Tab⟧ until its icon is highlighted, then release the ⟦Alt⟧ key. Press ⟦Alt⟧⟦Spacebar⟧ and select Close.

Calendar

Calendar

Calendar is a scheduling program that allows you to enter information on a daily or monthly basis. With the use of an alarm, Calendar will also remind you of any scheduled appointment at a specified time. Calendar is located in the Accessories program group window. To use Calendar, double-click on its icon (shown to the left).

The untitled Calendar window will appear as shown in Figure 10.7. Calendar contains one-hour time intervals for the current date. It also has an appointment area that allows you to enter any appointments that you make.

You can choose to display a monthly view of Calendar. To switch from the Day view to the Month view, select View from the Calendar menu and choose Month. The month view of Calendar appears as in Figure 10.8.

You can also switch quickly between Day view and Month view by double-clicking the date in the status line, or if using the keyboard by pressing the arrow keys to move to the date and pressing ⟦Enter⟧.

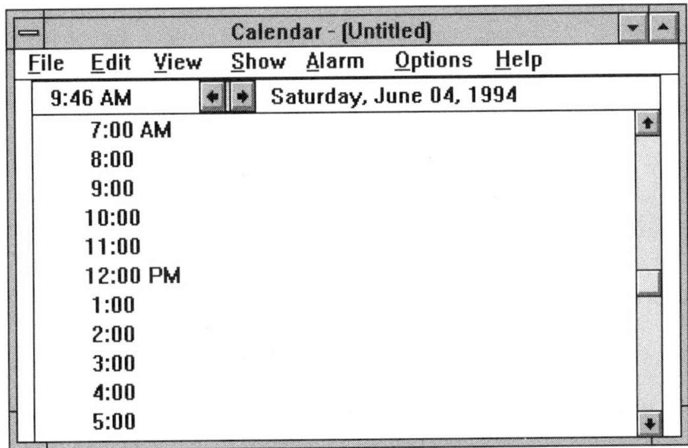

FIGURE 10.7
The initial Calendar window in Day view

You can enter appointments, display appointment days, set an alarm to remind you of appointments, and customize your Calendar so that it displays in other than 60-minute intervals. For example, you can use a 24-hour clock or a starting time other than 7 a.m. Appointments can be removed by using the Remove command from the Edit menu in Calendar. The Remove dialog box will appear as in Figure 10.9.

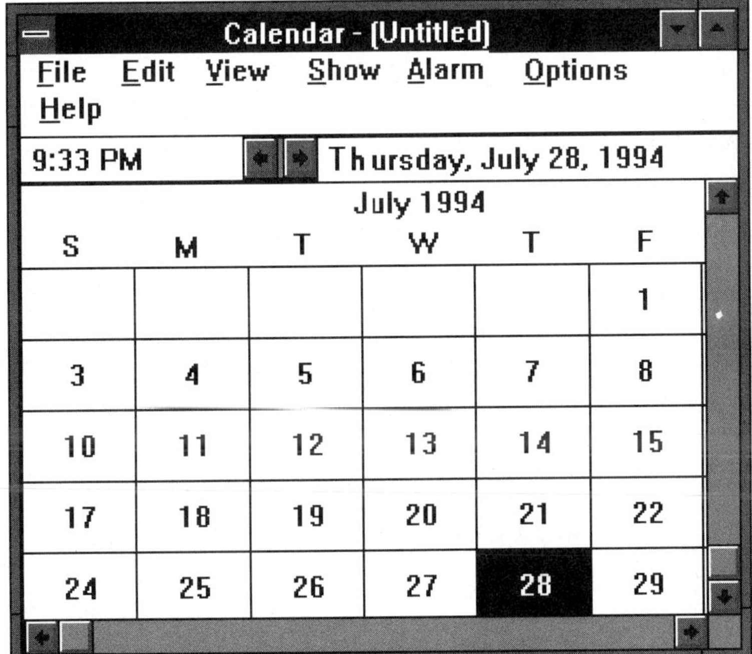

FIGURE 10.8
The Calendar in Month view

Entering Appointments

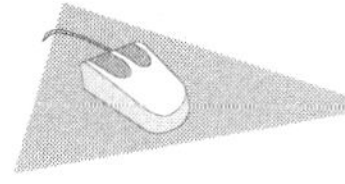

1. Open Calendar from Accessories in Program Manager.

2. Click on Show and then on Date.

3. Type the date 6/28/94. Click on OK.

4. Click on Options, and then on Day Settings.

5. Leave the Interval for the hour bar at 60 minutes.

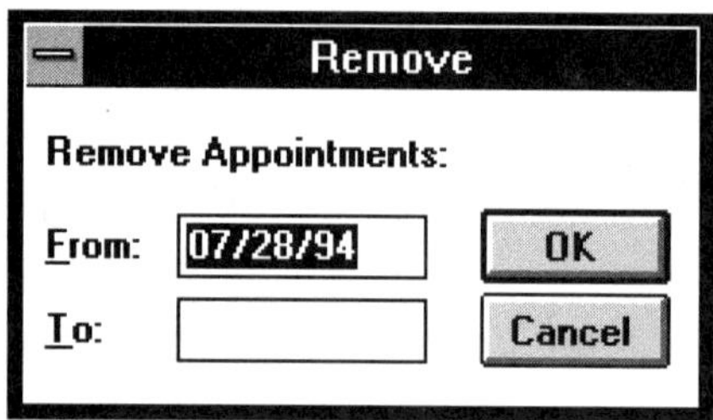

6. Change the Starting time to 6:00 AM. Confirm this entry by choosing OK.

7. Click on Options and then on Special Time. Set this special time for 12:15 PM.

8. At the insertion point (the time should be 12:15), type:

   `Lunch at El Rialto with Monica`

9. Set an alarm for this important appointment by pressing F5 (the menu command is Alarm Set).

10. Make an additional entry next to 2:00 by clicking on that line. Enter:

    `Call Steve Ross about project`

11. Set an alarm for this appointment.

12. Save these entries by clicking on File and then on Save As; when you are prompted for a file name, use your last name (the first eight letters). Be sure to save the file on your data disk or in another directory as appropriate.

GUIDED ACTIVITY 10.8

Entering Appointments

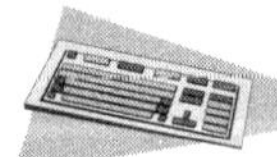

1. Open Calendar from Accessories in Program Manager.

2. Press Alt S for Show, and then select Date.

3. Type the date 6/28/94. Press Enter.

4. Press Alt O for Options, and then select Day Settings.

5. Leave the Interval for the hour bar at 60 minutes.

6. Change the Starting time by pressing Alt S and typing 6:00AM. Press Enter.

7. Press Alt O for Options, and then select Special Time. Set this special time for 12:15 PM (Alt P).

8. At the insertion point (the time should be 12:15), type:

   `Lunch at El Rialto with Monica`

9. Set an alarm for this important appointment by pressing F5.

10. Make an additional entry next to 2 : 00. Use ⬇ to move to that line. Type:

```
Call Steve Ross about project
```

11. Set an alarm for this appointment.

12. Save these entries by pressing [Alt][F] and selecting Save As; when you are prompted for a file name, use your last name (first eight letters). Be sure to save the file on your data disk by typing A : or another directory as appropriate before the file name.

Printing the Calendar

To print entries in Calendar, select the File menu and then Print. The dialog box will appear as in Figure 10.10.

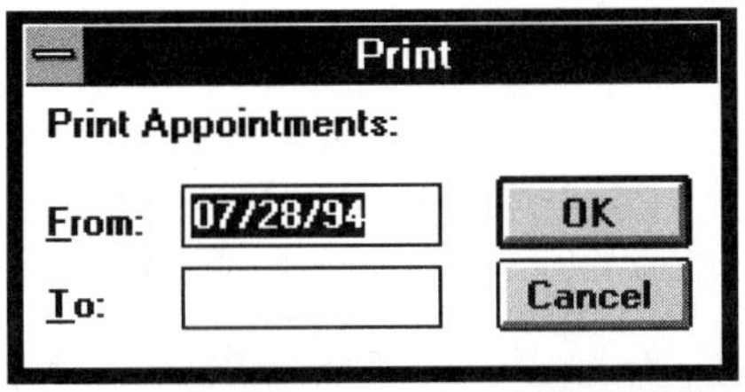

You can add *headers* or *footers* to your appointments before you print. Headers or footers can be used to add explanatory notes to your appointments. For example, you can include a page number or the file name as a header or footer on a printed page. To add headers and footers, select Page Setup from the File menu. The Page Setup dialog box will appear as in Figure 10.11.

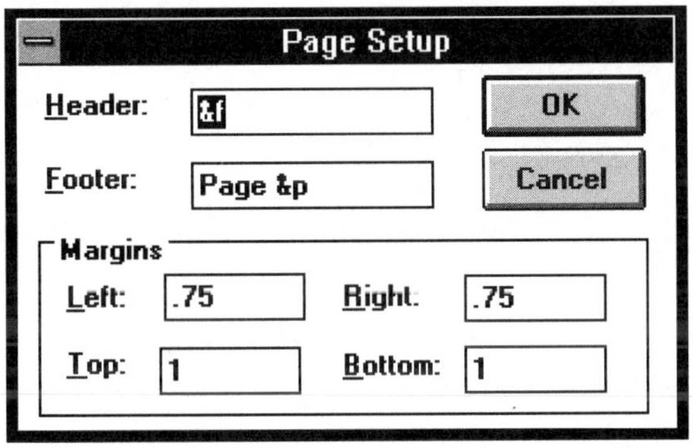

You will notice that the Header and Footer boxes contain special codes that can be used, as shown in Figure 10.11. These codes consist of the "&" (ampersand) sign and a single letter. The following codes can be used:

FIGURE 10.10
The Calendar Print dialog box

FIGURE 10.11
The Calendar Page Setup dialog box

Code	Explanation
&d	Enter the current date
&t	Enter the current time
&p	Enter page numbers
&f	Enter the current file name
&l	Left-align the text
&r	Right-align the text
&c	Center the text

When you are ready to print, click or choose OK.

Closing Calendar

When you are finished with your session and want to close Calendar, single-click its icon at the bottom of the screen or on the Control Menu box in the upper-left corner, as shown in Figure 10.12. The drop-down dialog box will appear; click on or choose Close.

If Calendar has not been reduced to its icon, you can close it by single-clicking on the control panel and choosing Close. Calendar can be easily closed by pressing Alt F4 on the keyboard.

FIGURE 10.12
The Calendar Control menu

GUIDED ACTIVITY 10.9

Printing Appointments

1. Print the appointments that you entered in Guided Activity 10.7 by clicking on File and then on Print.

2. You will be prompted to enter two dates. The entries made between those two dates will be printed. Click on OK to print.

3. Save by selecting Save from the File menu.

4. Close Calendar by clicking on the Control Menu box and then on Close.

GUIDED ACTIVITY 10.10

Printing Appointments

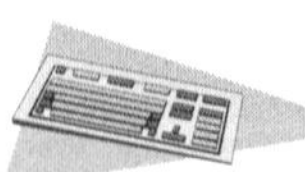

1. Print the appointments that you entered in Guided Activity 10.8 by pressing Alt F for File and selecting Print.

2. You will be prompted to enter two dates. The entries made between those two dates will be printed. Press Alt T to enter the To date. Press Enter to print.

3. Save by pressing Alt F and then selecting Save.

4. Close Calendar by pressing Alt Spacebar and then selecting Close.

Cardfile

Cardfile

Cardfile is an electronic index card system. Cardfile is very similar to a Rolodex in that it contains information such as telephone numbers, addresses, names, titles, and the like. Cardfile is located in the Accessories program group window. Double-click on its icon (shown to the left) to start Cardfile.

FIGURE 10.13
A blank card

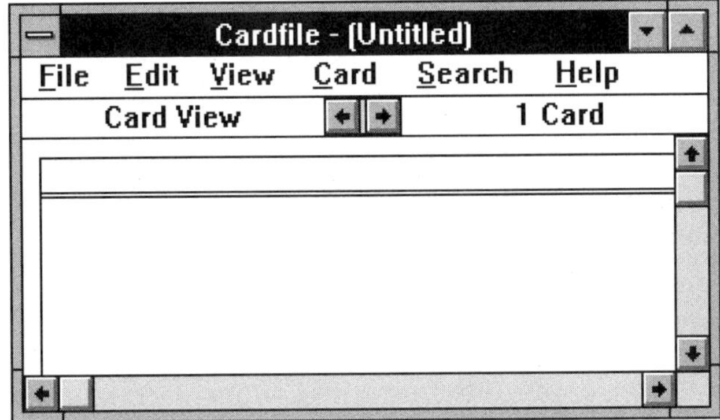

The untitled Cardfile window containing a single blank card appears as illustrated in Figure 10.13.

To add a new card, choose Add from the Card menu or press F7. The Add dialog box is illustrated in Figure 10.14. You create an index to the card file as you add cards. After you type the text of the index entry and select OK (or press Enter), a card is presented on which you can type several more lines of information, as in Figure 10.15). The top line of each card contains the index entry. To edit the index entry of an existing card, choose Index from the Edit menu or press F6. The Index dialog box will appear as in Figure 10.16.

FIGURE 10.14
Adding a card to the Cardfile (the information entered in this text box is the index entry)

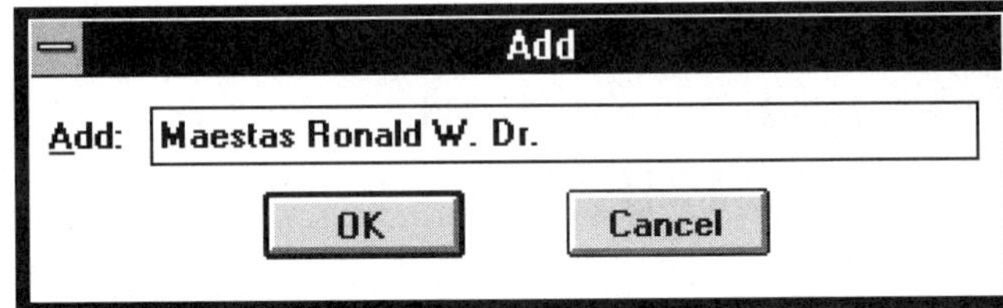

Cards are organized alphabetically. If you use a title, such as Dr. or Ms., it will be arranged accordingly, probably making the search for a specific person more difficult. We recommend that you use last name, first name, middle initial, and finally title in that order. Figure 10.17 shows a list of four cards in a file in which we entered the names incorrectly.

FIGURE 10.15
Entering information onto a card

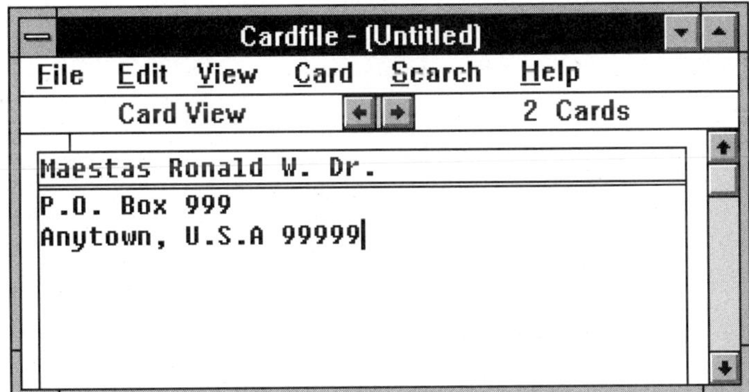

FIGURE 10.16
The Index dialog box

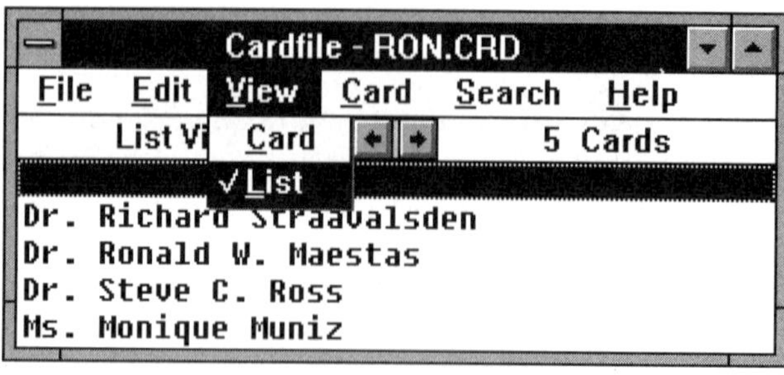

FIGURE 10.17
List of cards in the Cardfile (entered incorrectly)

Imagine the difficulty of finding a particular person in a list of 100 names if they were entered this way!

Cards can be deleted, duplicated, merged with other text, and printed. If you have a modem, Cardfile can be used to dial a phone number saved in a card.

If you want to print an individual card or the entire file, choose Print from the File menu. Your success in printing from Cardfile will depend on the system being used, particularly with networked environments. You may need to check with your instructor if you have any problems printing Cardfile.

Closing Cardfile

If Cardfile has been minimized to its icon, single-click its icon at the bottom of the screen. The drop-down menu will appear; click on or choose Close. If Cardfile has not been minimized, you can close by single-clicking the Control Menu box shown in Figure 10.18 and selecting Close. If you are using the keyboard, press Alt F4.

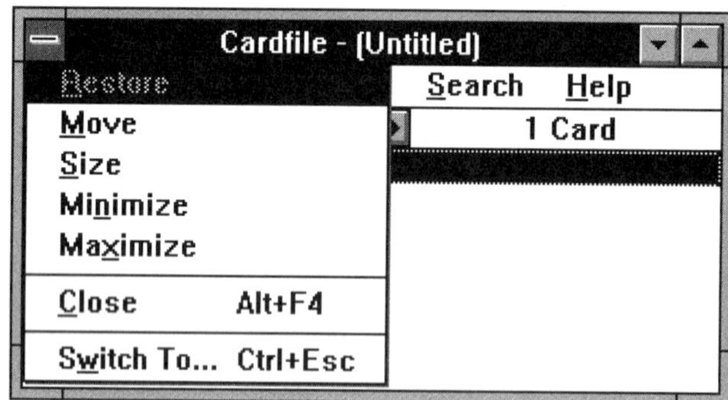

FIGURE 10.18
The Cardfile Control menu

Cardfile

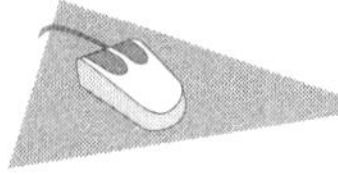

1. Open Cardfile from Accessories in Program Manager.

2. Click on Edit and then on Index. Enter the following text on the Index line and click on OK:

    ```
    Maestas Ronald W. Dr. 505-454-1234
    ```

3. Type the following address in the information area:

    ```
    Dr. Ronald W. Maestas
    P. O. Box 123
    Las Vegas, NM 87701
    ```

4. Add a new card by clicking on Card and then on Add. This time use your name and phone number on the Add line; click on OK. Type your address, city, state, and zip code in the information line.

5. Enter two more entries for your friends following the procedure in step 4.

6. Switch to the List View by clicking on View and then on List.

7. Search for Dr. Maestas's card by clicking on Search and then on Go To. Type Maestas in the Go To box. Do not use the title Dr.

8. Save your card file on your data disk under the name ADDRLIST by clicking on File and then on Save As.

9. Close Cardfile.

Cardfile

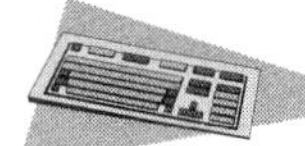

1. Open Cardfile from Accessories in Program Manager.

2. Press Alt E for Edit and then select Index. Enter the following text on the Index line and press Enter:

    Maestas Ronald W. Dr. 505-454-1234

3. Type the following address in the information area:

    Dr. Ronald W. Maestas
    P. O. Box 123
    Las Vegas, NM 87701

4. Add a new card by pressing Alt C for Card and then selecting Add. This time use your name and phone number on the Add line; press Enter. Type your address, city, state, and zip code in the information line.

5. Enter two more entries for your friends following the procedure in step 4.

6. Switch to the List View by pressing Alt V for View and then selecting List.

7. Search for Dr. Maestas's card by pressing Alt S for Search and then selecting Go To. Type Maestas in the Go To box. Do not use the title Dr.

8. Save your card file on your data disk under the name ADDRLIST by selecting Save As from the File menu.

9. Close Cardfile.

Clock

Clock

Windows' Clock was introduced in Unit 2. You may recall the discussion of minimizing and maximizing an icon. Clock is a convenient way to remind you of the time. Clock is available in the Accessories window; the clock icon is shown to the left. You can *display* Clock as an analog or digital clock. You cannot *change* the time using Clock. This is done using Control Panel as introduced in Unit 5.

Starting Clock

Open the Accessories window and double-click on the Clock icon, or choose Open from Program Manager's File menu. The icon must be highlighted if you use the latter procedure to start Clock.

The standard analog clock will appear, reflecting the computer's system time as in Figure 10.19.

To switch between the analog clock and a digital clock, click or choose Settings from the Clock menu shown in Figure 10.20.

The digital clock appears as in Figure 10.21. Whenever you start Clock, the last mode—analog or digital—will appear.

FIGURE 10.19
Analog Clock

FIGURE 10.20
The Clock Settings menu

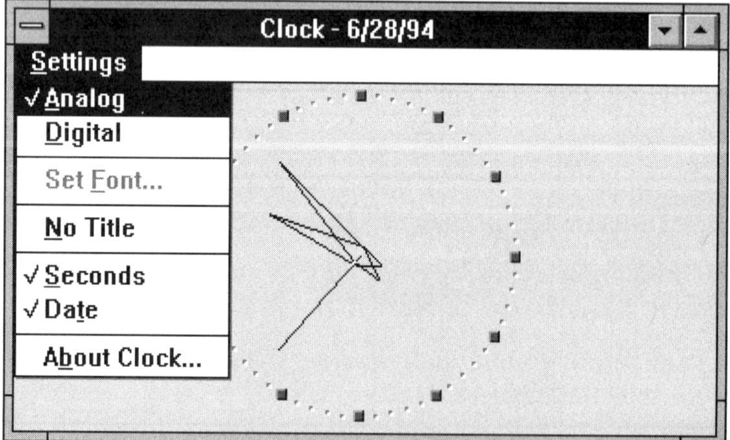

FIGURE 10.21
Digital Clock

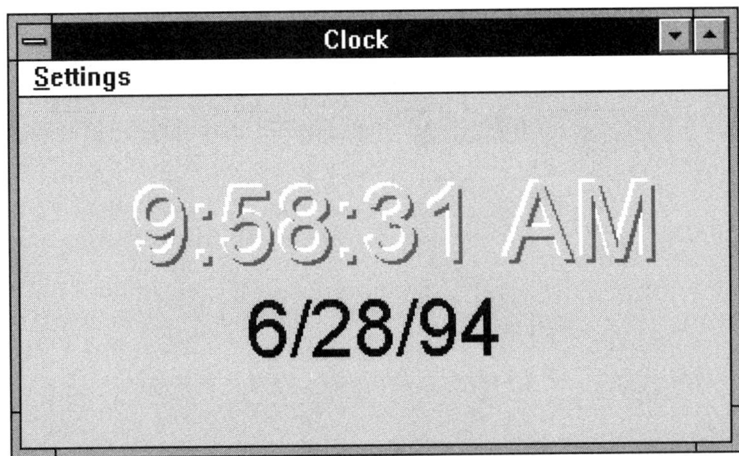

GUIDED ACTIVITY 10.13

Switching Clock

1. Open Clock from Accessories in Program Manager. The clock will display in analog mode the first time you start the application (but someone might have used the clock at your workstation earlier and set it to digital).

2. Click on Settings.

3. Click on the option that is not checked (Digital or Analog).

4. Click on the Control Menu box and then on Minimize. The Clock will be reduced to its icon in the lower portion of the screen. Notice that the minimized clock displays the current time.

GUIDED ACTIVITY 10.14

Switching Clock

1. Open Clock from Accessories in Program Manager. The clock will display in analog mode the first time you start the application (but someone might have used the clock at your workstation earlier and set it to digital).

2. Press [Alt][S] for Settings.

3. Select the option that is not checked (Digital or Analog).

4. Press [Alt][Spacebar] for the Control Menu and then select Minimize. The Clock will be reduced to its icon in the lower portion of the screen. Notice that the minimized clock displays the current time.

Closing Clock

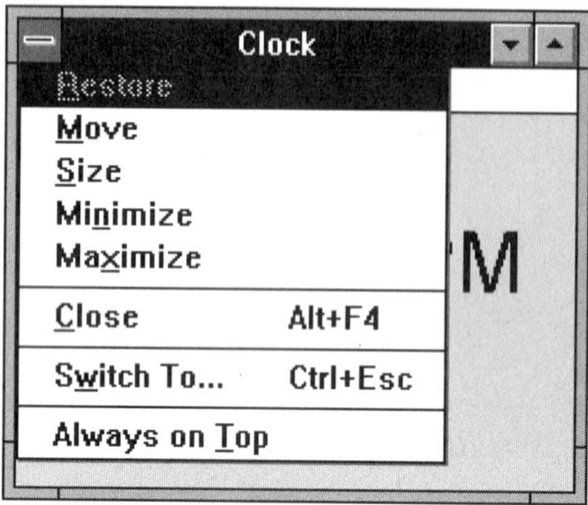

FIGURE 10.22
The Clock Control menu

If Clock has been minimized to its icon, single-click its icon at the bottom of the screen. The drop-down dialog box will appear; click or choose Close. If Clock has not been minimized, single-click on the Control Menu box (upper-left corner), shown in Figure 10.22, and choose Close. You can close Clock easily from the keyboard by pressing Alt F4.

Notepad

Notepad is a simple text editor that reads and writes plain *ASCII text files*—files that contain words and numbers but do not contain special formatting information. Notepad is very useful for jotting down notes and writing short memos, as well as creating, editing, and saving *batch files* (sets of MS-DOS instructions) that will run at the MS-DOS level. Notepad is also very useful for creating electronic messages that will be sent later via modem. In addition, Notepad can be used to read information files, such as PRINTERS.TXT or README.TXT, that are in the Windows directory.

Starting Notepad

Notepad

Notepad is included in the Accessories window. Double-click on its icon (shown to the left), or select Notepad and choose Open from Program Manager's File menu. Remember, the Notepad icon must be highlighted to perform the latter procedure.

The Notepad window (untitled) will appear as in Figure 10.23.

FIGURE 10.23
The Notepad window

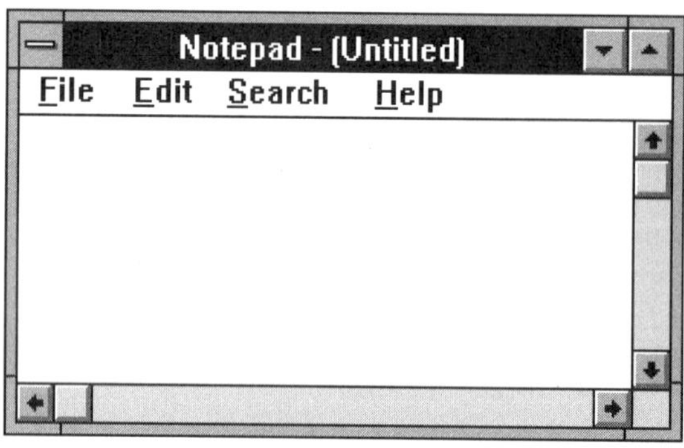

Entering Text

Text that you enter will start at the upper-left corner (insertion point) of the Notepad window. Text can be entered directly in the Notepad window. If you are entering long sentences or paragraphs, check Word Wrap. This option automatically wraps text to the next line when you reach the right border of the window. Word Wrap can be set from the Edit menu shown in Figure 10.24. Word Wrap remains on until you execute the command again—*toggle* it on, toggle it off.

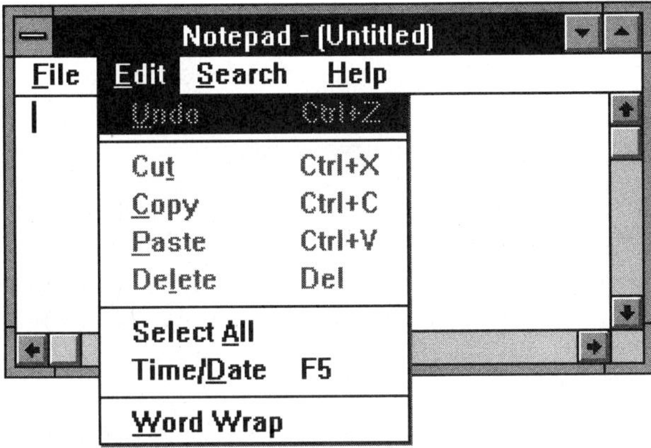

Closing Notepad

If Notepad has been minimized to an icon, single-click its icon at the bottom of the screen. When the drop-down dialog box appears, click or choose Close. If Notepad has not been minimized, single-click the Control Menu box shown in Figure 10.25 and choose Close. You can also close the file by selecting Exit from the File menu.

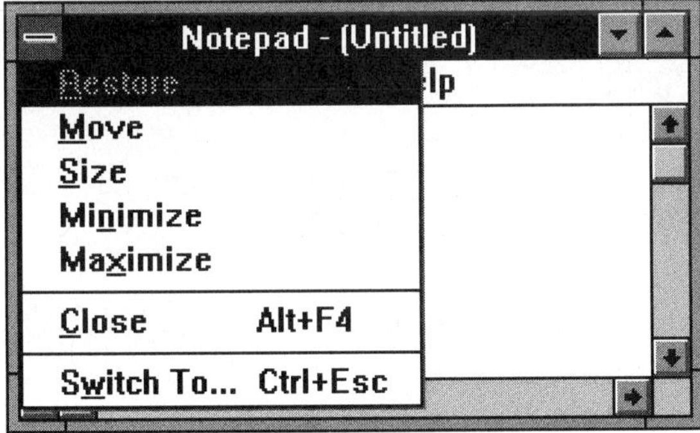

GUIDED ACTIVITY 10.15

Writing in Notepad

1. Open Notepad from the Accessories group in Program Manager.

2. Type the following text. *Do not press* Enter *after each line; instead, enter the text as a single long line.*

    ```
    Notes from Dr. Maestas's Information Analysis Class July
    16, 1994. Topic: Systems Development Life Cycle, review
    each step.
    ```

3. The notes will be hard to read because the lines extend beyond the right edge of the screen, so click on Word Wrap in the Edit menu. The text will fit within the borders of the window, and you will be able to read it.

4. The cursor will rest at the beginning of the document. For practice, check to make sure you typed the word systems. To search for the word, click on Find in the Search menu. Enter the word systems in the Find What box. Click on OK. You will see the word highlighted in Notepad. Close the dialog box.

5. Click on Print in the File menu to print the document.

6. Click on Save As in the File menu to save the document. Type NOTES in the Filename box. Be sure that you save the file on your data disk. Click on OK to complete the process.

7. Click on Exit in the File menu to leave Notepad.

GUIDED ACTIVITY 10.16

Writing in Notepad

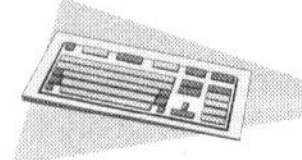

1. Open Notepad from the Accessories group in Program Manager.

2. Type the following text. *Do not press* Enter *after each line; instead, enter the text as a long line.*

    ```
    Notes from Dr. Maestas's Information Analysis Class July
    16, 1994. Topic: Systems Development Life Cycle, review
    each step.
    ```

3. The notes will be hard to read because the lines extend beyond the right edge of the screen, so press Alt E for the Edit menu and then select Word Wrap. The text will fit within the borders of the window, and you will be able to read it.

4. The cursor will rest at the beginning of the document. For practice, check to make sure you typed the word systems. To search for the word, press Alt S for Search and then select Find. Enter the word systems in the Find What box and press Enter. You will see the word highlighted in Notepad. Close the dialog box.

5. Press Alt F and then select Print to print the document.

6. Press [Alt][F] and then select Save As to save the document. Be sure you save the file on your data disk. Type NOTES in the Filename box and press [Enter].

7. Select Exit from the File menu to leave Notepad.

Creating a Time Log File

By entering .LOG in capital letters at the beginning of a Notepad file, as shown in Figure 10.26, you can create a log to keep track of how you spend your time. When you open this file again, Notepad automatically adds the current time and date to the end of the file. You can keep a log of how you spend your day by entering notes after each time and date.

FIGURE 10.26
A time log file

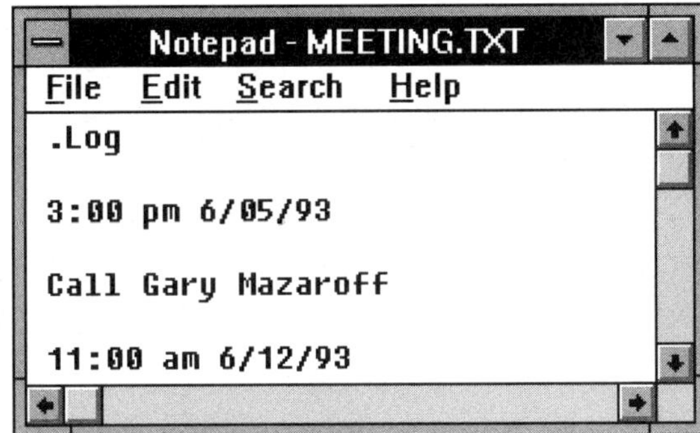

GUIDED ACTIVITY 10.17

Creating a Time Log File

1. Start Notepad.

2. In the empty Notepad window, type .LOG.

3. Click on Save As in the File menu and give the file name TIMELOG. Remember to save the file on your data disk.

4. Click on Open in the File menu to reopen the file you just saved. Below the word .LOG, you will see the current date and time.

5. Below the date and time stamp, type a list of tasks that you will perform today. For example, enter your class, study periods, work schedule, or any important appointments for the day.

6. Save the file again. Click on Save in the File menu. Click on Exit in the File menu to leave Notepad.

7. When you are finished with your tasks, start Notepad again and open your file. Notepad places the current date and time at the end of the file. You can now subtract the first time from the second to determine the amount of time you spent on this task.

8. Save the file again.

9. Close Notepad.

GUIDED ACTIVITY 10.18

Creating a Time Log File

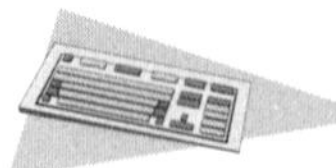

1. Start Notepad.

2. In the empty Notepad window, type .LOG.

3. Select Save As in the File menu and give the file name TIMELOG. Remember to save the file on your data disk.

4. Select Open from the File menu to reopen the file you just saved. Below the word .LOG, you will see the current date and time.

5. Below the date and time stamp, type a list of tasks that you will perform today. For example, enter your class, study periods, work schedule, or any important appointments for the day.

6. Save the file again. Select Save from the File menu. Select Exit from the File menu to leave Notepad.

7. When you are finished with your tasks, start Notepad again and open your file. Notepad places the current date and time at the end of the file. You can now subtract the first time from the second to determine the amount of time you spent on this task.

8. Save the file again.

9. Close Notepad.

Other Windows 3.1 Accessories

Object Packager (Figure 10.27) is used to embed one document in another (documents are word processing documents, spreadsheets, pictures, sound recordings, and so forth). For instance, you might develop an application that lists various airplanes your company sells. The basic list is in a Microsoft Word for Windows document, and you want the user of the program to be able to see a picture of the plane

FIGURE 10.27
Object Packager

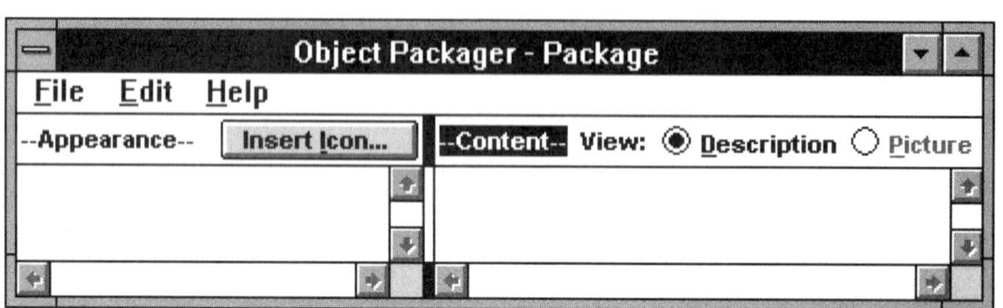

described in a paragraph by clicking an icon next to the description. Object Packager allows you to create such an application using the technique of "object linking and embedding" discussed in Unit 11.

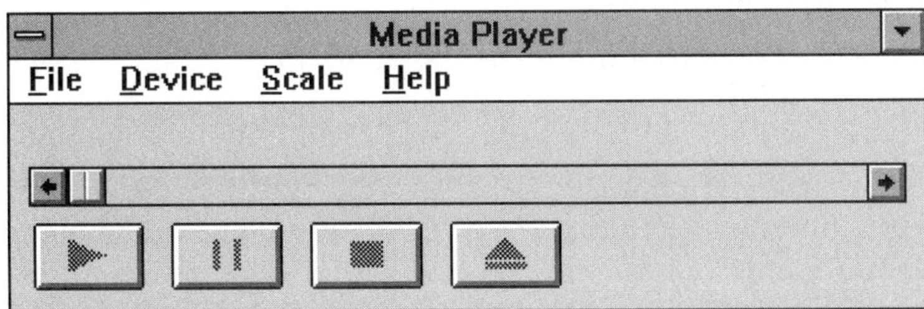

FIGURE 10.28
Sound Recorder

Sound Recorder (Figure 10.28) and Media Player (Figure 10.29) add the capabilities of audio to the primarily visual world of Windows. For both, you must have special hardware attached to your system that allows the recording and playback of specially coded sound files. With the right hardware, you can add your own voice or a measure from your favorite symphony to a Windows document.

FIGURE 10.29
Media Player

Character Map (Figure 10.30) is used to locate and insert special characters into documents, including characters from various type fonts (Figure 10.31).

FIGURE 10.30
*Character Map
of Symbols font*

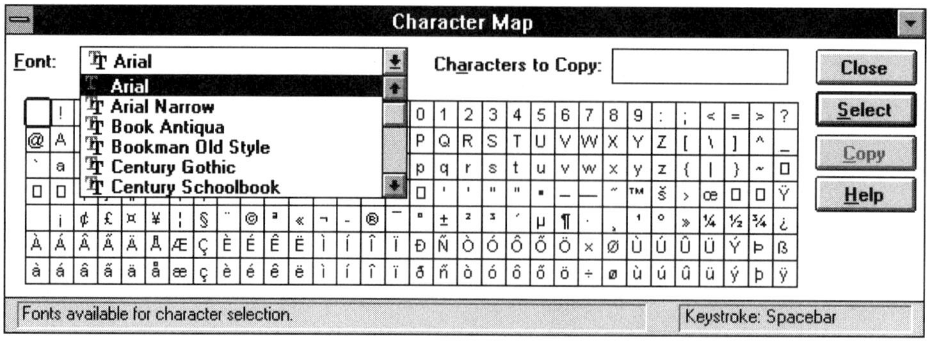

FIGURE 10.31
The Arial TrueType font as displayed in Character Map

Review Questions

*1. Which command(s) would be used to switch from a standard calculator to a scientific calculator?

2. State the Calculator key and keyboard equivalent used to perform each of the following functions:

   a. Perform a mathematical operation between two numbers.

   b. Clear the calculation.

   c. Display the square root of the displayed value.

   d. Delete the right-most digit of the displayed value.

3. When you are using the Statistics window, the Statistics box will overlap the calculator. How do you switch from one active area to the other, using a mouse? Using the keyboard?

*4. What is Calendar? List some of the functions that can be performed using Calendar.

5. What is Cardfile, and why is it similar to a Rolodex? Which command(s) can be used to remove a card from Cardfile?

6. Explain the difference between the analog clock and the digital clock.

*7. If you are using Notepad to create a memo, what should be done to prevent the text's going beyond the right edge of the window?

*8. How is a time log file created?

Key Terms

ASCII text file	Footer	Toggle
Batch file	Header	

Documentation Research

To answer the following questions, use Chapter 12, "Additional Accessories," of the *User's Guide*. Check the guide's index to find pages with the information needed. We recommend that you also write the relevant page number next to each question. For additional aid, you may need to use the on-line Help menu.

1. How do you copy the value in Calculator's display to the Clipboard?

2. How do you paste a number from the Clipboard to Calculator's display?

3. What command is used to set an alarm in Clock?

4. List the steps to open an appointment file as a read-only file.

5. What command is used to print an entire card file?

6. Using the on-line Help menu, what is the keyboard equivalent to activate Calculator's Statistics box?

7. Using the on-line Help menu, what is the keyboard equivalent to bring the first card in a file to the front?

8. Using the Notepad's on-line Help menu, how many procedure topics are listed?

The Windows Family of Products

This unit deals with four Microsoft software packages that you will probably encounter sometime in your work with the Windows environment. These products—Word for Windows, Excel, PowerPoint, and Project—have been designed to work with each other to provide a substantial "tool kit" on a personal computer. This unit focuses on the features of the products and gives a small demonstration of how they combine to support a decision-making task. Unlike other units in this book, this unit focuses on *what* can be done, rather than on *how* to do it. Other books in the West Microcomputing Series provide instruction in the use of Word for Windows and Excel, and references are available from other sources for the more sophisticated applications of PowerPoint and Project.

Learning Objectives

At the completion of this unit, you should know

1. the names and features of four prominent members of the Microsoft family of Windows products—Word for Windows, Excel, PowerPoint, and Project,

2. the three primary methods of sharing data among Windows applications.

At the completion of this unit, you should be able to

1. specify which of the products to use for a given application.

The Problem

To illustrate these software packages, we developed a simple problem. We have decided to build a cabin in the woods and want to plan our time to accomplish that feat. To solve our problem, we must plan a schedule to accommodate the tasks of building the cabin, which must be accomplished in a specific order. Microsoft Project will enable us to plan the schedule. Once the schedule is complete, we would like to produce a pie chart showing the proportion of time spent on each phase of the project. We will use Microsoft Excel to develop the chart. We plan to use the chart in two places: a letter to our father (created in Microsoft Word for Windows) and a set of overhead transparencies (created in Microsoft PowerPoint).

To begin, we list the steps to be accomplished and the relationship of these steps to other steps. You might do this on paper (as we did), or you can enter them directly into Project. Table 11.1 contains the task information. Some of the durations are in weeks (which, by definition, consist of five eight-hour days) and others are in days. The most complex part of this example is the constraints. Note that some tasks start after others are finished (for example, bidding cannot start until a week after the plans are finished, to give contractors time to study the plans), while other tasks start a certain number of days after another task has started (electrical work cannot start until after five days of framing). The most complex constraint is that for finishing, which cannot start until framing, electrical, and plumbing have reached certain stages of completion. Given the July 25 starting date, can you predict when the task will be finished?

TABLE 11.1
Task List

STEP	TASK	DURATION	CONSTRAINTS
1	Engineering Design	2 weeks	Start on 7/25/91 at 8:00 a.m.
2	Bidding	2 days	Start 1 week after completion of task 1.
3	Construction – Frame & Mech.	3 weeks	Start 4 days after completion of task 2.
4	Construction – Electrical	8 days	Start 5 days after start of task 3.
5	Construction – Plumbing	1 week	Start 7 days after start of task 3.
6	Finishing	2 weeks	Start after the following, whichever is latest: …3 days before completion of task 3; …2 days before completion of task 4; …completion of task 5.

Microsoft Project

The first step in analyzing our project requires using the software package Microsoft Project. We can enter information such as that contained in Table 11.1, whereupon Project will determine the starting and ending dates and times for each task. It

FIGURE 11.1
Microsoft Project task entry screen

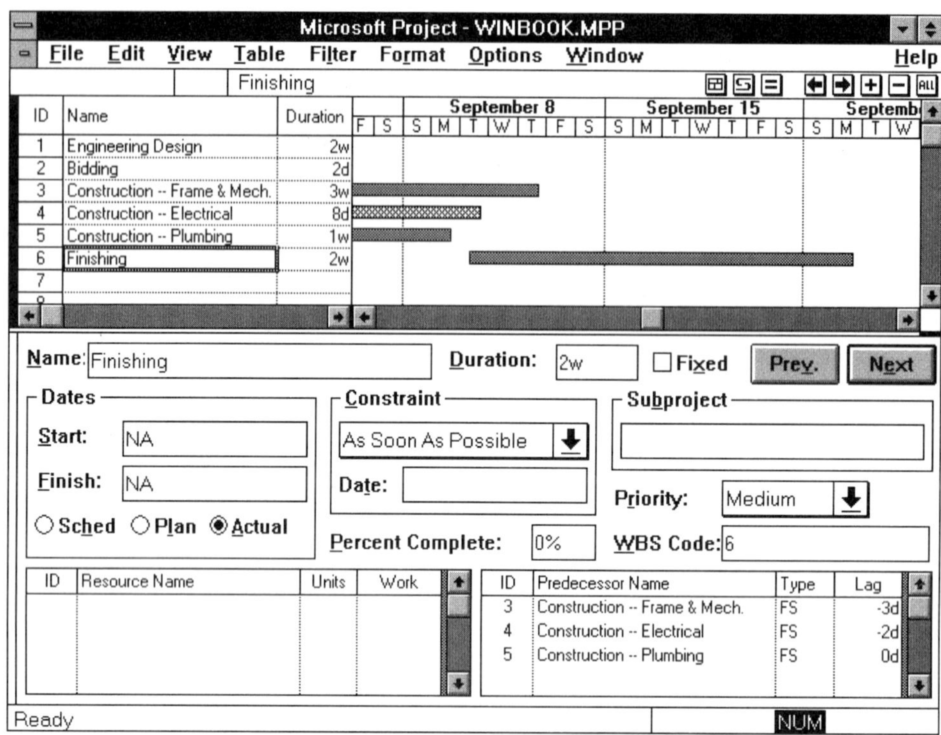

will also determine a *critical path*, the sequence of tasks that must be completed on time for the project as a whole to be completed on time.

Task information is entered on the multiwindowed screen illustrated in Figure 11.1. The upper-left window contains a list of the tasks already entered. The upper-right window contains a special type of bar chart, called a *Gantt chart* (named after the inventor), that shows the starting and ending times of each task. The bottom window is used for entering information about a task. Most of the information entered should be self-explanatory. Constraints are entered in the lower-right corner of this window. Unless you make a different entry, Project assumes that the constraint is a "finish before start" (FS) type of constraint. A negative number means that the current task can start that many days (or weeks, months, etc.) before the previous (antecedent) task ends. A positive number indicates a delay from the finish of the antecedent task to the start of the current task.

Project also allows the entry of resources that are associated with a task. Often, specific personnel must be scheduled for specific tasks, further complicating the planning process. We did not use the resource feature in this example, assuming that resources needed to build the cabin would be available from the contractors.

Once the tasks are entered, you can ask Project to display and print several items. Figure 11.2 contains the full Gantt chart. Tasks on the critical path are indicated by the diagonal hatching pattern. Figure 11.3 contains a diagram called a *PERT* (project evaluation and review technique) *chart*. Notice that information about the task is displayed in the box and that the relationship among tasks is displayed by their arrangement on the page. From both diagrams, we see that the scheduling of the electrical work is not critical, but that all other tasks are on the critical path and must be closely monitored if we are to finish our cabin on September 23.

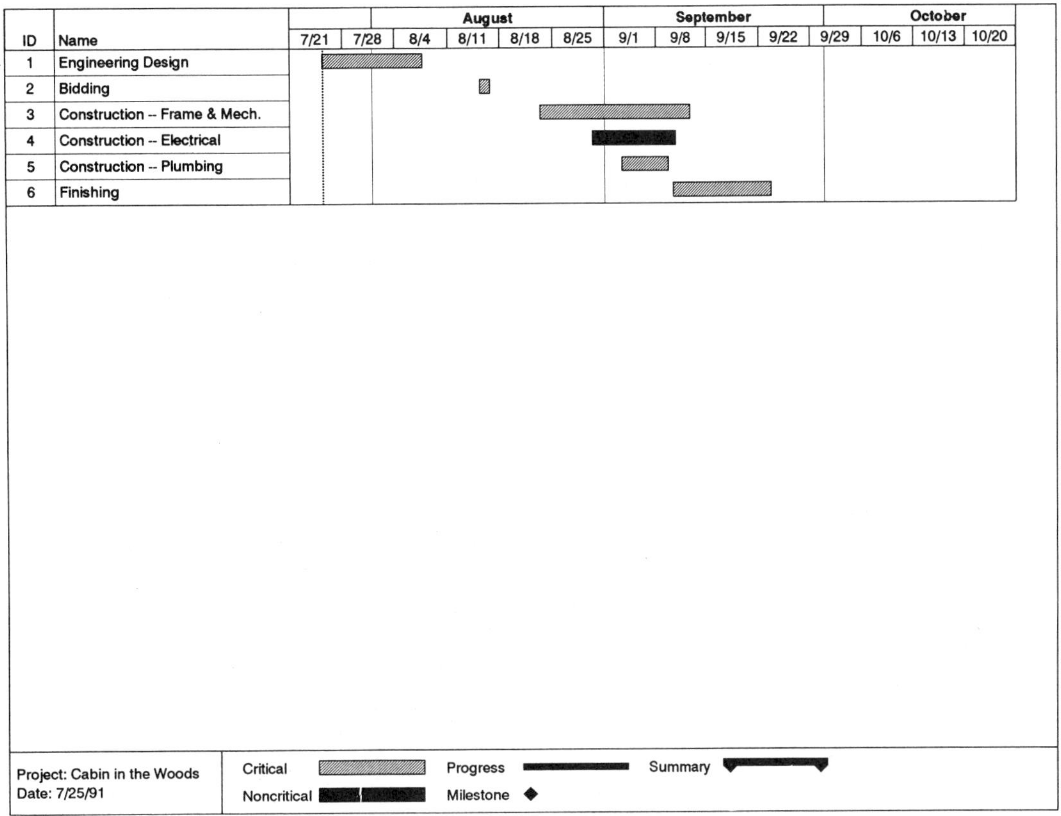

This illustration of Microsoft Project has visited only a few of its capabilities. One feature of the graphical user interface that project planners will appreciate is the ability to enter and edit information directly on the Gantt or PERT charts. Use the mouse to change the duration of a task on the Gantt chart, and all other parts of the project schedule adjust accordingly.

Sharing Information with Microsoft Excel

Once the project is planned, we want to use the spreadsheet package Microsoft Excel to create a graph. One of the methods for sharing information between Project and Excel is to *save in a different format*. Normally, Project saves information in a special format with an .MPP file extension. However, Project can also save the data in a file format that is directly transferable to Excel, the .XLS format. Once the data are saved in an Excel file, we can move to the next step of our project: creating a graph.

Microsoft Excel

Excel is the state-of-the-art spreadsheet package from Microsoft and the first popular PC package to use the graphical user interface extensively. Users familiar with other spreadsheet packages report that they are pleased with the power of Excel, the

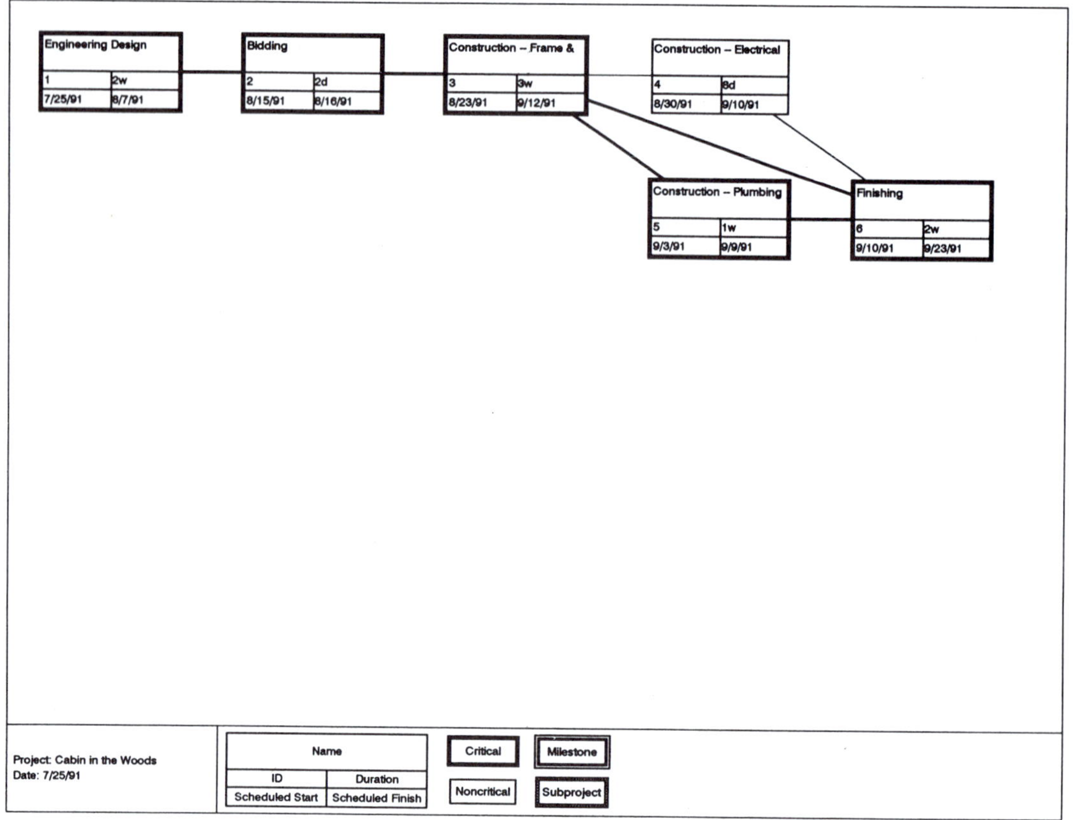

FIGURE 11.3
PERT chart

ease with which powerful models can be constructed, and the attractive output available using Excel's broad range of formatting options.

With Excel, you can display and link multiple spreadsheets on your screen. You can record macros as you work, store them on separate sheets, and apply them to any worksheet. You can check your figures with an array of advanced, built-in auditing tools as well. Excel for Windows has the capacity of 256 columns by 16,384 rows. In addition, it has 131 built-in worksheet functions and 224 macro functions. Excel operates with user-defined menus, dialog boxes, and on-line help for creating easy-to-use shortcuts and custom applications. Furthermore, Excel is compatible with Lotus 1-2-3 and Symphony, dBASE III Plus, and Microsoft Multiplan. For graphic display of numbers, a gallery of 44 built-in chart types plus customization is available in Excel. Further, Excel provides complete laser printer support for annual report-quality output, with multiple fonts, borders, shading, custom number, formats, and color.

Creating the Graph

After starting the Excel program, we opened the spreadsheet (.XLS) file saved by Project. To create the graph, we highlighted 12 spreadsheet cells containing the 6 task names and durations, used Edit Copy to copy them to the Clipboard, used File New Chart to create a chart of the data, and finally used Gallery 3-D Pie to select the type of chart we wanted. To produce the *pie chart* illustrated in Figure 11.4 took fewer than ten mouse clicks and no typing! Adding the *legend* explaining the shading

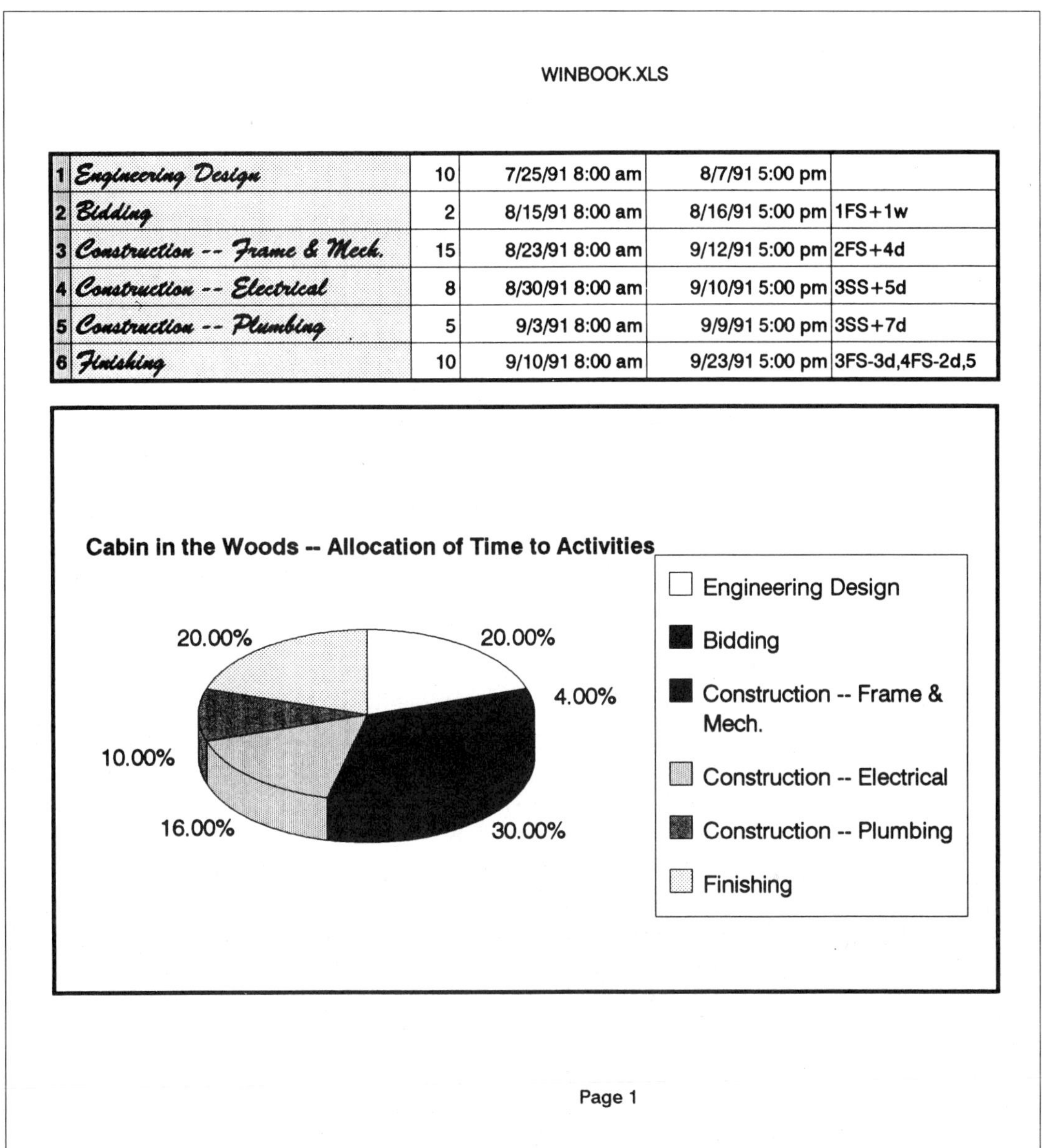

1	*Engineering Design*	10	7/25/91 8:00 am	8/7/91 5:00 pm	
2	*Bidding*	2	8/15/91 8:00 am	8/16/91 5:00 pm	1FS+1w
3	*Construction -- Frame & Mech.*	15	8/23/91 8:00 am	9/12/91 5:00 pm	2FS+4d
4	*Construction -- Electrical*	8	8/30/91 8:00 am	9/10/91 5:00 pm	3SS+5d
5	*Construction -- Plumbing*	5	9/3/91 8:00 am	9/9/91 5:00 pm	3SS+7d
6	*Finishing*	10	9/10/91 8:00 am	9/23/91 5:00 pm	3FS-3d,4FS-2d,5

patterns used required a few more mouse clicks. We did have to type the text of the title, but all other aspects of creating the graph and formatting the spreadsheet for printing were accomplished using the mouse.

Figure 11.4 contains the printed output we created using Excel. Both graph and spreadsheet data are printed on the same page. We used formatting features available in Excel to **highlight** (shade) the task number and task name columns, to draw the lines separating cells, and to specify a script typeface for the task name. The formatting was readily accomplished using the graphical user interface. The WYSIWYG (what you see is what you get) display on the screen provides the feedback that assures you that you are making the changes you intend to make.

The total time required to convert the file created by Project to the output displayed in Figure 11.4 was about 15 minutes. The spreadsheet and the chart were saved in two separate files (the chart file has an .XLC extension). The next step, discussed in the following section, was to copy the chart to the Clipboard for insertion into a Word for Windows document.

Sharing Information with Microsoft Word for Windows

We will use the technique called *dynamic data exchange (DDE)* to share information between an Excel chart and a Word for Windows document. Before we leave the Excel program, we select the chart and copy it to the Clipboard. Selecting the chart is easy: Place the mouse pointer in an open area of the chart (for example, between the word Cabin and the 20.00% notation) and click once. Small hollow boxes appear around the perimeter of the chart: its titles and legends. Copying to the Clipboard is almost as easy: Issue the menu command EditCopy. The chart will stay on the Clipboard until you exit Windows or cut or copy something else to the Clipboard. Linking the chart to the word processing document is covered in the next section.

Microsoft Word for Windows

Word for Windows is the word processing package developed by Microsoft for the Windows environment (its icon is shown to the left). A similar package, Microsoft Word, exists for those users who are not using Windows. Word for Windows is often called "Winword" to distinguish it from the character-based Word, but in this unit we will just use the term "Word" to refer to the Windows product. Be aware of the difference if you intend to purchase one or the other.

Word for Windows is a sophisticated program that includes a *spell checker*, a *thesaurus, mail merge* capability, and other utilities. Other characteristics of Word include *annotation*, which allows you to add comments to a document; *automatic numbering*, which permits numbering and renumbering of headings in outlines or renumbering of items in a series in the body of a document; *autosave*, which preserves changes in your document at intervals you specify; and *bold, italic*, and other *character formats*, which add emphasis to text. Single and double underlining, strike-through, superscript, subscript, and hidden text are other character formats that Word supports.

Word contains a number of paragraph formats, which are helpful in setting up your text. A document can contain multiple formats to permit you to have a standard format, say double-spaced and justified, while reserving a special format for headings and important paragraphs. These special formats can have left, center, or right alignment; a unique typeface; extra spacing before, after, or in the middle of the paragraph; and numerous other characteristics. The possibilities for arranging text are almost as limitless as your imagination.

Indexing is another helpful Word capability. Word can locate text that you have marked for index entries and then generate an index from these entries. The index can be created in multiple-column format, with continuous page referencing, special capitalization and indentation, and any other formatting feature you want. Clearly, such features are very useful in performing desktop publishing.

Word permits the importing of pictures, charts, and stylized text directly into a document. The *graphics* capabilities of Word enable you to include layout features within text. For example, you can create a company logo using Paintbrush, then import it into every page of your text. Or, as we shall do here, an Excel graph can be put in a Word document and linked to the original spreadsheet.

Linking the Chart to the Document

Once we started Word, we immediately pasted the chart into our document. (We could have waited until we typed the letter, but the chart was already on the Clipboard so we decided to paste it before starting on the text of the letter.) To accomplish the dynamic data exchange, we choose the Edit Paste Link command in Word, and indicate that the link should be updated automatically. This *dynamic* data exchange means that the chart in the word processing document will change whenever the data in the spreadsheet file change. If we desired a *static* data exchange, we would have used the EditPaste command. The benefit of a *static data exchange* is that it is faster to accomplish initially; it also permits a more rapid opening of the file in the future because there is no link between the document and the spreadsheet. A dynamic link requires that the spreadsheet program (Excel) be started whenever the document is opened. By contrast, a static link preserves the values of the data at the time the link is made. Subsequent updates to the data will not be reflected in the word processing document unless you redo the cut and paste.

Once the chart was in place, we typed the remainder of the letter. After typing, we used the mouse to highlight words and boldface or italicize them. We also changed the typeface of two phrases to highlight them. As with Excel, this is an easy process, requiring but a few mouse movements. A portion of the letter as printed appears in Figure 11.5.

Microsoft PowerPoint

PowerPoint for Windows provides a fast, easy way for you to create and manage high-quality overhead transparency and 35mm slide presentations. With PowerPoint (its screen icon is to the left), you do not need to be an artist to create professional-looking overheads and slides. Because PowerPoint uses the WYSIWYG technology of Windows, you see your material on the screen exactly as it will appear when printed or converted to 35mm slides. Changes can be viewed instantly, as well.

Creating the Slides

We created three slides for our presentation. Figure 11.6 contains the first two slides, printed in a *handout* format. Figure 11.7 shows a full-page version of the third slide, the one with our famous graph. Notice that a consistent pattern is printed on the left side of the slide and that the slide titles are in the same type style—but different sizes—and in a shaded box. PowerPoint makes it easy for you to design a *master slide* that carries common design elements from one slide to the next. The effects in black and white are interesting, but the effects in full color are fantastic!

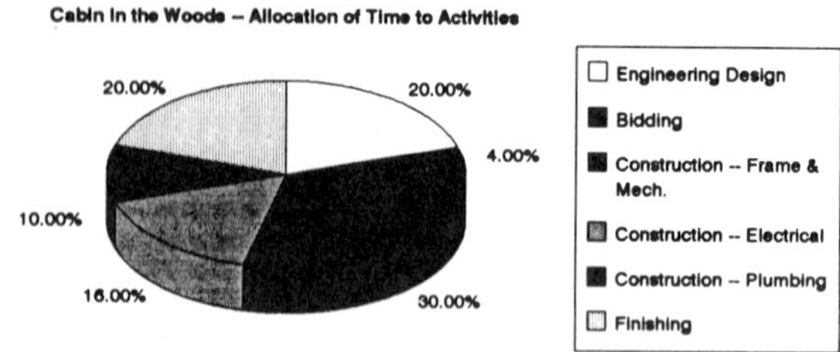

Dear Dad,

The following chart shows the allocation of time to the various activities involved in building our *Cabin in the Woods*.

We will start the engineering design on **July 25** and expect to finish the cabin on **September 23**. We're hoping that you will come up to visit us during the "fall colors" festival in October. Our cabin should be the *perfect* base for your activities.

. . .

Love,

The Kids

The text on slide 2 was copied to the Clipboard from the Excel spreadsheet, then pasted onto the slide. The diamond-shaped *bullet* characters were added after the paste. The chart on slide 3 required more sophisticated treatment. We wanted to be able to edit the chart if necessary while we were working on the PowerPoint presentation. The chart was brought into the PowerPoint slide with the command File/Insert/Excel/Chart. As explained below, this command links both the chart and the program that created it to the slide.

Some Windows products support a technique called *object linking and embedding*, or *OLE*. The premise of OLE is that an object (here, the chart) will appear as part of the receiving program (PowerPoint), but that all editing of that chart will be done using the originating program (Excel). OLE goes beyond the dynamic data exchange (DDE) method we used to link the chart to the Word document. Not only will the chart change when the original data are changed in Excel (common to both DDE and OLE), but, with OLE, we can initiate editing of the chart from within PowerPoint. By contrast, with DDE we would have to leave Word and enter Excel to edit the chart. With OLE, we initiate editing of the chart from within PowerPoint, by double-clicking the object to be edited. If Excel is not open, it will be started, the appropriate spreadsheet and accompanying chart will be loaded, and editing can commence. When we are finished editing the chart (changing the legend, for instance), we are taken back to the PowerPoint slide.

OLE as demonstrated in the PowerPoint/Excel link might not seem such a big deal, but future Windows software, both from Microsoft and from other companies,

FIGURE 11.6
Two slides in handout format

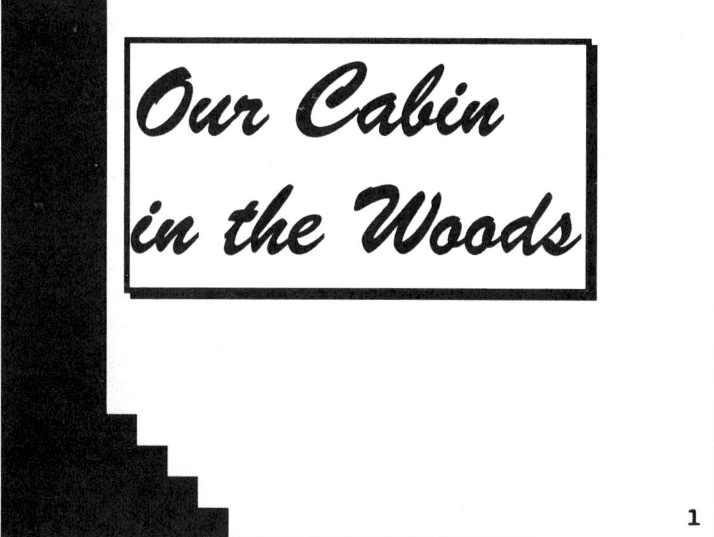

FIGURE 11.7
A full-page slide

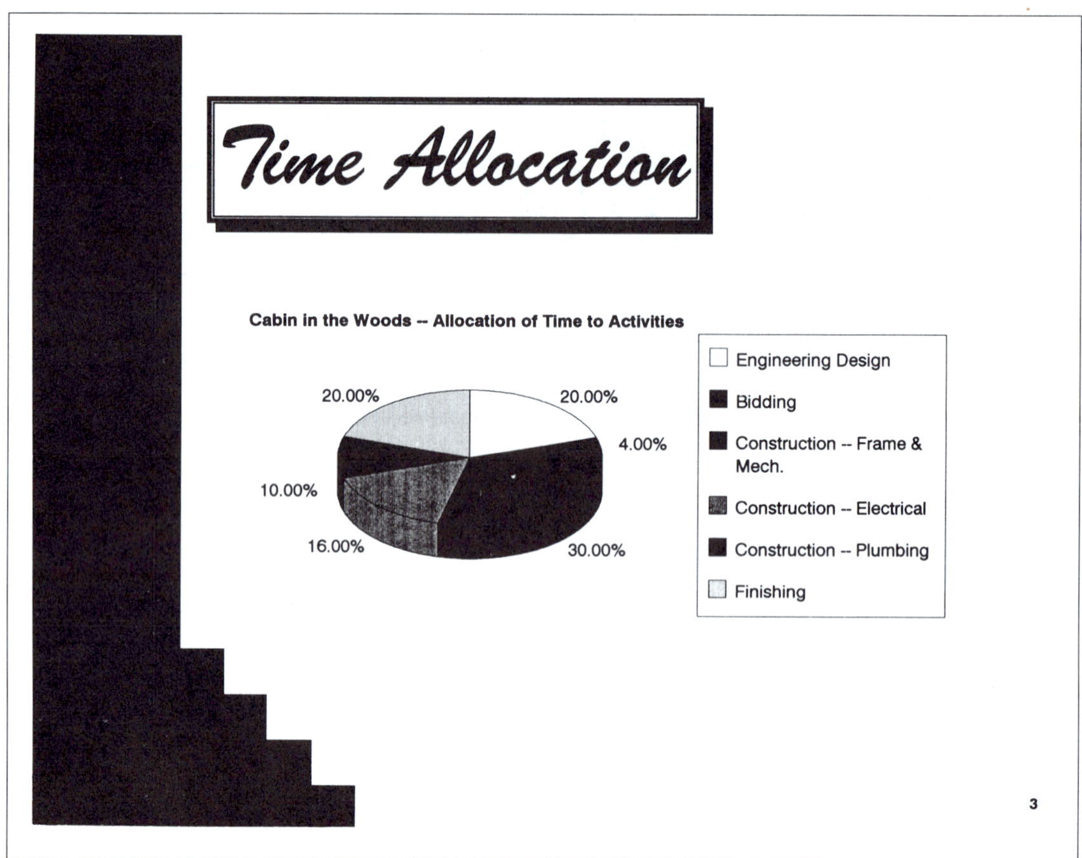

will make great use of this feature to further integrate their products. OLE is one example of *object-oriented programming* (*OOP*), a new technique that enables objects to contain both data (such as the numbers behind the chart) as well as the procedures necessary to display the data (for instance, Excel's charting program). You will see OOP techniques applied more and more in Windows as well as other operating systems as programmers become more familiar with their use.

Review Questions

*1. Increasing numbers of users are starting to benefit from the Windows family of products. Identify those products that are mentioned in this unit, and give a brief description of each.

2. Describe the three methods of transferring data from one Windows application to another. What are the advantages and disadvantages of each?

*3. Identify the product associated with each set of terms:

    a. macros, columns, spreadsheets

    b. slide creation, WYSIWYG technology, overheads

    c. spell checker, superscripts, annotations

    d. PERT chart, Gantt chart, critical path

Key Terms

Annotation
Automatic numbering
Autosave
Bold
Bullet
Character format
Critical path
Dynamic data exchange
  (DDE)
Gantt chart

Graphics
Handout
Highlight
Indexing
Italic
Legend
Mail merge
Master slide
Object linking and
  embedding (OLE)

Object-oriented
  programming (OOP)
PERT chart
Pie chart
Save in a different format
Spell checker
Static data exchange
Thesaurus

Advanced Windows Applications

III

■ **PART THREE** In this section we discuss advanced Windows applications. Such applications include Recorder, PIF Editor, Customizing Windows, Program Manager and Control Panel, and Clipboard. While the last three topics have been presented earlier, here we provide additional information on the advanced features of each.

Unit 12 covers the Windows application Recorder, which is designed to capture a sequence of keystrokes and mouse actions, save these sequences in a file, and play them back with a single keystroke or keystroke combination. This process is referred to as a macro. Unit 13 introduces PIF editor, which allows you to use non-Windows applications that have been written for MS-DOS while you are in the Windows environment. Units 14 and 15 cover advanced topics in customizing and optimizing Windows. Finally, Unit 16 explains how to use Clipboard to transfer information between applications.

Recorder

Recorder is a Windows application for creating macros. A ***macro*** is a sequence of keystrokes and mouse actions that are recorded, then played back at a later time. You use a macro to take the place of longer step-by-step sequence commands, such as entering text, saving files, or loading applications. These keystrokes or key combinations are entered in a file, saved, and ultimately executed at the appropriate time. You can automate many Windows tasks with macros. Since macros can be complex, they are best used by more experienced users.

Learning Objectives

At the completion of this unit, you should know

1. what a macro is,

2. the macro recording options available in Recorder.

At the completion of this unit, you should be able to

1. start and close Recorder,

2. record, create, and use a macro.

Starting Recorder

Recorder

Recorder is contained in Program Manager's Accessories program group. To start Recorder, double-click on its icon. If you are using the keyboard, highlight Recorder using the arrow keys, and choose Open from the Program Manager's File menu. The Recorder icon resembles a camcorder (as shown to the left). An untitled Recorder window appears as in Figure 12.1.

FIGURE 12.1
The initial Recorder window

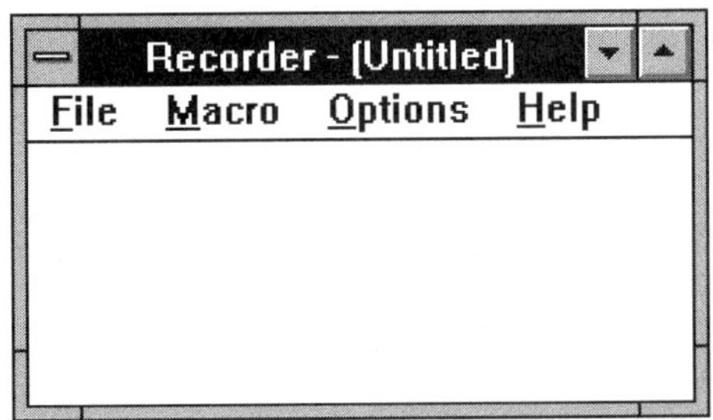

The workspace on the Recorder window is blank until you create and save a macro. Macros are saved in files with an .REC extension. Each .REC file contains one or more macros. There is a limit to the number of macros that can be entered into a file, as the macro file cannot exceed 64KB. You can create as many macro files as you need, but only one file can be open at a time.

Macros can be simple or complex, depending on what you want to record. Your evolving skill in using the Windows environment may lead to programs' requiring multiple windows and multiple applications. As you become more sophisticated in your use of the Recorder, you should refer to the Microsoft Windows 3.1 *User's Guide* for a more detailed discussion of it.

Recording a Macro

To record a macro (after you have started Recorder), you must open the application where the macro will run. For example, if you want a macro to run one or more commands in Write, you will need to start Write and make sure that you have an open window in Write. Then, switch to the Recorder window (using Alt Tab or clicking on the window as usual). From the Recorder menu, select the Macro command, then select Record. The Record Macro dialog box will appear as in Figure 12.2.

In the Record Macro Name box, enter a name for the macro (up to 40 characters) that identifies the purpose of the macro, plus a *Shortcut Key* combination. The Shortcut Key combination is used to play back or *run* the macro. The Ctrl, Shift, or Alt key in combination with any other single letter key can be used for the macro. Ctrl is the default setting. To change this default setting, click on either the Shift or Alt box. Next, click the Start box to begin recording the macro. The Recorder icon will start to blink. Enter the keystrokes and mouse actions you want to record.

NOTE *It is best to use command key sequences rather than mouse actions when recording the macro, because the macro may not operate properly on a system that uses a different kind of display.*

When you want to stop recording, click the blinking Recorder icon at the bottom of the screen or press Ctrl Break. The drop-down dialog box shown in Figure 12.3 will appear, prompting you to save the macro, resume recording, or cancel recording. Select Save Macro and OK to complete the recording.

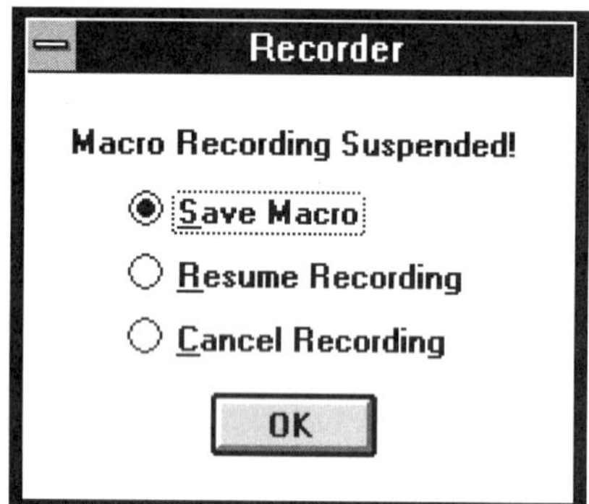

Creating a Macro

The following discussion demonstrates the creation of a simple macro that displays the Calendar in the monthly mode. Proceed as follows:

1. Start Recorder from the Accessories program group and minimize Recorder to its icon.

2. Start Calendar as an open application window.

3. Double-click on the Recorder icon at the bottom of the screen.

4. Choose the Record command on Recorder's Macro menu.

5. In the Record Macro Name box, type the following:

```
To View Monthly Calendar
```

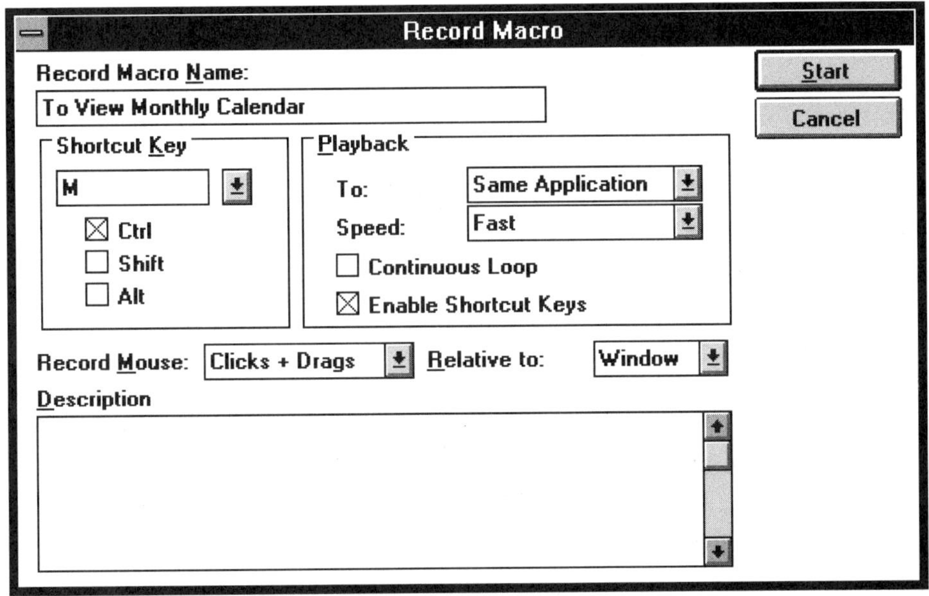

6. In the Shortcut Key box, type M. Since the Ctrl box (default) is checked, the keyboard shortcut will be Ctrl M; see Figure 12.4 for the Record Macro dialog box.

7. Click Start.

8. Make the Calendar window current by clicking on its window or pressing Alt Tab.

9. Press Alt V, M to select View and Monthly from the Calendar's menu. This is the command that we want to record for later use.

10. Click on the Recorder icon or press Ctrl Break.

11. A drop-down dialog box will appear, asking if you want to save, resume, or cancel. Select Save Macro and click OK to complete the recording. (You can use the mouse pointer at this time, since this action is not part of the macro itself.)

12. To save the macro in a file, restore the Recorder window by double-clicking its icon at the bottom of the screen, choose File Save As, select the proper disk or directory, and enter a file name such as STEVES.REC for your personal set, or WRITE.REC for macros that work with a specific program.

13. Run the macro by pressing Ctrl M.

Figure 12.5 illustrates the macros created and saved in a file named NOTEPAD.REC. The left column lists the shortcut keys for each macro and the right column lists the macro's description. To run the macro, use the shortcut key combination (here, Ctrl M; press and hold Ctrl, then press M).

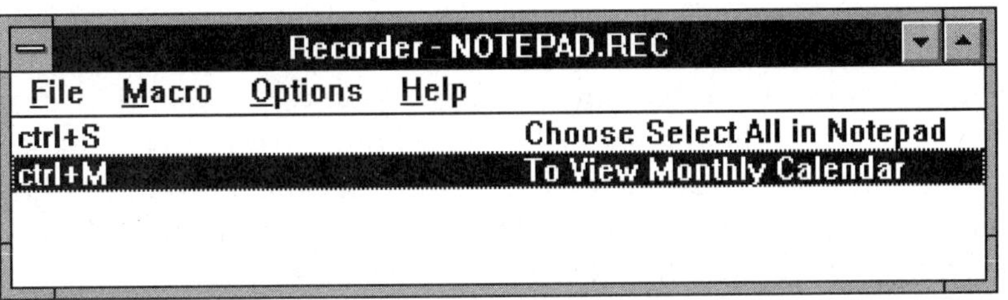

Using a Macro

When you have created and saved a macro, you can use it to automate your work in Windows. To use a macro, you have to begin the macro at the time and place it will be used. For example, if you want to run the "Monthly Calendar" macro, you must have its application, Calendar, open in a window (not minimized). Press Ctrl M. This macro will not run in any application other than the Calendar application unless you change default options.

A macro can be played back by using the shortcut key (Ctrl M) or by using the Run command in the Macro menu. If you have not assigned a shortcut key to a macro, you must use the Run command to play back the macro. You can use this procedure to invoke the macro if you do not remember the shortcut key. To stop a macro while it is running, press Ctrl Break. A drop-down dialog box will appear, asking you to confirm the cancellation.

Record Options

Beyond the basic steps for creating, saving, and running a macro, there are additional options while using Recorder. These options allow you to do the following:

- Specify whether mouse movements will be recorded and whether they are relative to the entire screen or only to the window (change the "Record Mouse" and "Relative to" lists)

- Play back the macro only in the application where you recorded it or play it back in any application—an example of the latter being a "global" macro for the File Save command found in most Windows applications (change the "Playback To" list)

- Play the macro back quickly or at the speed at which it was recorded (change the "Playback Speed" list)

- Make the macro play continuously until you press Ctrl Break (check the "Continuous Loop" box)

- Invoke other macros from the macro you are recording (if "Enable Shortcut Keys" is checked, another macro can be invoked in the midst of the macro being recorded)

Review the Record Macro window illustrated in Figure 12.4. You will notice the lists for each of these options. For more information on these advanced options, refer to Microsoft's Windows 3.1 *User's Guide*.

Using Recorder Files

Recorder files can contain many macros. However, as mentioned earlier, Recorder will stop when the file uses 64KB of memory. You can create other Recorder files, but only one file can be opened at any given time. If you have created and saved your favorite macros in two different files, you can combine them into one file (up to the 64KB limit) with the File Merge command.

Macro Properties

Macro **N**ame:

To View Monthly Calendar

OK

Cancel

Shortcut **K**ey

M

☒ Ctrl
☐ Shift
☐ Alt

Playback

To: Same Application

Speed: Fast

☐ Continuous Loop
☒ Enable Shortcut Keys

Mouse Coordinates Relative To: Window
Contains no mouse messages.
Description

Changing a Macro

You can change the Properties of a macro that you record. Most of the options mentioned above can also be changed. To change the Properties, load the macro file that contains the macro you want to modify by using the Open command from the File menu. You will see a window like that in Figure 12.5. Click on the macro to be changed, then select Properties from the Macro menu. The drop-down dialog box will appear as in Figure 12.6.

Closing Recorder

If Recorder has been minimized to an icon, single-click its icon at the bottom of the screen. The drop-down dialog box will appear; select Close. If Recorder has not been minimized, select either Exit from the File menu or Close from the Control Menu box (upper-left corner as in Figure 12.7). Finally, Recorder can be closed quickly by using the keyboard combination Alt F4.

Recorder - NOTEPAD.REC

GUIDED ACTIVITY 12.1

Making a Macro

1. Start Write from the Accessories group in Program Manager.

2. Switch to Program Manager by double-clicking on its icon, and open Recorder from the Accessories group.

3. Click on Record in the Macro menu. In the dialog box, enter the following settings:

   a. Macro Name: Heading

   b. Shortcut Key: H; confirm that Ctrl is checked, not Shift or Alt

   c. Playback To: Same Application

   d. Playback Speed: Fast

   e. Enable Shortcut Keys: Confirm that this box is checked

   f. Mouse Coordinates Relative to: Window

4. Click on Start. You will be returned to your original Write window.

5. Type the following:

   ```
   To:
   From: (your name)
   Date:
   Subject:
   ```

6. Click on the blinking Recorder icon at the bottom of the screen to suspend the recording of the macro.

7. Click on Save Macro and then on OK.

8. While in Write, click on New in the File menu. (Choose "No" from the "save current changes" dialog box.) To run your macro, press [Ctrl][H], the shortcut key you assigned to the macro. Thus, your heading will be typed out automatically.

9. Save the Recorder file on your data disk with the name WRITE.REC by clicking on Save As from the File menu.

10. Close Recorder by clicking on Exit in the File menu.

11. Close Write without saving the file.

GUIDED ACTIVITY 12.2

Making a Macro

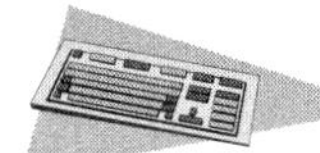

1. Start Write from the Accessories group in Program Manager.

2. Switch to Program Manager by pressing [Alt][Tab] until its icon is highlighted, then releasing [Alt]. Press [Alt][W] for Window and select Accessories. Highlight the Recorder icon and press [Enter].

3. Select Record from the Macro menu. In the dialog box, enter the following settings:

   a. Macro Name: Heading; press [Tab] to move to the next box

   b. Shortcut Key: H; confirm that Ctrl is checked, not Shift or Alt

   c. Playback To: Same Application

   d. Playback Speed: Fast

   e. Enable Shortcut Keys: Confirm that this box is checked

   f. Mouse Coordinates Relative to: Window

4. Press [Alt][S] for Start. You will be returned to your original Write window.

5. Type the following:

   ```
   To:
   From:  (your name)
   Date:
   Subject:
   ```

6. Press [Ctrl][Break] to suspend the recording of the macro. A Recorder dialog box will appear.

7. Press [Alt][S] for Save Macro and then press [Enter]. The Recorder icon will stop blinking. This does not save the macro on disk; it only allows you to invoke the macro during the current session.

8. While in Write, select New from the File menu. (Choose "No" from the "save current changes" dialog box.) To run your macro, press [Ctrl][H], the shortcut key you assigned to the macro. Thus, your heading will be typed out automatically.

9. Save the Recorder file on your data disk with the name WRITE.REC by selecting Save from the File menu.

10. Close Recorder by selecting Exit in the File menu.

11. Close Write without saving the file.

Review Questions

*1. What does the shortcut key name do?

*2. What is the basic purpose of a macro?

 3. Review the procedures for creating a macro to view the Calendar in the monthly mode.

*4. If a macro is created for Write, can it be used in Calendar? Why or why not?

 5. List the options available in Recorder that were mentioned in this unit.

*6. What are the properties of a macro that can be changed? How are the changes made?

Key Terms

Macro   Run   Shortcut key

Documentation Research

To answer the following questions, use Chapter 12, "Additional Accessories," of the *User's Guide*. Check the guide's index to find pages with the information needed. We recommend that you also write the relevant page number next to each question. For additional aid, you may need to use the on-line Help menu.

1. How do you maintain the Recorder window at playback?

2. Why is it best to keep recording of mouse movements to a minimum?

3. What are some guidelines for creating macros?

4. Using Recorder's on-line Help menu, how many procedure topics are listed?

5. Using Recorder's on-line Help menu, how do you create a new file?

To use non-Windows applications (such as DOS versions of Lotus 1-2-3, dBASE IV, or Quattro Pro) with Windows, you will need a program information file (PIF). A program information file contains special information regarding Windows' requirements to run an application. You can create or edit a PIF by using PIF Editor.

Learning Objectives

At the completion of this unit, you should know

1. what a PIF (program information file) is.

At the completion of this unit, you should be able to

1. start and close PIF Editor,

2. set PIF options.

Program Information Files

Each "Windows" application program—such as Write, Paintbrush, Word, Excel, and others that we have discussed to this point—contain instructions to Windows as to how the program is to be treated. These instructions include the amount of memory required to run the program, the size of the window, the video display requirements, and so on. "Non-Windows" applications programs, such as Lotus 1-2-3 (release 3.4 and lower) and WordPerfect (release 5.1 and lower) do not contain such information. **PIF Editor** is used to instruct Windows how to deal with an MS-DOS application that you want to run in the Windows environment. The settings are saved in a **program information file (PIF)** that has a .PIF extension. Normally, you will create a PIF file for each program (some program publishers furnish a PIF file with their software). MS-DOS programs that do not have an associated PIF file will be assigned to use the file named _DEFAULT.PIF (the underscore is part of the file name).

Starting PIF Editor

PIF Editor

To start PIF Editor, either double-click on the icon (shown to the left) from either the Main or the Accessories program group in Program Manager, or highlight the icon and select Open from Program Manager's File menu. PIF Editor, with a new, untitled window, appears as in Figure 13.1.

FIGURE 13.1
*Untitled PIF
Editor window*

You will notice the default (standard) settings. These include *Video Memory* requirements and *XMS Memory*. The other settings are entered at the time you Open or Edit a PIF file. If you want to edit an existing PIF, choose Open from the File menu, and select the file you wish to edit. A list of PIF files will appear in a dialog box, as shown in Figure 13.2. For example, if you want to edit the Lotus PIF, click on its file name and then on OK. The window for the file you choose will appear as in Figure 13.3. (Modes of Windows operation are discussed in Unit 15 of this book.)

NOTE *PIF settings in your system may be different from those illustrated here. Your system manager may have established a different PIF file for Lotus, or it may not be on your system. Ask your instructor about the settings in your system.*

You can change or edit the Program Filename, Window Title, Optional Parameters, and Start-up Directory. Figure 13.3 contains the PIF settings for Lotus 1-2-3 (not the Windows version), with its Program Filename as C:\123R2\LOTUS.EXE. The Window Title is Lotus Access Menu and the Start-up Directory C:\123R3.

Open

File Name: Directories:
*.pif   c:\windows

_default.pif   c:\
dbase.pif   windows
dosprmpt.pif   apw_data
edit.pif   lotustmp
edit00.pif   msapps
lharc.pif   rplot
lotus.pif   system
ni.pif

List Files of Type: Drives:
PIF Files (*.PIF)   c:

OK
Cancel

PIF Editor - LOTUS.PIF

File   Mode   Help

Program Filename: LOTUS.EXE

Window Title: Lotus Access Menu

Optional Parameters:

Start-up Directory: C:\123R3

Video Memory: ● Text   ○ Low Graphics   ○ High Graphics

Memory Requirements: KB Required 128   KB Desired 640

EMS Memory: KB Required 0   KB Limit 1024

XMS Memory: KB Required 0   KB Limit 1024

Display Usage: ● Full Screen   Execution: ☐ Background
                  ○ Windowed   ☐ Exclusive
☒ Close Window on Exit   Advanced...

Press F1 for Help on Program Filename.

GUIDED ACTIVITY 13.1   *(OPTIONAL)*

Using PIF Editor (TO BE DONE ONLY AT THE DIRECTION OF THE INSTRUCTOR!)

1. Start PIF Editor from the Main or the Accessories Group in Program Manager.

2. In the Program Filename Box, type the path and executable file name of a non-Windows application. For example, to use WordPerfect, type `C:\WP\WP.EXE`.

   This entry is intended only as an example. Your entry will depend on the non-Windows application that you wish to install.

3. Type `WordPerfect` in the Window Title box.

Advanced Options

Multitasking Options
Background Priority: 50   Foreground Priority: 100   OK
☒ Detect Idle Time   Cancel

Memory Options
☐ EMS Memory Locked   ☐ XMS Memory Locked
☒ Uses High Memory Area   ☐ Lock Application Memory

Display Options
Monitor Ports: ☐ Text   ☐ Low Graphics   ☒ High Graphics
☒ Emulate Text Mode   ☐ Retain Video Memory

Other Options
☒ Allow Fast Paste   ☐ Allow Close When Active
Reserve Shortcut Keys: ☐ Alt+Tab   ☐ Alt+Esc   ☐ Ctrl+Esc
☐ PrtSc   ☐ Alt+PrtSc   ☐ Alt+Space
☐ Alt+Enter
Application Shortcut Key: None

Press F1 for Help on Priority.

4. Do not change any of the other settings.

5. Save the file by clicking on Save As in the File menu. Name the file MYWP.PIF or another name as directed by your instructor.

6. Exit PIF Editor by clicking on Exit in the File menu.

GUIDED ACTIVITY 13.2 *(OPTIONAL)*

Using PIF Editor *(TO BE DONE ONLY AT THE DIRECTION OF THE INSTRUCTOR!)*

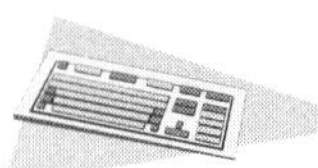

1. Start PIF Editor from the Main or the Accessories Group in Program Manager.

2. At the Program Filename Box, type the path and executable file name of a non-Windows application. For example, to use WordPerfect, type `C:\WP\WP.EXE`.

    This entry is intended only as an example. Your entry will depend on the non-Windows application that you wish to install.

3. Press `Alt` `T` to enter the Window Title box. Type `WordPerfect`.

4. Do not change any of the other settings.

5. Save the file by selecting Save As from the File menu. Name the file MYWP.PIF or another name as directed by your instructor. Press `Enter` to complete the process.

6. Exit PIF Editor by selecting Exit from the File menu.

PIFs and Program Manager

Once the PIF is set up, it must be added to the Program Manager. Techniques for adding PIF files and other program files and groups are discussed in Unit 14 of this book.

Understanding the Options

This section briefly explains Standard mode options. The options for 386 Enhanced mode are similar, although some of the following are on the Advanced Options screen—see the section following. (Standard and 386 Enhanced modes are discussed in detail in Unit 15.) These options are determined by the non-Windows application being installed.

PROGRAM FILENAME Used to store the path and file name of the file that starts the application. Use the complete name, including the extension. The file will usually contain the extension .EXE or .COM.

WINDOW TITLE A descriptive name that is usually associated with the particular application you are using. For example, Lotus Access Menu; this entry is optional but highly recommended since it will appear with the icon in Program Manager displays.

OPTIONAL PARAMETERS Any parameters required by the application. These parameters are similar to parameters you would use after the application's file name, usually following a slash character (/) when starting the program from MS-DOS.

START-UP DIRECTORY Used to indicate the drive and directory that you want Windows to make current for the application you are using. You can use this feature to have WordPerfect always default to drive A: by entering A:\ in this box.

VIDEO MEMORY (This option appears when you are running Windows in Standard mode; see Figure 13.4. If you are running in 386 Enhanced mode on a 386SX or better computer, Video Memory is an advanced option and does not appear on the basic options screen; see Figure 13.3.) Indicates how the application uses the display. The three video modes that are available are Text, Low Graphics, and High Graphics. Use Text if your application runs only in text mode. Use Low Graphics if the application runs in graphics mode or if it uses multiple "screen pages" in text mode. High graphics is used when you wish to reserve enough memory to display the application initially in high-resolution graphics mode. When you switch from a non-Windows application to a different non-Windows application or back to the Windows desktop, Windows saves the contents of your screen so that it can restore your context when you switch back. Windows has to reserve a certain amount of memory for this purpose. Saving a graphics mode screen takes considerably more memory than saving a text mode screen.

MEMORY REQUIREMENTS Specifies how many kilobytes of conventional memory must be free to begin an application.

EMS MEMORY When running in 386 Enhanced mode, Windows simulates expanded memory for applications that use it.

Use EMS Memory options to specify the amount of expanded memory to allocate to an application.

NOTE   *When running in virtual mode, Windows allocates EMS and XMS memory from the same memory pool, using the application's memory strategy: either the Lotus/Intel/Microsoft (LIM) Expanded Memory Specification or the Lotus/Intel/Microsoft/AST eXtended Memory Specification.*

This option specifies KB Required—The minimum amount of expanded memory in kilobytes (KB) that your application requires. Check the requirements for your application. If you don't know how much EMS memory is required, leave the setting as it is.

If you are running other applications and Windows cannot provide the specified amount of memory, a message appears. You may need to free some memory before continuing. Use a setting of 0 for applications that do not require expanded memory.

KB Limit specifies the maximum amount of expanded memory your application is allocated. This option prevents an application from taking more expanded memory than it needs.

The default setting is 1024. A setting of –1 allocates as much expanded memory to an application as it requests, up to the limit of system memory. This can slow down the rest of your system. A setting of 0 prevents the application from using EMS memory.

XMS MEMORY FOR STANDARD MODE   Type the amount of extended memory to reserve for the application. If your computer's extended memory conforms to the Lotus/Intel/Microsoft/AST eXtended Memory Specification, version 2.0 or later, you can use these settings. You can usually leave these settings at their default values.

This option specifies KB Required—the minimum amount of required extended memory in kilobytes (KB). Check the system requirements for your application. If you don't know how much is required, leave the setting as it is.

Use a setting of 0 for applications that do not use extended memory. If you are running other applications and Windows cannot provide the specified amount of memory, a message appears. You may need to free some memory before starting Windows.

KB Limit specifies the maximum amount of extended memory in kilobytes allocated to the application.

This setting prevents applications using XMS memory from tieing up all available extended memory blocks when they are not going to use them all. The default setting of 0 prevents the application from using any extended memory, except in the high memory area (HMA). A setting of –1 allocates as much extended memory to an application as it requires, up to the limit of system memory; in general, it's not a good idea to use a setting of –1 because this can slow down your system dramatically.

DISPLAY USAGE   Use these options to control how the application is initially displayed. Full Screen is used to start the application in a full screen. Running an application in a full screen saves memory. You switch between a full-screen application and the Windows desktop by pressing [Alt][Tab]. You cannot share information between full-screen applications and other applications as easily as you can when they are running in a window. (You can press [Alt][PrtSc] to copy an image of the entire screen onto the Clipboard when an application is running in a full screen.)

Windows is used to start the application in a window. Running an application in a window uses more memory. However, you gain the advantages of running in a window, including easily sharing information between applications. To switch an application from a full screen to a window, or vice versa, press [Alt][Enter]. Some applications can only run in a full screen because they display graphics or have direct access to the part of memory used by the screen. In these cases, a message is displayed when you try to switch from a full screen to a window.

EXECUTION EXCLUSIVE Select this check box if you want the application to have exclusive use of resources when it is the active application. If you select this option, no other applications, including those with the Background option set, can run when this application is active.

You can select this option both for applications that run in a window and those that run in a full screen. However, an application running in a window does not receive all the computer's resources. Windows reserves some resources for itself and for running Windows applications.

BACKGROUND AND FOREGROUND PRIORITY When you specify Background and Foreground priority, you are determining how CPU (processor) resources are allocated to the applications. The numbers you specify set the priority of the application relative to the other applications that are running. (Therefore, these numbers cannot be translated into a fixed percentage of CPU time.) The higher the priority an application has, the more CPU resources are allocated to it. Priorities range from 0 to 10,000. Default foreground priority is 100. Default background priority is 50. The *Foreground Priority* is the application's priority when it is the active application. For example, to ensure that an application receives all of the processing time it needs without interruption, set this option to 10,000. The *Background Priority* is the application's priority when it is not the active application.

NOTE *When an application is running in a window, you can also change its priorities by using commands on the Control menu.*

CLOSE WINDOW ON EXIT Clear this check box if you want the window (or screen) to remain open when you quit the application. This is especially useful if you are running a command or application that displays output on the screen. If the window closes too quickly, you won't see the output. By default, the window closes when you quit the application.

PIF Editor Advanced Options

If you are using Windows in 386 Enhanced mode, the options fall into two categories: basic and advanced. Most of the *basic options* are presented in the preceding discussion. *Advanced options* are available by selecting or clicking on the Advanced box in the window that is displayed in Figure 13.3. The Advanced Options dialog box will appear (Figure 13.4).

These Advanced options are organized into four groups: Multitasking, Memory, Display, and Other options.

Multitasking refers to the simultaneous operation of more than one application. Multitasking Options specify how the application will run in relation to other applications. You can specify Background Priority to indicate how much processor time the application should receive when it is running in the background (i.e., when another window is active).[1] Specify a value from 0 to 10,000; the default value is 50. Foreground Priority is used to indicate how much processor time the application should receive when it is running in the foreground with the same value range (0 to 10,000); the default value is 100. The exact allocation depends on how many applications are open, their status (foreground or background), and the specific values entered here. Detect Idle Time allows Windows to give system resources to other applications while this application is idle, waiting for input from you.

Memory Options control how the application uses the computer's available memory. You can specify the required amount and limit of *EMS Memory Locked* and *XMS Memory Locked*; set these as illustrated in Figure 13.4 unless the documentation with your application specifically states otherwise. Also for best performance, unless the documentation with your application specifically states otherwise, you should check Uses High Memory Area. We discuss the types of memory in more detail in Unit 15 of this book.

Display Options detail how the application appears on the screen and how Windows manages memory for the application's display. Display options include Monitor Ports, Emulate Text Mode, and Retain Video Memory. Normally you should indicate the most sophisticated level of graphics in the Video Memory line; for example, High Graphics for a program that uses EGA or VGA graphics. Normally you do *not* select any of the Monitor Ports boxes, as these are needed only by certain software that bypasses the normal DOS display techniques. Checking *Emulate Text Mode* will speed up some applications. Checking Retain Video Memory will ensure that Windows will always be able to display the program in the highest resolution checked in the Video Memory line.

Finally, Other Options permit you to customize the way applications run in Windows in 386 Enhanced mode. These options allow for Fast Paste of information from the Clipboard, Close When Active, Reserve Shortcut Keys, and Application Shortcut Key. Be cautious about checking the Close When Active box, because if you do so you will be able to close the window and exit Windows without properly exiting the application. Since most applications (e.g., dBASE IV, Lotus, and WordPerfect) warn you about the risk of losing unsaved work before exiting, it is generally a good idea to ensure a normal exit by leaving this box unchecked.

The Microsoft Windows 3.1 *User's Guide* contains more detailed explanations of these standard and enhanced settings.

Review Questions

*1.   What is a program information file (PIF)?

2.   Review each of the following standard options:

   a.   Program Filename

   b.   Window Title

---

1 The "Background" box on the basic options screen (386 Enhanced mode) must be checked for an MS-DOS application to run in the background.

    c. Optional Parameters

    d. Start-Up Directory

    e. Video Memory Mode

    f. Memory Requirements

    g. EMS Memory

    h. XMS Memory

    i. Close Window on Exit

3. What advanced options are available in PIF Editor?

*4. How are the advanced options organized? Briefly describe each group (do not list commands—a brief one-sentence description is sufficient).

Key Terms

Advanced options	Emulate Text Mode	Program information file
Background Priority	Foreground Priority	(PIF)
Basic options	Multitasking	Video memory
EMS memory	PIF Editor	XMS memory

Documentation Research

To answer the following questions, use Chapter 8, "PIF Editor," of the *User's Guide*. Check the guide's index to find pages with the information needed. We recommend that you also write the relevant page number next to each question. For additional aid, you may need to use the on-line Help menu.

1. On what page(s) of the *User's Guide* do you find information on PIFs and PIF Editor?

2. What type of applications utilize PIFs? Explain why.

3. Explain the memory requirements when specifying basic PIF options for 386 Enhanced mode.

4. List the structure of PIF Editor's on-line Help menu. How many categories of help are available?

5. Using PIF Editor's on-line Help menu, Advanced Options for 386 mode, what is the normal background-foreground priority number?

6. Using PIF Editor's on-line Help menu, Standard Options (optional parameters), what command would you use to run Microsoft Word in character mode?

Customizing Windows

You can customize Windows to your particular taste using Control Panel in the Main Program Group. The default settings in Windows are recorded in a file called WIN.INI (for WINdows INItialization). With earlier versions of Windows you would make changes directly in the .INI file using Notepad, Write, or some other text editor. You can still use this approach to customize Windows 3.1; however, most custom changes can be accomplished more easily through Control Panel, Program Manager, or File Manager.

Control Panel was presented in Unit 5. You may wish to review that unit before proceeding. In addition to the changes (color, desktop, keyboard speed, and the like) presented in Unit 5, you can use Control Panel for more advanced customization of Windows. This unit also deals with the management of programs and program groups in Program Manager.

Learning Objectives

At the completion of this unit, you should know

1. how to customize Windows 3.1.

At the completion of this unit, you should be able to

1. select background patterns,

2. choose a custom wallpaper,

3. define country options,

4. select or deselect sound,

5. add, delete, and rearrange programs and program groups in Program Manager.

Customizing the Desktop

The *desktop* consists of that area of the Windows screen that is outside any particular window or icon. It is also the background area where you create and work with Windows applications. Control Panel's Desktop icon is used to change or customize the appearance of your desktop. The options available for customizing the Desktop include Pattern, Applications, Screen Saver, Wallpaper, Cursor, and spatial dimensions.

Pattern lets you cover your desktop with a repeating dot pattern. You can create the pattern yourself or use a pattern furnished by Windows.

If your computer has sufficient memory, you can add an interesting *wallpaper* background to your desktop for a more artistic design. Windows is furnished with many wallpaper choices and also allows you to design your own wallpaper.

Spatial options enable you to control the distances between objects on your desktop.

You can disable Fast "Alt+Tab" Switching. We recommend that you do not, retaining the ability to switch among applications by holding down the [Alt] key while you tab to the application you want. You can specify a *screen saver*, a moving pattern or picture that displays after you have not used the computer for a period of time. This avoids damage to the screen from displaying the same image for extended periods.

Starting Desktop

Desktop

To customize Desktop, open the Main Program Group through Program Manager, double-click on the Control Panel icon, then double-click the Desktop icon (shown to the left). If you are using the keyboard, select Settings from the Control Panel menu and choose Desktop. The Desktop dialog box will appear as in Figure 14.1. The standard (default) settings for Pattern Name and Wallpaper File appear as (None) until you make a change, as in Figure 14.2. The other settings that can be customized include Icons Spacing, Cursor Blink Rate, Screen Saver, and Sizing Grid. The spacing and grid options are measured in pixel units, a *pixel* (picture element) being a dot on the screen. Some screens have resolutions as low as 320 pixels (wide) by 200 pixels (high), while others are as high-resolution as 1024 by 768. Standard VGA resolution is 640 by 480. The amount of space occupied by a single "dot" is therefore quite variable, dependent on both the resolution of the screen and the size of the screen. Most of the figures in this book were captured from a standard VGA screen.

Change the icon spacing to spread or condense the icons on the desktop. (The spacing does not take effect until you give the Window/Arrange Icons command. Then all icons in the active window are arranged according to the spacing dimension.) Change Sizing Grid Granularity to a number higher than zero to put an invisible grid on the screen. When you move or resize windows or icons, they will "snap" to the nearest grid line and be better aligned. Border Width affects the width of the borders around most windows.

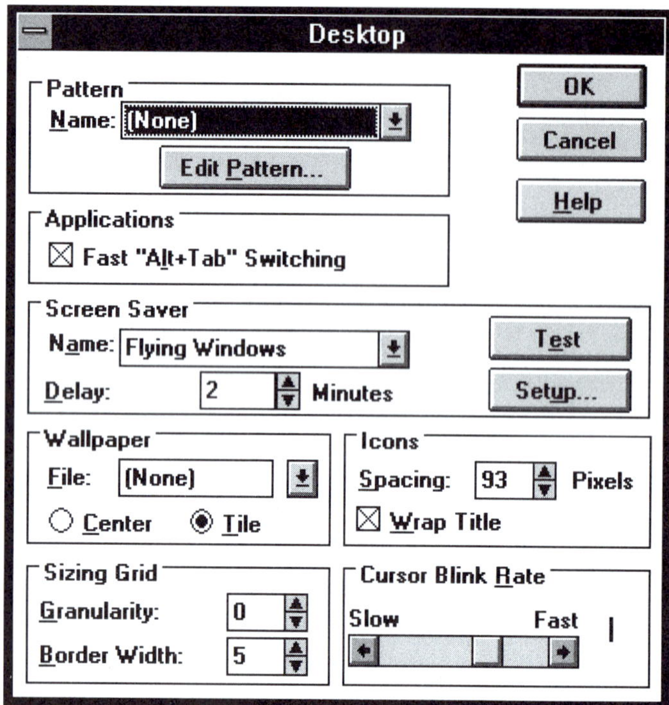

GUIDED ACTIVITY 14.1

Looking at the Desktop

1. Open the Control Panel by double-clicking on its icon from the Main program group in Program Manager.

2. Double-click on the Desktop icon.

3. Observe the Desktop dialog box. The Pattern Name box may read as (None), or may list one of the other available patterns installed on your version of Windows.

4. If the Wallpaper File reads (None), proceed with Guided Activity 14.3. If it does not:

   a. Click on the list box arrow next to Wallpaper File.

   b. From the list that appears, click on (None). You might have to scroll to the top of the list to find this selection.

   c. Choose OK to exit the Desktop dialog box.

GUIDED ACTIVITY 14.2

Looking at the Desktop

1. Open the Control Panel from the Main program group in Program Manager by highlighting its icon and pressing [Enter].

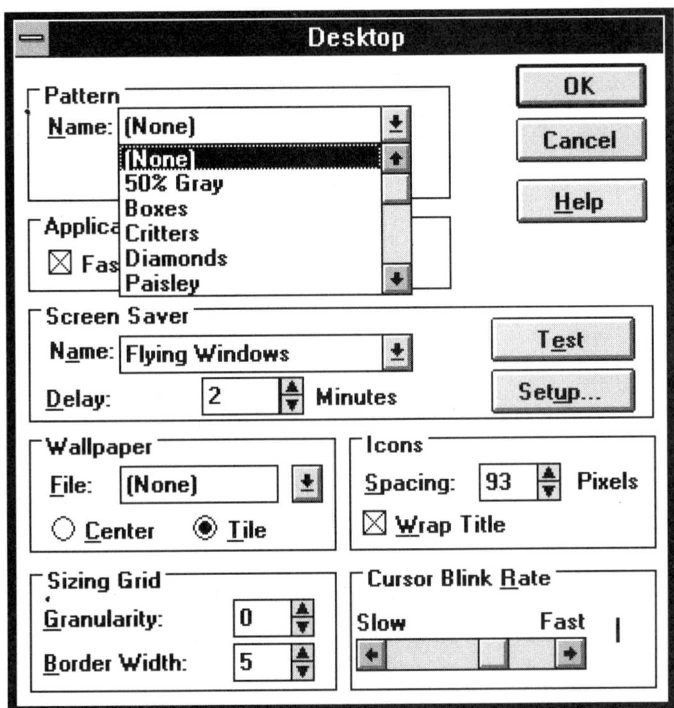

2. Press [Alt][S] for the Settings menu and then select Desktop. You may highlight the Desktop icon and press [Enter] to avoid using a menu to open Desktop.

3. Observe the Desktop dialog box. The Pattern Name box may read as (None), or may list one of the other available patterns installed on your version of Windows.

4. If the Wallpaper File reads (None), proceed with Guided Activity 14.4. If it does not:

   a. Press [Alt][F] to move to the Wallpaper File list box and press [Alt][↓] to open the list.

   b. From the list that appears, highlight (None). You might have to scroll to the top of the list to find this selection.

   c. Press [Enter] to exit the Desktop dialog box.

Customizing Background Pattern

To customize the background pattern on your desktop, click on the down arrow in the Pattern box as shown in Figure 14.2.

Patterns that are available include 50% Gray, Boxes, Critters, Diamonds, and so forth. If you want to view any pattern without actually selecting it, click on the Edit Pattern button in the Pattern box (visible in Figure 14.1). An Edit Pattern dialog box will appear as shown in Figure 14.3.

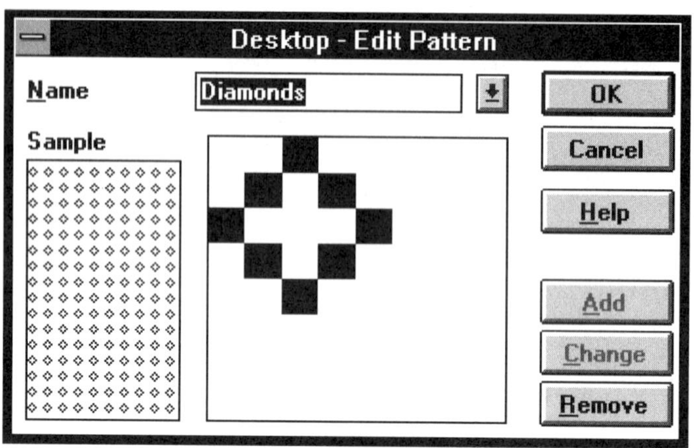

Press the arrow button, and you will see the pattern list, as well as a sample of each. For example, the illustration in Figure 14.3 contains the Diamonds pattern. To complete the pattern selection, click on OK.

You can edit a background pattern, as well as add a new background pattern. Using the mouse, click on a spot where you want to add or remove a dark dot. You cannot edit the pattern using the keyboard. If you create a new pattern, select the Add button, and the pattern will be included on the list. Double-click the mouse to apply this pattern to your desktop.

GUIDED ACTIVITY 14.3

Selecting Patterns

1. Open Control Panel from the Main program group. Double-click on the Desktop icon.

2. Change the Name in the Pattern box to Critters by clicking on the down arrow that is to the right of the Name box. When the list appears, click on Critters. You can see a sample of your choice by clicking on the Edit Pattern box. The pattern will appear in the Sample box. Click on OK when you want to continue.

3. Click on OK to complete the choice. You will return to Control Panel.

4. Reduce Control Panel to an icon by clicking on the minimize button in the upper-right corner. Your desktop should have a pattern of critters on it. (You have to use some imagination to see them.)

GUIDED ACTIVITY 14.4

Selecting Patterns

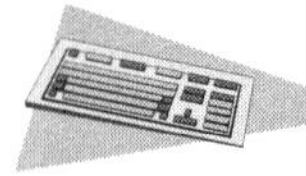

1. Open Control Panel from the Main program group. Select Desktop from the Settings menu.

2. Change the Name in the Pattern box to Critters by using the arrow keys to go through the list. You can see a sample of your choice by pressing [Alt][P] for the Edit Pattern box. The pattern will appear in the Sample box. Press [Enter] when you want to continue.

3. Press [Enter] to complete the choice. You will return to Control Panel.

4. Reduce Control Panel to an icon by pressing [Alt][Spacebar] and then selecting Minimize. Your desktop should have a pattern of critters on it. (You have to use some imagination to see them.)

Customizing Wallpaper

You must have sufficient memory (at least 2MB) to use Wallpaper. If you want to change the desktop to a different background, use the wallpaper option. This option allows you to display a picture as a backdrop to everything you do in Windows. Figure 14.4 shows an example of a "Cars" background. Several other choices are available, including Arcade, Arches, Argyle, Castle, Egypt, Marble, Redbrick, Rivets, Squares, Tartan, Thatch, and Zigzag.

To customize the desktop with a wallpaper option, click on the Desktop icon on the Control Panel. When the dialog box appears, click on arrow in the Wallpaper box. If you are using the keyboard, press [Alt][F] followed by [Alt][↓]. A list box of available wallpaper files will appear. Each wallpaper file has a .BMP extension, which means that the file's contents "maps" the position of each visible bit in the image. To complete your choice of wallpaper, select OK.

If the picture is large enough, the Wallpaper will cover the entire screen. If the picture is large, click on the Center option box to display one copy of the picture in the center of the screen; otherwise, click on Tile to display side-by-side as many copies as will fit on the screen.

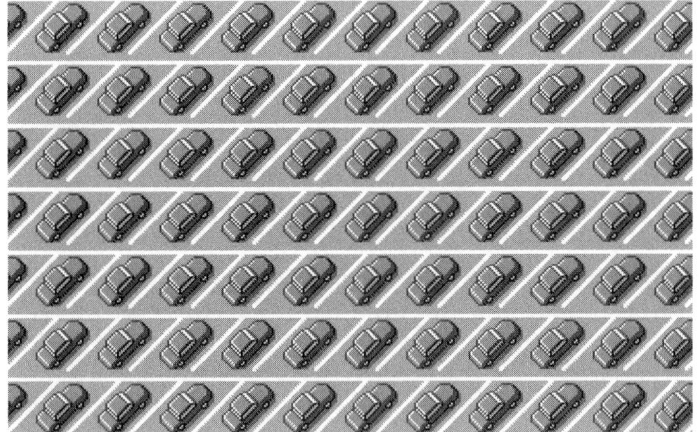

FIGURE 14.4
"Cars" wallpaper

Even More Custom Wallpaper

If you want to get really fancy, you can make your own wallpaper using Paintbrush or any other program that creates .BMP files. Or you might acquire a wallpaper file from a friend, as *shareware,* or from a public bulletin board. The ultimate thrill is to take a color photograph or picture to a copy shop that has a color scanner (we went to the Kinko's in our town) and ask the operators to create a scanned image. Tell them you want the image to be 640 by 480 (or whatever your screen resolution is) and ask them to save it in .BMP image format if possible. If they can't do .BMP, ask for .PCX. You can retrieve the .PCX image in Paintbrush and Save As a .BMP file. Make sure you get a disk in an IBM-PC format, not Apple Macintosh format.

Regardless of how you obtain the .BMP file, put it on your hard disk in the WINDOWS directory. It will then appear among your choices when you select Wallpaper.

GUIDED ACTIVITY 14.5

Applying Wallpaper

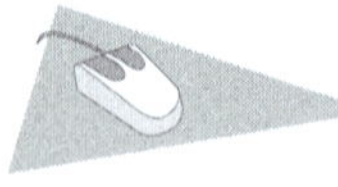

1. Restore Control Panel from its icon by double-clicking on it. Open Desktop.

2. View the list of wallpaper images by clicking on the down arrow button to the right of the File box in the Wallpaper section.

3. Select PAPER.BMP from the list in the File box. You may have to scroll down the list to find the selection. Choose Tile or Center by clicking on the particular option.

4. Click on OK to complete the choice.

5. Close Control Panel.

GUIDED ACTIVITY 14.6

Applying Wallpaper

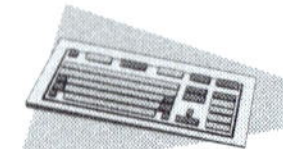

1. Restore Control Panel from its icon by pressing [Alt][Tab] until it is highlighted. Select Desktop from the Settings menu. Press [Alt][F] to enter the Wallpaper section.

2. View the different names of wallpaper images by using the arrow keys to scan the list.

3. Select PAPER.BMP from the list in the File box. You may have to scroll down the list to find the selection. Choose Tile or Center by pressing [Alt][T] or [Alt][C], respectively.

4. Press [Enter] to complete the choice.

5. Close Control Panel.

Customizing Country Options

The International section of Control Panel allows you to customize your system for a wide variety of countries. You can customize Windows for international currency symbols, dates and times, or measurement systems.

Windows 3.1 default settings are those commonly used in the United States. However, with the International option you can change these other settings as desired. Perhaps you will find yourself corresponding with an international associate. You can customize your desktop to accommodate your needs.

Starting International

International

To change Windows's international settings, double-click on the *international icon* in the Control Panel (shown to the left), or select Settings from the Control Panel menu and choose International. The International dialog box will appear as in Figure 14.5.

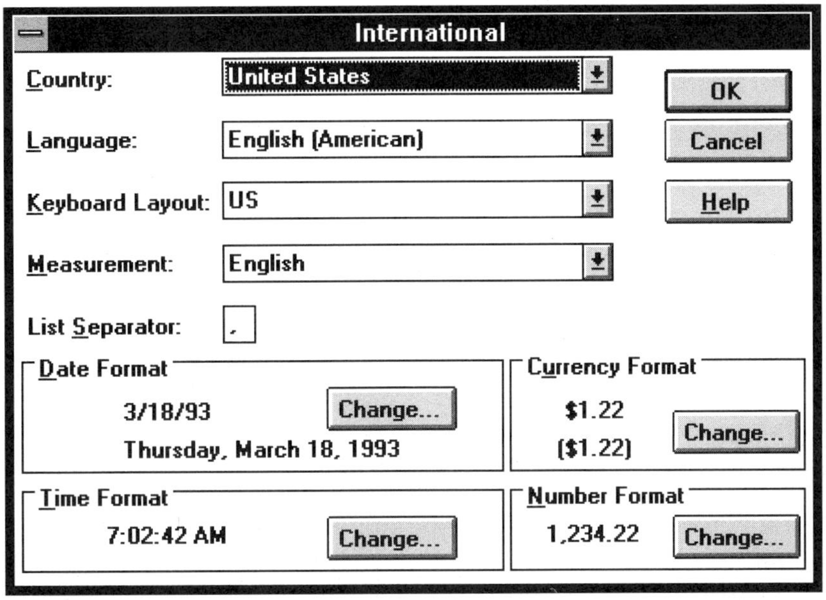

FIGURE 14.5
*The Control
Panel
International
dialog box*

This dialog box contains individual boxes to change Country, Language, Keyboard Layout, Measurement, and List Separator, as well as Date, Time, Currency, and Number formats.

To customize Windows, choose the Country drop-down list box. The default Country setting is the United States. Other country choices include Sweden, Switzerland (in French, German, or Italian), Taiwan, and United Kingdom, to name a few. After you select a particular country, Control Panel automatically adjusts the settings of Measurement, Date Format, Time Format, Currency Format, and Number Format.

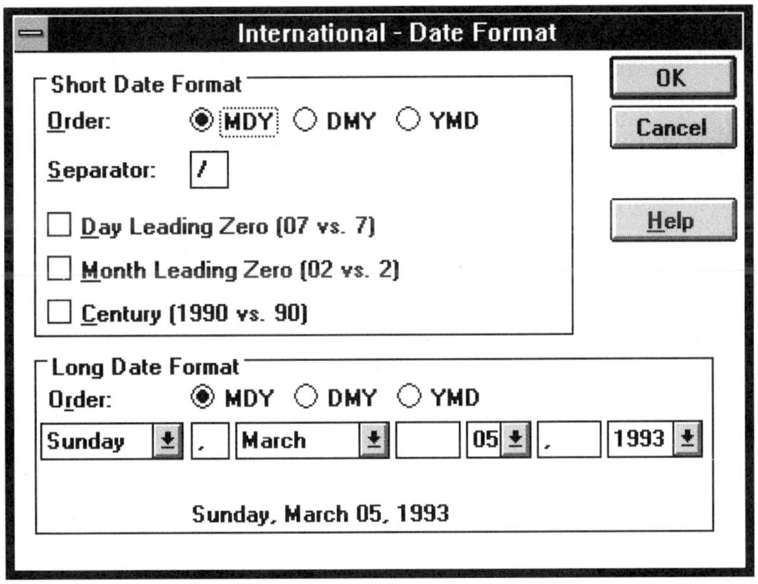

FIGURE 14.6
*The Control
Panel
International–
Date Format
dialog box*

If for some reason the settings are not what you want after selecting a country, you can make the desired changes by clicking on the Change button for that particular setting. Each Change button has its own dialog box. Figure 14.6 shows an example of using the Change dialog box of a particular setting, in this case Date Format.

Going International

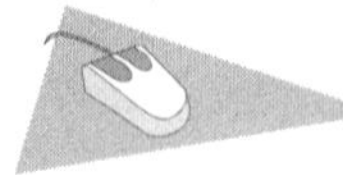

1. Open International by double-clicking on its icon from Control Panel in the Main program group.

2. Change the current Country setting (United States) to Sweden. You will have to click on the down arrow to the right of this box to see the list. Notice how the numeric formats change for date, time, and currency.

3. Change the Language box to Swedish.

4. Change Keyboard Layout to Swedish.

5. Click on OK to complete the action. You might be asked to insert one of the Windows Setup disks. Do so, or click cancel.

6. Before you close Control Panel, be sure to change the settings back to their original values—by default, United States country, English (American) language, US keyboard, English measurement, and comma as list separator. Close Control Panel.

Going International

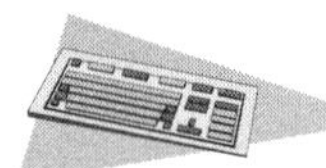

1. Open Control Panel from the Main program group. Select International from the Settings menu.

2. Change the current Country setting (United States) to Sweden. You will have to press [Alt][C] to enter this setting. Use the arrow keys to scan the list. Notice how the numeric formats change for date, time, and currency.

3. Change the Language box (press [Alt][L]) to Swedish.

4. Change Keyboard Layout (press [Alt][K]) to Swedish.

5. Press [Enter] to complete the action. You might be asked to insert one of the Windows Setup disks. Do so, or click cancel.

6. Before you close Control Panel, be sure to change the settings back to their original values—by default, United States country, English (American) language, US keyboard, English measurement, and comma as list separator. Close Control Panel.

Using Sound

If you do not have a sound card installed in your computer, which is usually the case as we write this text, then most of the features on the Sound dialog box are unavailable to you and will appear gray when you invoke this item. The "Enable

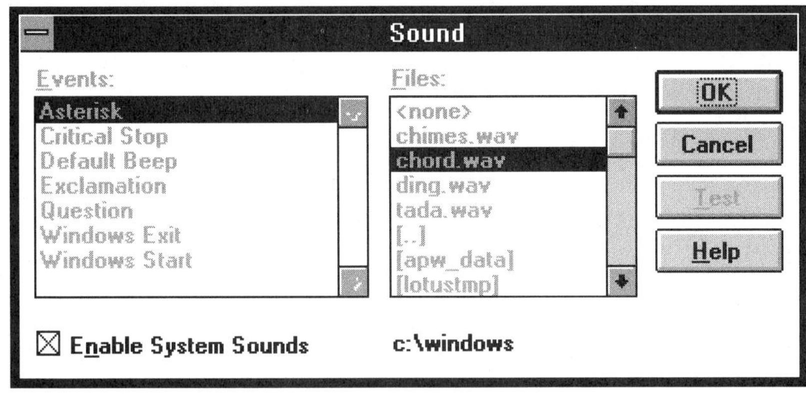

FIGURE 14.7
The Control Panel Sound dialog box

System Sounds" check box will turn the beep on or off. If you have a sound card installed, then you can assign different sounds (stored in .WAV files) to different events. The new Compaq Deskpro computers contain a feature called "Business Audio" that allows the recording and playback of sounds. In the future, expect to see more computers equipped with sound capabilities.

Windows sounds a warning beep when you select a command that is not valid. Sound can be turned on or off. If you do not hear the warning beep, you may need to turn the sound on.

Sound

To change Sound, either double-click on its icon in Control Panel (shown to the left), or select Settings from the Control Panel menu and choose Sound. The Sound dialog box will appear as in Figure 14.7.

In this figure, the "X" in the Enable System Sounds box indicates that Sound is on. To change this current choice, place the mouse pointer in the box and click. The "X" will then disappear.

GUIDED ACTIVITY 14.9

Turning Sound Off

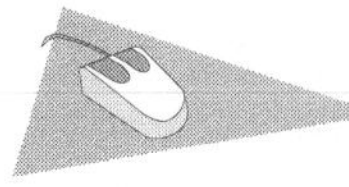

1. Open Control Panel from the Main program group.

2. Double-click on Sound.

3. The Enable System Sounds option may be marked with an "X", which will indicate that Sound is on. If an X is present, click on Enable System Sounds to turn Sound off. Click on OK to complete the process.

4. Close Control Panel.

GUIDED ACTIVITY 14.10

Turning Sound Off

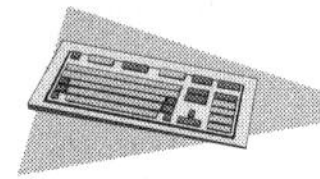

1. Open Control Panel from the Main program group.

2. Select Sound from the Settings menu.

3. The Enable System Sounds option may be marked with an "X", which will indicate that Sound is on. If an "X" is present, press `Alt` `W` to turn Sound off. Press `Enter` to complete the process.

4. Close Control Panel.

Working with Program Groups and Programs in Program Manager

You can rearrange the programs and program groups displayed by Program Manager. For instance, you can move Paintbrush from the Accessories to the Windows Applications program group if you wish. Or you can delete the games group entirely.

CAUTION *Before you make any changes in a school or business situation, check with your instructor or lab manager. A few minutes spent changing things can undo many hours of setup work.*

As the caution above implies, you can cause great distress if you are not careful in making changes. We recommend that you (or your organization) keep a "standard" copy of two files—WIN.INI and SYSTEM.INI—on a floppy disk so that you can recover from inadvertent changes. Use the techniques discussed in Unit 4 to copy these files from the WINDOWS directory to a floppy disk before attempting any of the techniques discussed here. In a school, your instructor might prohibit you from doing any of the following. We present the information here so you will know how to modify your Windows environment on your (own) personal computer.

Program Properties

We start with the simplest changes: those to the *properties* of a single program. First, highlight the program group and program that you wish to change. Then choose Properties from the File menu in Program Manager. Figure 14.8 illustrates the properties of the program Microsoft Word. The Description is the text that will appear on the Program Manager screen, under the icon for the program. (You cannot change the name that appears under the icon when it is minimized, for that is determined by Windows.)

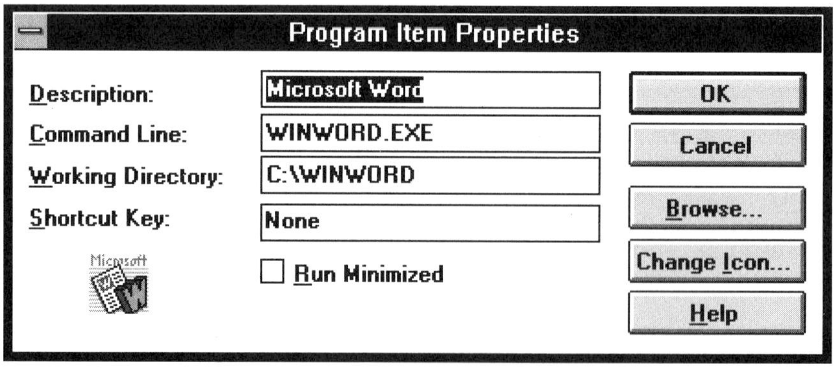

The Command Line contains the file name and extension, including directory, of the program to be run when the icon is chosen. The Program Item Properties dialog

FIGURE 14.8
The File Properties dialog box

box allows the setting of a Working Directory. In Figure 14.8, C:\WINWORD is the default directory that appears when one user chooses File Open or File Save As in Word. The next time the user starts Word and gives the File Open command, the directory will be the one specified in Properties.

If you do not remember the exact file name, enter the directory in the Command Line box and select the Browse button. A list of all .EXE (*executable*) files will appear. To see other types of files—in Windows, all of the following are legitimate program file extensions: .COM, .EXE, .BAT, and .PIF—change the extension in the file name box.

Most users of Windows 3.1 have the opportunity of selecting from additional icons for their applications. After pressing the Change Icon button (illustrated in Figure 14.8), change the File Name selection to C:\WINDOWS\ MORICONS.DLL as illustrated in Figure 14.9. This file contains many colorful new *built-in icons*, some of which are appropriate to specific programs (for example, Paradox 3.5) and others that are more generic in nature, such as those illustrated in Figure 14.9. If you like the icon, select OK. You can abort any File Properties changes by pressing the Cancel button.

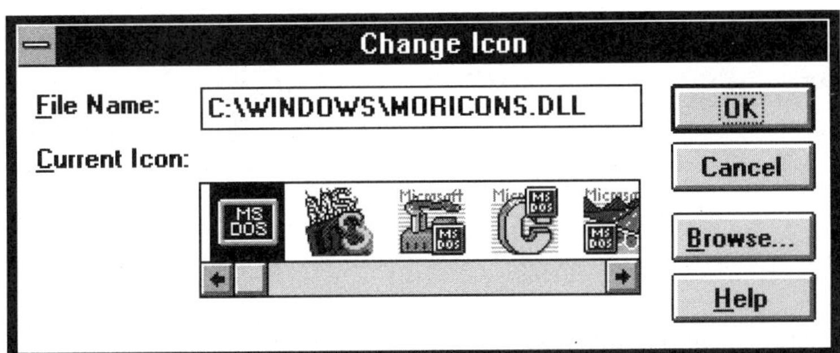

FIGURE 14.9
The Change Icon dialog box

Adding a File Icon to a Program Group

Windows 3.1 allows you to place an icon representing a file in a program group. When the file icon is clicked, the associated application program is opened and the file is loaded. Thus, you could place an icon representing an Excel spreadsheet that you use often in a program group. Double-clicking that icon will start Excel and then load your spreadsheet. The easiest method for adding a file icon to a program group is to open both File Manager and Program Manager, then "drag" the file icon from File Manager and "drop" it into the appropriate Program Manager group.

Moving and Copying Programs from One Group to Another

The graphical user interface of Windows makes moving or copying a (program) icon from one group to another quite easy. Before moving or copying, open both the program group window containing the icon and the program group window that is to receive it.

To use the mouse to *move* a program, simply drag the icon from one window to the other (that is, position the pointer on the icon, press and hold the mouse button, drag the icon, then release the mouse button). The icon will disappear from its original window and appear in the other.

To use the mouse to *copy* a program, press and hold [Ctrl] while you drag the icon from one window to the other. The icon will continue to appear in its original window and will also appear in the other. The program can now be started from either window.

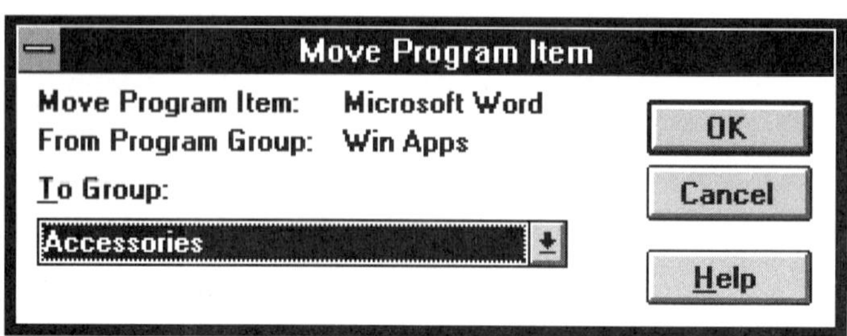

If you are using the keyboard, both Move and Copy are choices in the File menu. Before giving the command, highlight the program icon title using the usual techniques. Then enter the File/Move (or File/Copy) command. A dialog box like those illustrated in Figures 14.10 and 14.11 will appear. Choose the new group from the list box and then choose OK.

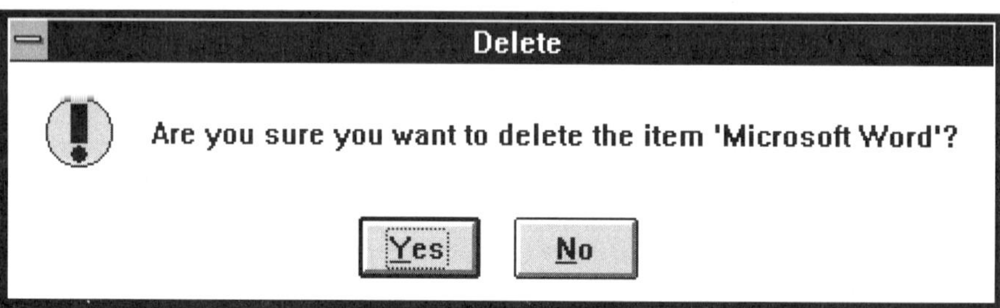

Deleting Programs

To *delete* a program icon from a program group window, highlight the icon using either mouse or keyboard, then press [Del] or choose Delete from the File menu. Windows will ask you to confirm your intention, as illustrated in Figure 14.12.

Delete

Are you sure you want to delete the item 'Microsoft Word'?

Yes   No

Adding New Programs or Program Groups

The File/New command allows you to add program items or program groups, as shown in Figure 14.13. Select Program Group if you want to add an entire new group (the equivalent of Accessories, Windows Applications, and so on). Select Program Item if you want to add a new program to an existing program group.

The New Program Group Properties dialog box is illustrated in Figure 14.14. Use this to create a special window; in a work situation, you might create a window for special accounting programs.

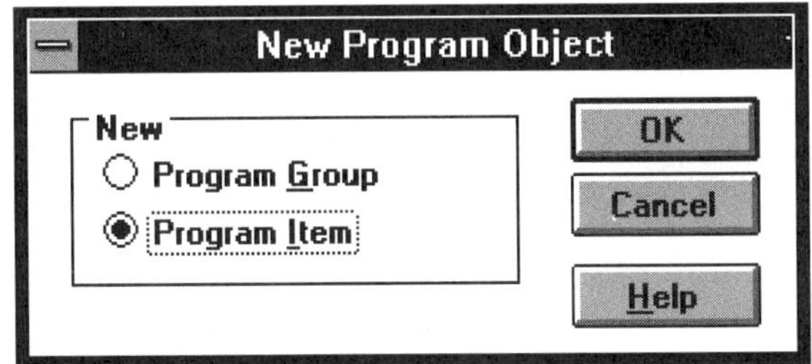

FIGURE 14.13
The New Program Object dialog box

FIGURE 14.14
The New Program Group Properties dialog box

FIGURE 14.15
The New Program Item Properties dialog box

The New Program Item Properties dialog box is illustrated in Figure 14.15. The entries are similar to those discussed earlier in this unit in the section "Program Properties." New Program Item is the place where you add the information in a .PIF file (see Unit 13) to Program Manager. Enter the name of the .PIF file, including the directory path and .PIF extension, on the Command Line. If you are a sophisticated user of MS-DOS and have developed *batch files* to automate some of your work, you can enter a .BAT file name on the Command Line. You can also enter program names of both Windows and non-Windows programs. A batch file or non-Windows program will use the file _DEFAULT.PIF to determine its operating parameters, while all Windows programs contain a full complement of operating parameters in themselves and communicate that information to the Windows program.

Saving Your Changes

Some of the changes you make using the File menu are not saved unless Save Settings or Exit is checked on the Options menu of Program Manager.

Review Questions

*1.   What is the Desktop?

*2.   List and briefly describe the options available for customizing Desktop.

3.   What command(s) will allow you to view a pattern without actually selecting it?

4. What can be done to the International section of Control Panel?

5. What are the Change boxes, used when customizing the International section?

*6. What indicates that Sound is off?

7. What are the properties of a program?

8. How do you

   a. move a program item from one group to another?

   b. copy a program item from one group to another?

   c. delete a program item from a group?

9. Describe the process by which you would create a new program group window on your screen, copy some programs from other groups to the new group, and add new programs not previously part of your Windows environment to the new group.

Key Terms

Batch file	Executable file	Properties
Built-in icon	International icon	Screen saver
Copy	Move	Spatial options
Delete	Pattern	Shareware
Desktop	Pixel	Wallpaper

Documentation Research

To answer the following questions, use Chapter 5, "Control Panel," of the *User's Guide*. Check the guide's index to find pages with the information needed. We recommend that you also write the relevant page number next to each question. For additional aid, you may need to use the on-line Help menu.

1. How do you change the Sizing Grid?

2. If you want to install a new printer, what steps are necessary?

3. Explain the purpose of the Timeout Options.

4. List the steps to connect and disconnect a network printer.

5. Using Control Panel's on-line Help menu, how many categories of help are listed?

6. Using Control Panel's on-line Help menu, how many steps are listed to create a desktop pattern?

Optimizing Windows

Optimizing means customizing the computer system so that it uses its resources most efficiently. These system resources include disk space and memory. In Windows, these available resources can affect the following:

- Which applications you can run

- How many applications you can run simultaneously

- How fast Windows and Windows applications run

- How much data you can store between one session and the next

Optimizing your computer for Microsoft Windows 3.1 is intended to "balance" how your computer will accommodate speed, capacity, and free disk space. By speed, we mean the ability to run programs quickly, whether in the foreground or in the background. By capacity, we mean the ability to run many programs at the same time. By free disk space, we mean the amount of space on the drive not used by files. You can improve Windows' performance by configuring your computer system's memory properly.

Two ways in which you can optimize Windows are to free up conventional memory and to perform routine maintenance on your hard disk.

Learning Objectives

At the completion of this unit, you should know

1. what resource management techniques are used to optimize Windows.

At the completion of this unit, you should be able to

1.   check disk space,

2.   modify the CONFIG.SYS and AUTOEXEC.BAT files,

3.   perform routine maintenance,

4.   improve Windows' performance by balancing system memory and disk resources.

Windows' Modes of Operation

Throughout this book we have alluded to the modes of operation of Windows 3.1, without really defining them. For most operations, the mode is irrelevant because your computer and Windows will operate at the most advanced mode possible without any direction from the user. For instance, if you do not have a 386 or better microprocessor in your computer, Windows 3.1 will not operate in *386 Enhanced mode*. Even if you do have a 386 or better microprocessor, Windows 3.1 requires a certain amount of memory, usually *more than* 2 *megabytes* (*MB*), before it will operate in 386 Enhanced mode. What, then, is 386 Enhanced mode, and what does Windows do if it cannot operate in that mode?

The 386 Enhanced mode is one of two operating modes of Windows 3.1. The other is Standard mode. These are defined as follows:

- 386 Enhanced mode is the most advanced operating mode, enabling Windows to use the *virtual memory* capabilities of the 80386 (and newer) microprocessor. Virtual memory is a technique that makes use of disk storage to mimic RAM memory, thereby allowing programs to operate as if there were more RAM available than is physically installed in the computer. In 386 Enhanced mode, Windows can operate more than one non-Windows application at a time (say, multitask Lotus 1-2-3 Release 3.1 with WordPerfect 5.1), and it is also more efficient in its operation of Windows applications.

- Standard mode is defined as the normal mode for Windows. If your computer does not have a 80386 microprocessor or 2MB of RAM, but does have an Intel 80286 microprocessor and 1MB of RAM, then Windows will usually operate in this mode. This mode provides access to extended memory (defined later in this unit). In Standard mode, you can switch among non-Windows applications, but only one of them at a time will be "running." If your computer has 3MB or less RAM, you might find that Standard mode is faster than 386 Enhanced mode for running Windows applications.

When you start Windows by typing WIN, the software will automatically calculate the optimal operating mode and Windows will start in that mode. To learn in what mode Windows is running, choose About Program Manager from the Program Manager Help menu. The resulting dialog box indicates the mode, as shown in Figure 15.1.

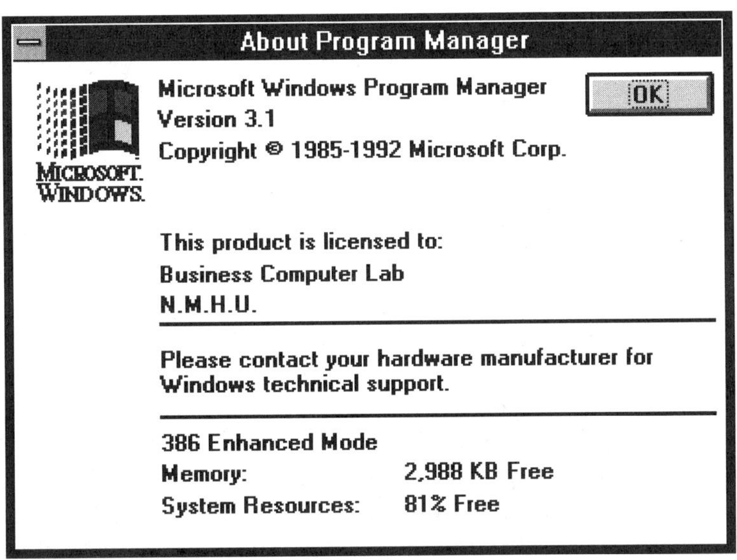

FIGURE 15.1
The Help About Program Manager dialog box

To start Windows in a mode that you specify, type one of the following:

Command	*Mode*
WIN/S	Standard mode
WIN/3	386 Enhanced mode

Memory

Memory provides temporary storage for applications and data. Memory resides on your computer's motherboard or can be added on. All applications must be loaded into memory in order to run.

The more memory you have installed on your computer, the more applications you can run with Windows. Memory can be increased on your computer by installing a memory board into a slot inside the machine. A personal computer can have three types of memory: conventional, extended, and expanded. Understanding what each type of memory is and what it is used for is necessary in order to configure your own computer system.

Conventional Memory

The first 640KB (kilobytes) of memory on any computer that uses an 8086, 8088, 80286, 80386, 80386SX, or 80486 microprocessor is called *conventional memory* (or main memory). Conventional memory is used to load the Disk Operating System (DOS).[1] Device drivers, network software, and other memory-resident programs might also use conventional memory.

---

1 Both the latest versions of DOS (5.0 and above) and some memory managers available from vendors other than Microsoft (such as QEMM 6.0 from Quarterdeck Software) allow for DOS to be partially loaded in memory other than conventional.

Windows 3.1 requires at least 380KB of conventional memory. Since most computer systems have only 640KB of memory available, it is important to keep as much of this memory as possible available for Windows.

Extended Memory

Extended memory (sometimes called *XMS* memory) is memory in excess of the 640KB that is standard on most newer computers. It is an extension of the computer's conventional memory. Normally, 80286 and higher class computers come with 640KB of conventional memory and 384KB or more extended memory, for a total of at least 1 megabyte (MB) of memory.

To use extended memory you must install a special program called an *extended memory manager*. An extended memory manager administers the use of your system's memory so that several programs will not attempt to use the same memory at the same time. An extended memory manager is required to run Windows in Standard or 386 Enhanced mode. Windows includes an extended memory manager called HIMEM.SYS.

Extended memory is very fast and extremely efficient for application use. However, not all non-Windows applications are designed to use extended memory.

Expanded Memory

Before the advent of extended memory, Lotus, Intel, and Microsoft developed a system called *expanded memory* (or *EMS* memory) as a way to add memory in excess of 640KB to a computer. Expanded memory exists apart from the system's conventional and extended memory. As is the case with extended memory, you must install a special program called *expanded memory manager*, which usually comes with the expanded memory board.

When a program uses expanded memory, it can access only a small portion of this memory at a given moment. Each time a different portion of expanded memory is needed, the program must request that memory from the expanded memory manager.

Expanded memory can be used on any computer that runs on MS-DOS, regardless of its microprocessor, although only those applications that are written with expanded memory can take advantage of this enhancement. Windows can use expanded memory, but it runs more efficiently with extended memory. In addition, expanded memory is slower and more cumbersome to use than extended memory. The program EMM386.SYS (provided with Windows and later versions of MS-DOS) allows extended memory to behave as if it were expanded memory.

Checking Disk Space

To determine how much conventional memory you have, as well as how much free disk space is available, use the DOS command *CHKDSK*. Before using this program, you should quit Windows. At the DOS prompt, type `CHKDSK`, and press Enter.

NOTE *If you use DOS version 4.0 or later, you can use a program called MEM instead of CHKDSK.*

You will see on the monitor the results of CHKDSK similar to the following:

```
C:\>chkdsk
Volume Serial Number is 2023-08F8

68046848 bytes total disk space
   75776 bytes in 3 hidden files
  264192 bytes in 92 directories
62818304 bytes in 1741 user files
 5038080 bytes available on disk

    2048 bytes in each allocation unit
   33226 total allocation units on disk
    2460 available allocation units on disk

  655360 total bytes memory
  526224 bytes free
```

The last two lines in the CHKDSK report provide memory information. The "total bytes memory" number tells you how much conventional memory your system starts out with when you turn on the computer. The "bytes free" number indicates how much conventional memory is available for Windows to use. If you have at least 640KB of memory, the first number should be approximately 655360. (There are actually 1,024 *bytes* in a *kilobyte*.) To optimize operations, you want to make the "bytes free" number as high as you can. In addition, if CHKDSK reports any "lost allocation units" or "lost clusters," you have a problem with the logical structure of your hard disk. For optimal performance in Windows, you need to correct the problem. The DOS command CHKDSK/F (the "F" parameter stands for " fix") will convert these lost allocation units or lost clusters to one or more files with names such as FILE0000.CHK. You can then ERASE the files with the .CHK extension. (Consult your DOS manual or your instructor for any questions you may have on lost clusters.)

The difference between "total bytes memory" and "bytes free" represents the memory claimed by DOS and the other components of your system before you start Windows. You cannot eliminate DOS from your system, but you may be able to eliminate other items to free up some memory for Windows.

Some of the items that you may have on your computer can be set aside to increase the available conventional memory. They include the following:

- Network software

- Device drivers

- Memory-resident "pop-up" programs

- Memory-resident DOS commands

GUIDED ACTIVITY 15.1

Doing a CHKDSK

1. Quit Windows by closing Program Manager.

2. At the C:> prompt type CHKDSK/F and press ⏎Enter.

3. If you find lost clusters, convert them to files.

NOTE *Check with your instructor or laboratory supervisor about deleting these files.*

References

This unit presents a very quick overview of an extremely complex topic. The authors and others have spent several days researching the proper setup of Windows on their systems. Before you do anything other than *look* at the various system files, we recommend that you obtain the following references:

- *Microsoft Windows User's Guide,* which should have come with your copy of Windows

- *The Windows Resource Kit,* which you can order from Microsoft (1-800-642-7676)

- *Running Windows,* published by Microsoft Press, available at many bookstores

Editing System Files

Device drivers, memory-resident programs, and so on are normally placed in memory by commands stored in the CONFIG.SYS or AUTOEXEC.BAT files. The easiest method for viewing and editing these files is to use a program called SYSEDIT that is furnished with Windows.

NOTE *Before you make any changes in a school or business situation, check with your instructor or lab manager. A few minutes spent changing things can undo many hours of setup work.*

As the note above implies, you can cause great distress if you are not careful in making changes. It is possible to inadvertently modify AUTOEXEC.BAT and CON-FIG.SYS to the point where your computer will not operate. We recommend that you (or your organization) make an "emergency boot disk" containing the disk operating system and the original copies of AUTOEXEC.BAT and CONFIG.SYS.[2] In a school, your instructor might prohibit you from doing any of the following. We present the information here so that you will know how to modify your Windows environment on your (own) personal computer.

---

2 To make the emergency boot disk: Format a floppy disk in drive A: using the command FORMAT A:/S. Then copy the following files to the disk: COMMAND.COM, AUTOEXEC.BAT, CONFIG.SYS.

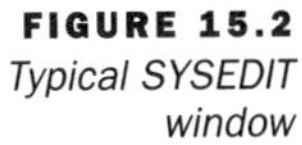

FIGURE 15.2
Typical SYSEDIT window

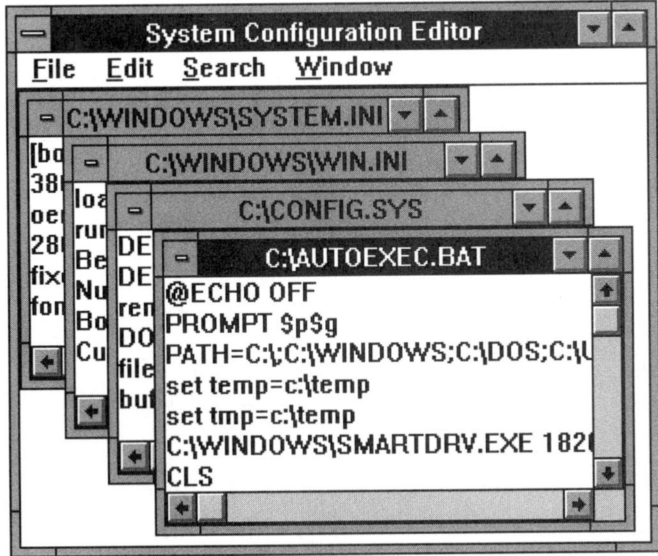

To use the SYSEDIT program, make the Program Manager window active. From the File menu, choose Run, type SYSEDIT in the Command Line, and press Enter. If the command is available on your system, you will see a display similar to that in Figure 15.2. The specific contents of each file will vary from system to system. If you expect to do a lot of tinkering with Windows (*advanced users only, please*), you can add SYSEDIT to one of the Program Manager program groups, perhaps Accessories.

GUIDED ACTIVITY 15.2

Start SYSEDIT (TO BE DONE ONLY AT THE DIRECTION OF YOUR INSTRUCTOR!)

1. Start Windows and Program Manager.

2. On Program Manager's File menu, choose Run, type SYSEDIT on the Command Line, and press Enter. You should see a display similar to Figure 15.2. If you get an error message, someone has removed or hidden SYSEDIT so that you cannot use it.

3. Click the title bar of the CONFIG.SYS document window. (With a keyboard, choose this document window from the Window menu.) You will be able to compare your CONFIG.SYS file with the description in the following section.

The CONFIG.SYS File

The following example lists some items that you need and don't need in your **CONFIG.SYS** file, such as files, buffers, and *stacks*. This example is not intended to tell you *exactly* what you need on your system, but merely to suggest how to optimize Windows. You may need to consult your MS-DOS manual or your computer support technician for assistance.

Items Necessary in CONFIG.SYS	*Comment*
`FILES=30`	Allows 30 files to be open at once
`BUFFERS=20`	Reduce to 10 if you are using SMARTDrive
`STACKS=9,192`	Only if using DOS 3.2
`STACKS=0,0`	If using DOS 3.3 or later
`DEVICE=C:\HIMEM.SYS`	If running Windows in Standard mode or 386 Enhanced mode[3]
`DEVICE=C:\WINDOWS\EGA.SYS`	If your system uses an EGA display and you are running non-Windows applications in Real mode or Standard mode

Items you *might* need in your CONFIG.SYS file include:

- A line that installs memory-resident network software (only if using a network)

- A line that installs SMARTDRV.SYS

- A line that installs EMM386.SYS

- A line that installs SHARE.EXE

- A line that begins with `SHELL=`

- A line that begins with `LASTDRIVE=`

- One or more lines installing device drivers (such as a scanner) that work with Windows software

SMARTDRV.SYS enables you to take advantage of SMARTDrive, the Windows disk cache utility. EMM386.SYS is used only if you have an 80386 or 80486 computer and want to use expanded memory when Windows is not running or when Windows is running in Real mode. SHARE.EXE is needed on some computers that use disks larger than 32MB. You can include this file in the AUTOEXEC.BAT file if needed. `SHELL=` increases the size of the DOS environment. If the CONFIG.SYS file has a `SHELL=` line with a `/E` parameter, you can reduce the number that follows the `/E` to reclaim some memory. `LASTDRIVE=` allows you to use drive letters higher than E for devices, such as RAM disks or network drives. To conserve memory, the letter that follows `LASTDRIVE=` should not be higher than necessary. This number should reflect the maximum number of devices (drives) that are available.

Items you *may not* need in the CONFIG.SYS file include:

- Lines that install device drivers you can do without

- A line that installs FASTOPEN.EXE

---

3 You might have a memory manager other than HIMEM.SYS installed. One popular program is QEMM386.SYS from Quarterdeck Software.

You can do without any line that installs a mouse driver, provided you do not need the mouse in any non-Windows applications. Windows provides its own mouse driver for use within Windows.

The AUTOEXEC.BAT File

The **AUTOEXEC.BAT** file is designed to automatically run programs or execute specified DOS commands each time you start or **reboot** (reset) your computer. One of the items most likely found in this file is a line beginning with PATH. This tells DOS what directories to search for if you start a program that is not located in the current (root) directory. The PATH line does not reduce available memory. Other commands that are usually included in the AUTOEXEC.BAT file include: CD or CHDIR, DATE, ECHO or @ECHO, GOTO, IF, PAUSE, PROMPT, REM, SET, TIME, VER, and a command to start Windows. The following items reduce available memory and *might* be unnecessary:

- A command that runs a mouse driver (such as MOUSE.COM)

- APPEND, FASTOPEN, SUBST, ASSIGN, JOIN, MODE

- Any command that starts a memory-resident program

- Any command that starts a DOS shell

The DOS commands APPEND and FASTOPEN reduce available memory and do not enhance Windows performance. SUBST, ASSIGN, and JOIN are not recommended for use with Windows. Memory-resident programs (such as SideKick, Hotline, and the like) should be run *after* you have started Windows, within a window. DOS **shell programs**, such as XTree and Norton Commander, are convenient for running non-Windows applications and issuing DOS commands. However, they should only be used *after* you have started Windows so that you do not reduce the memory available to Windows.

Routine Maintenance

To optimize how Windows runs on your system, you need to understand how the amount of free disk space can affect your system's performance and capacity. In addition, it is important to know how the information on your disk can be structured as efficiently as possible. To free up disk space, you may wish to delete unnecessary files. You may also want to delete lost files and compact your hard disk.

From time to time, you will need to "clean up" your hard disk (a chore called "housekeeping"). Begin by removing or backing up any files that you no longer need or are not currently using. You can back up these files on floppy disks for later use. Files that are furnished with Windows but not absolutely necessary for its operation include the following:

- *.BMP files (wallpaper files, but don't delete the one you're using)

- SOL.EXE, SOL.HLP, REVERSI.EXE, REVERSI.HLP, WINMINE.EXE, WINMINE.HLP (games and their help files)

- MSDOS.EXE, PBRUSH.EXE, PBRUSH.HLP, WRITE.EXE, WRITE.HLP, CALENDAR.EXE, and the like; these files are the programs in the Accessory and Main program groups and their help text (be selective here, but you can probably delete Write if you have Word for Windows, and so on)

Temporary files that are created while working with Windows can be deleted. Normally, these files are deleted when you quit Windows. If your computer "locks up," or if for some reason you accidentally turn off your computer before exiting Windows properly, one or more of these types of files may be left behind on your disks. Temporary files used by Windows applications begin with the tilde (~) and have an extension of .TMP. If you find any of these files on your disk when you are not running Windows, you should delete them. However, *do not delete any temporary files while Windows is running.*

Use the CHKDSK/F DOS command and parameter described earlier in this unit to check for **lost clusters**. (Do not run CHKDSK within Windows—exit to DOS first.) Clusters are lost when a program ends in an abnormal manner (such as when a storm cuts off the power, or you reset the computer, or the software "hangs" due to a circumstance the manufacturer did not anticipate).

Finally, over time, as applications are read from and written onto different sectors of your hard disk, information can become fragmented. *Fragmentation* occurs when a file, instead of being stored in a single location, is stored in different locations on the disk. Fragmentation does not affect the validity of the information—your data remain intact when you read a fragmented file into an application—but it takes longer to read the file from the disk. Also, more time is needed to write files back to the disk. Fragmentation is corrected by compacting the disk.

To *compact* your hard disk, run a disk compaction utility that comes with your computer, or one from a third party such as Norton Utilities. Follow carefully the manufacturer's instructions for disk compacting. Compacting a disk should be done directly from MS-DOS.

WARNING *DO NOT run a disk compaction utility from Windows since, by doing so, you could damage the files on your hard disk.*

Swap Files

Windows 3.1 uses a technique called *swap files* to temporarily hold information. When in Real or Standard modes, Windows 3.1 creates application swap files to hold information from non-Windows applications. These are erased when you exit Windows using normal procedures discussed in Unit 1. When in 386 Enhanced mode, Windows 3.1 uses either a permanent swap file or a temporary swap file as part of its virtual memory technique. To establish or change a swap file, choose 386 Enhanced from the Control Panel window, which brings forth the dialog box illustrated in Figure 15.3, then click the Virtual Memory button, which brings forth the dialog box illustrated in Figure 15.4. Click the Change button to alter the current settings. This

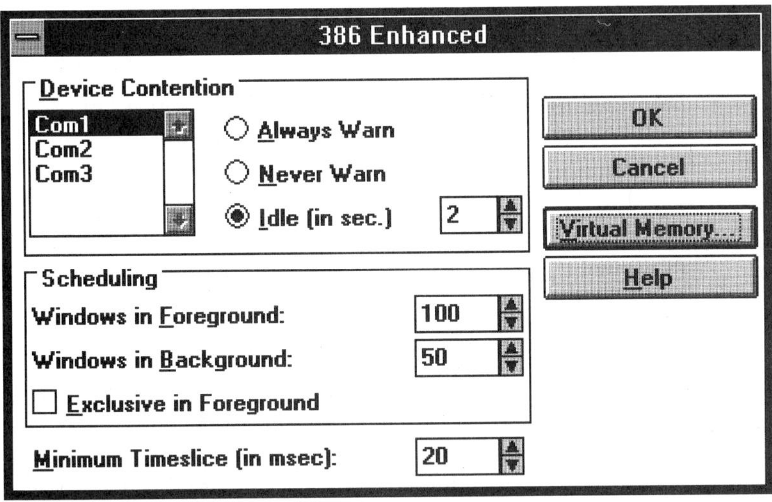

FIGURE 15.3
Control Panel's 386 Enhanced window

section discusses how to set up a permanent swap file, which is usually the more efficient of the two.

Whenever Windows is started in 386 Enhanced mode, it checks to see whether a permanent swap file has been established. If there is none, Windows will create a temporary swap file from available disk space. When Windows is exited using normal procedures, the temporary swap file is deleted. Temporary swap files do not have a permanent effect on your available disk space. But because Windows must create them out of available disk space each time the program is started, access to the disk is less efficient since the file is spread out over the disk.

FIGURE 15.4
The Virtual Memory dialog box

A better solution than using temporary swap files is to establish a permanent swap file. This file is set up by Windows in a contiguous (physically adjacent) part of the hard disk. Access is thereby made faster because all the swap file data are in one place and Windows can directly access the data; it need not go through DOS. The main disadvantage of a permanent swap file is that it represents a permanent decrease in available hard drive space. (If you discontinue using Windows, however, the file can be removed—"permanent" in this case means that you must consciously remove the file.)

If you have more than 10MB of space available on your disk and do a lot of work using Windows, you should normally set up a permanent swap file. To create a permanent swap file (as in Figure 15.4), do the following:

1. Exit Windows.

2. If possible, compact the files on your disk, as discussed in the previous section. This will leave a larger amount of contiguous space for your swap file.

3. Start Windows.

4. Close any applications that are automatically started with Windows (such as Clock and File Manager). Only Program Manager should be in operation.

5. From the Program Manager File menu, choose Run, enter the program name SWAPFILE, and click OK (or press Enter) to execute the program.

6. If there is already a permanent swap file on your disk, you will be given the option of deleting it and creating a new one, or simply deleting the one you have.

7. Swapfile will report on your disk and recommend a size for the new swap file. Use Windows' recommendation, or enter your own size, and choose Create to accomplish the change.

To learn more about swap files and the SWAPFILE program, consult Chapter 14, "Optimizing Windows," in the *User's Guide*.

Review Questions

*1. Briefly, explain conventional memory, extended memory, and expanded memory.

2. What is meant by "optimizing" Windows? Give an example.

*3. Describe the procedure to determine disk space.

*4. What can be done to increase available conventional memory?

5. Explain fragmentation. What can be done to correct "fragmented" files?

Key Terms

386 Enhanced mode	Expanded memory manager	Memory-resident program
AUTOEXEC.BAT		
Byte	Extended memory (XMS)	Reboot
CHKDSK	Extended memory manager	Shell program
Compact		Stack
CONFIG.SYS	Fragmentation	Standard mode
Conventional memory	Kilobyte (KB)	Swap file
Device driver	Lost cluster	Temporary file
Expanded memory (EMS)	Megabyte (MB)	Virtual memory

Documentation Research

To answer the following questions, use Chapter 14, "Optimizing Windows," of the *User's Guide*. Check the guide's index to find pages with the information needed. We recommend that you also write the relevant page number next to each question. For additional aid, you may need to use the on-line Help menu.

1. What performance factors are used to optimize Windows?

2. How does Windows simulate additional memory in 386 Enhanced mode?

3. If you need to configure an 80386 or 80486 computer, how many FILES and BUFF-ERS should the CONFIG.SYS file contain?

4. When can you optimize your system using SMARTDrive?

5. How can you improve the efficiency of your hard disk?

6. List some recommendations for streamlining your CONFIG.SYS and AUTOEXEC.BAT files.

Transferring Data Using Clipboard

Clipboard is a utility program that acts as a temporary storage area for information being transferred between applications during a Windows session. You can cut or copy information from an application onto the Clipboard, and then transfer that information from the Clipboard into other applications or elsewhere in the same application.

Information you cut or copy onto the Clipboard remains there until you clear the Clipboard, cut or copy new information to the Clipboard, or exit from Windows. Clipboard can be used to transfer information from all windows except Clock and from most non-Windows applications. Clipboard retains its contents until you change them. Thus, you can paste the information into the designated area whenever you want to, as well as paste the same information repeatedly.

Clipboard provides a fast and convenient way to gather all the information required to complete a project in one place at one time. It can be used to move data between applications not specifically designed for Windows. Thus, it is a flexible and powerful tool for increasing your productivity.

Learning Objectives

At the completion of this unit, you should know

1. how to use Clipboard,

2. the formats used to transfer information using Clipboard.

At the completion of this unit, you should be able to

1. start and exit Clipboard,

2. copy, cut, and paste information,

3. use Clipboard Viewer,

4. open and close the File, Edit, and Display menus.

Clipboard

Clipboard

Clipboard is an area of memory in Windows that holds information that can be transferred from one application to another. If you have used a word processor, you will appreciate the ability to move or copy text and graphics from one location to another. This process is known as "cut and paste."

The procedures involved in using Clipboard are the same for all Windows applications. To cut or copy information from a Windows application:

1. Select the information you want to copy.

2. Choose the application's Cut or Copy command. (The *Cut* command is used if you want to move the information, while the *Copy* command is used to make a duplicate copy of the information.)

3. Switch to where you want the information copied. This might be elsewhere in the same document (or spreadsheet or graphic), to a different document in the same application, or to a different application.

4. Position the cursor or insertion point at the location where the information is to be placed.

5. Choose the receiving application's *Paste* command.

Copy, Cut, and Paste Commands

Almost all Windows applications have an Edit menu with Copy, Cut, and Paste commands. One of the few applications that does not have these commands is Clock, since it is not able to receive any kind of user input.

These commands work the same way in all applications. Copy puts the selected information on the Clipboard without removing it from the original document. Cut, on the other hand, puts the information on the Clipboard and at the same time deletes it from the source. Paste puts a copy of the Clipboard's contents into a designated area without removing anything from the Clipboard.

If you have not selected any information in the source document, the application's Copy and Cut commands will appear in gray. The Paste command will also appear in gray. Once you select information, the Cut and Copy commands will appear in the Edit menu as black. Once you have "cut" or "copied" to the Clipboard, the Paste command will be black.

GUIDED ACTIVITY 16.1

Cutting and Pasting

1. Open the Accessories program group in Program Manager.

2. Open Notepad from Accessories by double-clicking on its icon.

3. Click on Open in the File menu in Notepad.

4. Double-click on the file SETUP.TXT.

5. Mark the first few lines of this file by dragging the mouse over the text. You should see the text selected as highlighted.

6. Click on Copy in the Edit menu.

7. Close Notepad.

8. Open Write from Accessories.

9. Click on New in the File menu.

10. Click on Paste in the Edit menu. The text copied from Notepad should now appear.

11. Click on Save in the File menu. Type a file name and click on OK to save the file.

12. Close Write.

GUIDED ACTIVITY 16.2

Cutting and Pasting

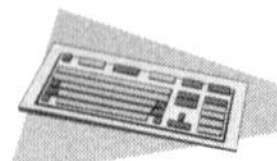

1. Open the Accessories program group in Program Manager.

2. Open Notepad from Accessories by highlighting its icon and pressing [Enter].

3. Select Open from the File menu in Notepad.

4. Using the arrow keys, highlight the file SETUP.TXT and press [Enter].

5. Mark the first few lines of this file by pressing and holding down [Shift] while using the arrow keys to highlight the text.

6. Select Copy from the Edit menu.

7. Close Notepad.

8. Open Write from Accessories.

9. Select New from the File menu.

10. Select Paste from the Edit menu. The text copied from Notepad should now appear.

11. Select Save from the File menu. Type a file name and press [Enter] to save the file.

12. Close Write.

COPY ENTIRE SCREEN

To copy the image of the entire screen to the Clipboard, press the Print Screen key (sometimes labeled PrtSc or Print Scrn). The Clipboard contents can then be pasted into Paintbrush or another graphics program for editing, then cutting and pasting into a word processing document. That is the technique we used to reproduce the various program icons that you see in this text. To copy only the active window to the clipboard (for example, the Virtual Memory window), press and hold the [Alt] key before you press [PrtSc].

The Clipboard Viewer

Clipboard Viewer lets you see what is contained in Clipboard before you paste. To open Clipboard Viewer, double-click on its program item icon in Program Manager, normally in the Main program group, as shown in Figure 16.1. The Clipboard window will appear as in Figure 16.2. The Clipboard window contains the usual parts: title bar, Control Menu box, sizing buttons, scroll bars, menu bar, and the workspace.

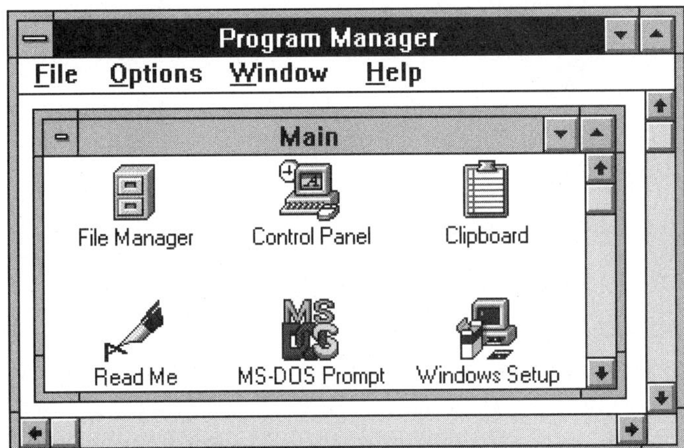

FIGURE 16.1
Program Manager Main program group

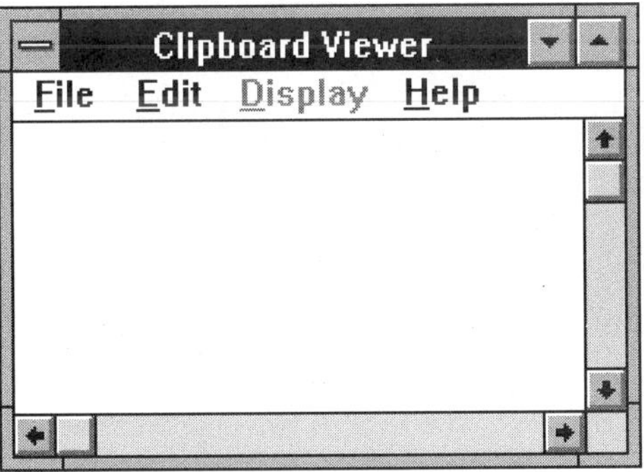

FIGURE 16.2
The Clipboard window

Starting Clipboard Viewer

1. Start Notepad from the Accessories program group.

2. Click on Open in the File menu and open a file by double-clicking on it.

3. Mark the text to be copied.

4. Click on Copy in the Edit menu.

5. Minimize Notepad to an icon by clicking on the minimize button in the upper-right corner of the window.

6. Double-click on the Clipboard icon from the Main program group.

7. The text you marked in step 3 should now appear in the Clipboard Viewer. Figure 16.3 shows a sample of text that was copied from Notepad to Clipboard.

GUIDED ACTIVITY 16.4

Starting Clipboard Viewer

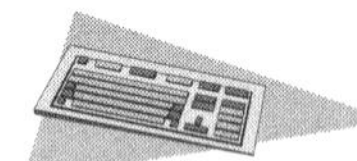

1. Start Notepad from the Accessories program group.

2. Select Open from the File menu (Alt F) and open a file by highlighting the file name and pressing Enter.

3. Mark the text to be copied. Remember, pressing and holding down the Shift key will allow you to highlight the text that is to be copied.

4. Select Copy from the Edit menu.

5. Minimize Notepad to an icon by pressing Alt Spacebar for the Control menu and selecting Minimize.

6. Open Clipboard from the Main program group. To open Clipboard, press Alt Tab until the Program Manager icon is highlighted and release Alt. Press Alt W for Window, and then select Main. Highlight the Clipboard icon and press Enter.

7. The text you marked in step 3 should now appear in the Clipboard Viewer. Figure 16.3 shows a sample of text that was copied from Notepad to Clipboard.

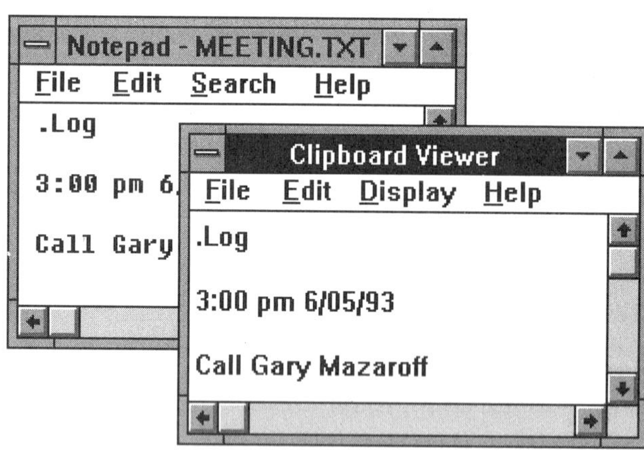

Clipboard Menus

Three of the menus in Clipboard—File, Edit, and Display—offer some flexibility in how you treat data or blocks of copy once they are on the clipboard.

The File Menu

Commands in the File menu, shown in Figure 16.4, allow you to save and to reuse the current contents of the Clipboard.

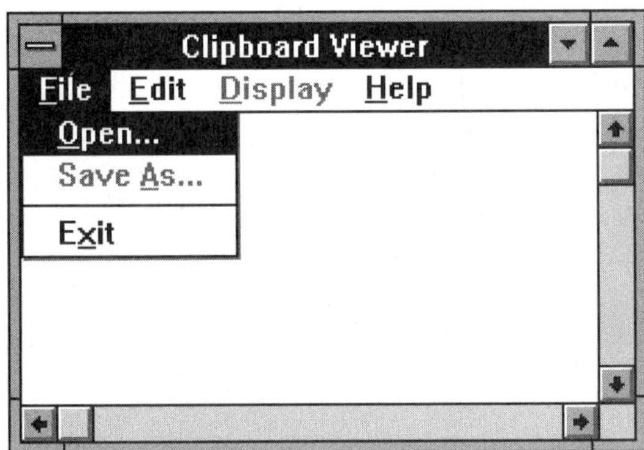

FIGURE 16.4
The Clipboard File menu

Use the Save As command to store the current Clipboard contents to a disk file. Clipboard automatically adds the file extension .CLP. The Open command is used to replace the current contents of the Clipboard with an existing .CLP file. The File menu's Exit command closes Clipboard, as does the Close command from the Control Menu. Clipboard files are useful when creating and storing graphic images that can be placed several times within a document.

The Edit Menu

The Edit menu has only one command, Delete, which deletes the contents of the Clipboard. Information on the Clipboard uses a great deal of memory, thereby reducing the amount of available memory for other applications. If you get a warning message

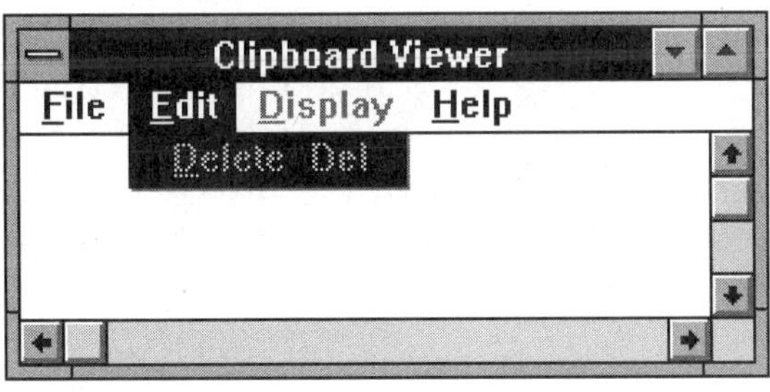

FIGURE 16.5
The Clipboard Edit menu

indicating that you do not have enough memory to carry out a command, or if you notice your applications are running slower than normal, you should use Clipboard's Delete command to delete the current contents of Clipboard, as shown in Figure 16.5. If there is nothing on the Clipboard, the Delete choice will be gray as in Figure 16.5.

As you use the Delete command, a drop-down dialog box will appear, requesting that you confirm your selection. If you feel that you need to save the contents of Clipboard for future use, use the File menu's Save As command to create a disk file. You can now safely delete the contents of the Clipboard.

The Display Menu

The Display menu lets you change the format by which Clipboard displays its contents. When you transfer data from one location to another through Clipboard, Windows attempts to maintain formatting. For example, if you copy text from a Write document to the Clipboard, and then paste it into another Write document, the paragraph retains all of its formatting characteristics. But if you copy text into another application that does not contain the same type of formatting characteristics, such as Notepad, the actual transfer will be in plain text without the special formatted characteristics.

In the same manner, if you copy a drawing created in a *vector format* (a format that records a set of commands by which the drawing can be recreated), the source program supplies the selection in at least two versions, in vector format and as a bitmap (a format that records only the actual positions and colors of each dot in the drawing). The vector format is the more information-rich of the two, but if the receiving program uses only bit maps, the Clipboard transfers a bitmap.

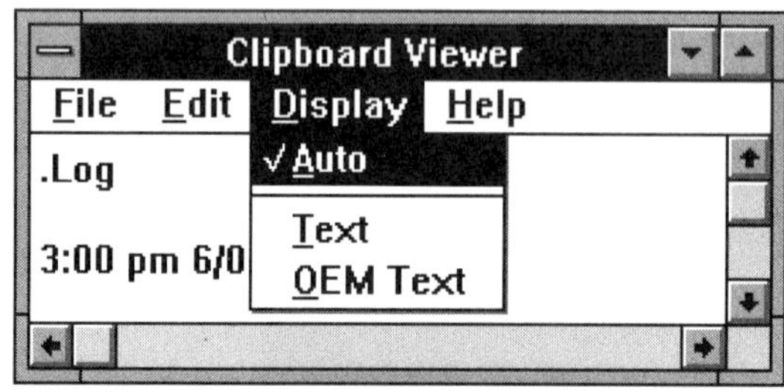

FIGURE 16.6
The Clipboard Display menu for text

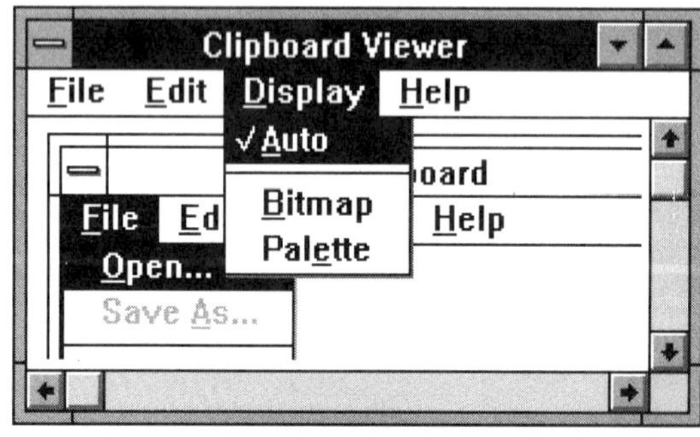

FIGURE 16.7
The Clipboard Display menu for a graphic image

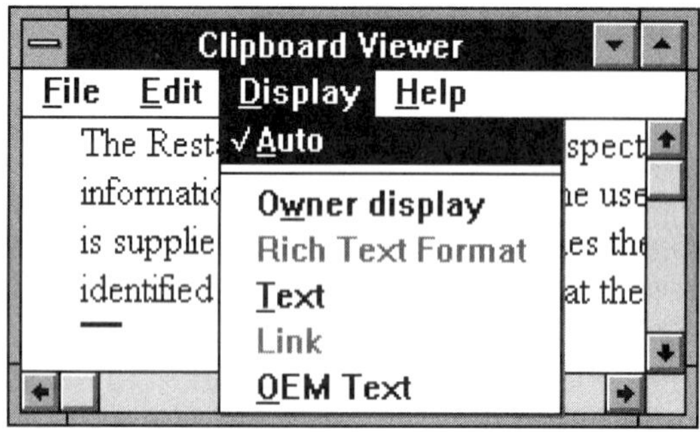

FIGURE 16.8
The Clipboard Display menu for a text file

When a selection has been sent to the Clipboard in multiple formats, you can see what formats are available by viewing Clipboard's Display menu, shown in Figure 16.6.

For example, if you want to duplicate (copy) a document from Word for Windows with multiple fonts to Clipboard, Clipboard's Display will appear as Auto. The other selections on the Clipboard Display menu include Text and OEM Text.

A second type of Display viewer allows transferring of graphic images. Figure 16.7 shows the available options: Auto (default choice), Bitmap, or Palette.

If you transfer copy from a Microsoft Word document, the Display menu will appear as in Figure 16.8. This allows you to transfer data in Auto, Owner display, Text, and OEM Text formats.

Owner display refers to the way the information is sent to the Clipboard from Word for Windows with all formatting information intact. Text is the plain text version that Windows will transfer to a single font application, such as Notepad. *OEM Text* is a format that Windows will use if you transfer Clipboard's contents to a non-Windows application.

Clipboard with Non-Windows Applications

You can use the Clipboard to transfer information in and out of applications that were not designed specifically for Windows 3.1, although a few restrictions do apply. You can copy information from a non-Windows application to the Clipboard, but you cannot cut information from a non-Windows application to Clipboard. Also, if you are running Windows in either Real mode or Standard mode, your non-Windows applications will use the entire screen (you will not be able to run them in a window). Therefore, you will only be able to copy the entire screen to the Clipboard at a given time. Finally, you cannot copy information to the Clipboard from a non-Windows application that runs in graphics mode unless you are running Windows in 386 Enhanced mode.

Review Questions

*1. Explain the purpose of Clipboard.

*2. What is the difference between Cut and Copy?

3. How do you activate Clipboard Viewer?

*4. Explain the importance of multiple formats while transferring information.

5. How would you transfer data from an Excel worksheet?

Key Terms

Clipboard	Cut	Paste
Copy	OEM text	Vector format

Documentation Research

To answer the following questions, use Chapter 2, " Application Basics," and Chapter 7, "Non-Windows Applications," of the *User's Guide*. Check the guide's index to find pages with the information needed. We recommend that you also write the relevant page number next to each question. For additional aid, you may need to use the on-line Help menu.

1. Can you copy an entire screen for a non-Windows application that is running in graphics mode?

2. Using Clipboard's on-line Help menu, how many topics are available describing procedures?

3. Clipboard stores information in multiple formats so that you can transfer information between applications that use different formats. What command is used to view the Clipboard in another format? Use the on-line Help menu.

4. What command is used to return to the first format that was displayed?

5. How do you clear the Clipboard contents, thus freeing memory?

Windows Setup[1]

Windows Setup is a program that copies information from the original Windows disks, then creates initialization files that instruct Windows how to act. It is different from Control Panel (see Units 5 and 14), which affects what you see on the screen. You can use Windows Setup to change system settings, set up applications to use with Windows, and add or remove optional Windows components.

Adding Windows Components

Using Windows Setup, you can add any Windows components to your system that you may have chosen not to include when you first set up Windows. You can select all or only certain parts of a component. For example, you may want to set up some of the Accessories applications, but not others.

To Add a Complete Component

1. Select (check) the check box next to the Component description.

2. Choose the OK button.

To Add Specific Component Files

Choose the Files button for the component. Then complete the dialog box that appears.

For help, choose the Help button or press [F1] while using the dialog box.

---

1 Adapted from the on-line Help for the Windows Setup program. Portions of the following are copyright © 1990–1992 by Microsoft Corporation.

Changing System Settings

If you change to a system configuration that is different from the one you had when you set up Windows, you can use Setup to change your software and hardware settings. For example, you might want to change from an enhanced graphics adapter (EGA) to a video graphics adapter (VGA). You must have the appropriate hardware to support these changes. You can change your display (monitor), keyboard, mouse, or network settings.

NOTE *You will have to restart Windows or your system if you change settings by using Setup. For this reason, it is a good idea to close all your running applications before you use Setup.*

To Change Your Display, Keyboard, Mouse, or Network

1. Make sure that your hardware is set up to match the setting you are changing. Check your hardware documentation.

2. From the Options menu, choose Change System Settings.

3. Click the arrow at the right of the setting that you want to change to open the list. Or press [Alt][↓].

    Each list displays drivers or devices supported for that setting. Make sure your hardware is listed. Use the scroll bar or arrow keys to see more of the list.

4. Select the setting that you want.

5. Choose the OK button.

    Setup may prompt you to insert a Windows disk into drive A:. If it does, put the disk in drive A: and close the drive door, or type the path of the appropriate device-driver file. Then choose the OK button.

6. From the Options menu, choose Exit.

7. Make sure that there are no disks in any floppy disk drive, and then choose the Reboot button (if it appears) to restart your system. (After restarting your system, you can start Windows by typing WIN at the MS-DOS prompt.) Or choose the Restart Windows button.

    The next time you start Windows, the new settings will be in effect.

    Sometimes it may be necessary to run Setup from outside Windows. For example, if changes to your files prevent Windows from running correctly, you must run Setup from MS-DOS. For more detailed information, use a text editor to view the SETUP.TXT file, located on Disk 1 of your Windows disks.

To Run Setup from MS-DOS

1. Quit Windows.

   Do not use the MS-DOS Prompt icon in the Main group window, as this will result in an incorrect setup.

2. At the MS-DOS prompt, type SETUP, and then press [Enter].

To Completely Reinstall Windows

1. Quit Windows.

2. Delete the Windows directory and all the files and subdirectories contained in it.

3. Place your Microsoft Windows Disk 1 in drive A:, and then change to drive A:.

4. At the MS-DOS prompt, type SETUP, and then press [Enter].

5. Follow the Setup instructions on the screen.

Removing Windows Components

Using Windows Setup, you can remove several accessory applications and other components that were supplied with Windows but are not essential to running Windows. This is useful if your system has limited disk space. You can select all or only certain parts of a component. For example, you may want to set up some of the Accessories applications, but not others.

To Remove a Complete Component

1. Clear the check box next to the Component description.

2. Choose the OK button.

To Remove Specific Component Files

Choose the Files button for the component. Then complete the dialog box that appears.

For help, choose the Help button or press [F1] while using the dialog box.

Setting Up Existing Applications

After you install an application on your system, you can use Setup to make sure that it will run smoothly with Windows.

You can direct Setup to search:

- Local drives

- The current path

Setup creates an icon in a Program Manager group window for each application you add. However, Setup will add an icon for a non-Windows application only if the appropriate program information file (PIF) exists. Setup includes information for many applications, but not all. If Setup does not create a PIF for the application you want to add, you can create one by using PIF Editor. If you are adding just one Windows application, it might be easier to use Program Manager. If you are adding several Windows applications or one or more non-Windows applications, using Setup is the best method.

To Add an Application to Windows

1. From the Options menu, choose Set Up Applications.

2. Choose the OK button to search all your local drive(s) for existing applications.

3. In the list, select the locations you want Setup to search.

4. Choose the Search Now button.

    When Setup finishes its search, it displays in the left box the names of the applications it found. These names are from the application; they are not supplied by Setup. You must move each application that you want to set up from the left box to the right box.

5. Click each application you want to select. Or use the arrow keys to move to each application you want, and then press [Spacebar] to select it. When you select an application, Setup displays each application's path in the lower-left corner of the dialog box. Because more than one application can have the same name, check the path to make sure that the application is the one you want. Also, since Setup identifies each application by its program file name, at times it may display the wrong name. (For example, WordPerfect and Microsoft Multiplan both use the name WP.EXE.) Check the names of the applications Setup finds to verify that they are the correct applications.

6. Repeat step 3 to select additional applications.

    To cancel a selection, select it again.

7. To move selected applications to the right box, choose the Add button. Or press [Alt][A]. Or, to move all the listed applications to the right box, choose the Add All button. Or press [Alt][D].

    If you change your mind after adding an application to the right box, select the application, and then choose the Remove button. Or press [Alt][R].

8. Choose the OK button after you have added all the applications you want to set up.

Options Menu Commands

Change System Settings

Changes settings for your display (monitor), keyboard, mouse, and network.
If you change system settings, Setup prompts you to restart Windows so that the changes can take effect.

Set Up Applications

Sets up the applications already on your hard disk(s) so that they will run with Windows.

Add/Remove Windows Components

Installs optional Windows components, such as Readme files, Windows Accessories, and Windows Games on your system. Also deletes optional components from your system.

Exit

Quits Windows Setup.

Keyboard Commands[1]

This Appendix lists the key sequences to accomplish the primary activities in all the programs furnished with Windows. The programs are grouped in the typical program group structure. When you see two keys together, you should press and hold the first key while you press the second (for example, Ctrl S). Two keys separated by a comma indicate that the first key is to be pressed and released before you press the second key (for example, Shift F1, F2). The term "arrow keys" used in the following lists means any of the following: ↑, ↓, ←, or →.

System Keys

The following keys can be used from any window, regardless of the application you are using:

Key(s)	Function
Ctrl Esc	Switches to Task List.
Alt Esc	Switches to the next application window or minimized icon, including full-screen programs.
Alt Tab	Switches to the next application window, restoring applications that are running as icons.
PrtSc	Copies an image of the screen contents onto Clipboard.
Alt PrtSc	Copies an image of the active window onto Clipboard.

---

1 Adapted from the on-line Help for the Windows programs. Portions of the following are copyright © 1990–1992 by Microsoft Corporation.

Alt F4	Closes the active application window.
Ctrl F4	Closes the active document window.
F1	Starts Help and displays the Help Index for the application (see Help Keys).

Program Manager

Use the following keys in Program Manager:

Key(s)	Function
arrow keys	Move among items within a group window.
Ctrl F6 *or* Ctrl Tab	Moves among group windows and icons.
Enter	Starts the highlighted program.
Shift F4	Tiles the open windows.
Shift F5	Cascades the open windows.
Ctrl F4	Closes the active group window.
Alt F4	Exits Windows.

Main Program Group

File Manager Keys

Use the following keys in File Manager:

DIRECTORY TREE WINDOW

Key(s)	Function
Tab	Moves between the Directory Tree and disk drive icons.
Ctrl + disk drive letter	Moves to the disk drive icon that matches the specified letter.
← *or* →	Moves among disk drive icons when you are in the drive area.
Enter	Opens a directory or selects a drive.
↑ *or* ↓	Selects a directory above or below the current directory.
→	Selects the first subdirectory in the current directory.
←	Selects the next directory level up from the current directory.
Ctrl ↑	Selects the previous directory at the same level, if one exists.
Ctrl ↓	Selects the next directory at the same level, if one exists.

PgUp	Selects the directory one window up from the current directory.
PgDn	Selects the directory one window down from the current directory.
Home	Selects the root directory.
End	Selects the last directory in the list.
letter key	Selects the next directory whose name begins with the specified letter.

DIRECTORY WINDOWS

Key(s)	*Function*
PgUp	Selects the file or directory one window up from the current selection.
PgDn	Selects the file or directory one window down from the current selection.
Home	Selects the first file or directory in the list.
End	Selects the last file or directory in the list.
letter key	Selects the next file or directory whose name begins with the specified letter.
Shift + arrow keys	Selects multiple items.
Ctrl / (Slash)	Selects all items in the list.
Ctrl \ (Backslash)	Cancels the selection of all items in the list.
Shift F8	Causes the selection cursor to blink or stop blinking. Use Shift F8 with the arrow keys and Spacebar to select nonconsecutive items or to cancel the selections.
arrow key	Moves the cursor or scrolls to other items in the window.
Spacebar	Selects or cancels the selection of nonconsecutive items marked by a blinking cursor.
Enter	Opens a directory or runs a program.

Control Panel Keys

Use the following keys in Control Panel:

Key(s)	*Function*
Alt D	Makes the selected active printer the default printer in the Printers dialog box.
→ *or* ←	Moves the selected scroll box in the Desktop, Mouse, and Keyboard dialog boxes.

arrow keys	Moves among Control Panel icons.
arrow keys	Moves cursor among colors in Basic and Custom Colors palette.
Spacebar	Selects a color highlighted by the cursor in the Basic or Custom Colors palette.
Ctrl Esc	Opens the Task List dialog box.
Alt Esc	Switches to the next application window or application icon, including full screen applications.

Print Manager Keys

Use the following keys in Print Manager:

Key(s)	Function
Alt D	Deletes a file from the print queue.
Alt P	Pauses printing.
Alt R	Resumes printing.
Ctrl ↑	Moves a file up in a local print queue when the file has been selected.
Ctrl ↓	Moves a file down in a local print queue when the file has been selected.

Clipboard Keys

Use the following keys in performing tasks involving Clipboard:

Key(s)	Function
Shift Del	Cuts the selection from a Windows application and places it onto Clipboard.
Ctrl Ins	Copies the selection from a Windows application and places it onto Clipboard.
Shift Ins	Pastes the Clipboard contents into a Windows document.
Del	Clears the Clipboard contents.
PrtSc	Copies the entire screen onto Clipboard.
Alt PrtSc	Copies an image of the active window onto Clipboard.
Ctrl Esc	Opens the Task List dialog box.

Setup Keys

Use the following keys in Setup:

Key(s)	Function
F1	Starts Help and displays the Setup Help Index.
Alt Spacebar	Opens the Control menu.
Alt ↓	Opens a drop-down list box.
Alt ↑ or Alt ↓	Selects an item in a drop-down list box.
Tab	Moves from area to area within a dialog box.
Shift Tab	Moves from area to area in reverse order.
Alt + letter	Moves to the dialog box option whose underlined letter matches the one you type.
↑ or ↓	Moves among items in a list box.
Spacebar	Selects or cancels a selection in a list box.
Enter	Executes a command button, or chooses the selected item in a list box and executes the command.
Esc	Closes the dialog box without completing the command (same as Cancel).

Games

Solitaire

Use the following keys to play Solitaire:

Key(s)	Function
Tab	Moves among the deck, suit stacks, and playing row of stacks. Tab selects a stack only if that stack is applicable to the next move.
← and →	Moves to the next stack location.
↑ and ↓	Moves from card to card within the stack.
Enter or Spacebar	Picks up and releases a card or group of cards. Enter or Spacebar also turns over a new card in the deck or a stack, and turns over the deck itself.

Reversi

Use the following keys to play Reversi:

Key(s)	Function
arrow keys	Move the pointer.
Enter *or* Spacebar	Makes a move.

Minesweeper

The object of Minesweeper is to correctly mark all mines as quickly as possible without uncovering one. The following section explains how to play the game.

TO CHOOSE A SKILL LEVEL

From the Game menu, choose Beginner, Intermediate, or Expert. The higher the skill level, the larger the mine field.

TO START A NEW GAME

From the Game menu, choose New, or press F2. Or you can click the yellow "happy face" at the top of the game board.

TO LOCATE THE MINES

1. To uncover a square, select it using the left mouse button.

   If the square is a mine, you lose.

2. If the square isn't a mine, a number appears. This number represents the number of mines in the surrounding eight squares.

3. To mark a square as a mine, select it with the right mouse button. To mark a square you are uncertain about, point to it and click twice with the right mouse button. This marks the square with a question mark (?). Later, you can either mark the square as a mine, or uncover it.

Accessories

Write Keys

Use the following keys in Write. The 5 key is on the numeric keypad.

Key(s)	Function
5 →	Moves to the next sentence.
5 ←	Moves to the previous sentence.
5 ↓	Moves to the next paragraph.

Key(s)	Function
`5` `↑`	Moves to the previous paragraph.
`5` `PgDn`	Moves to the next page, according to the last repagination.
`5` `PgUp`	Moves to the previous page, according to the last repagination.
`Ctrl` `Enter`	Inserts a page break.
`Shift` `Del`	Cuts a selection and places it onto Clipboard.
`Ctrl` `Ins`	Copies a selection onto Clipboard.
`Shift` `Ins`	Pastes the Clipboard contents into a document.
`Alt` `Backspace`	Undoes the last action.
`Alt` `PrtSc`	Copies the entire screen onto Clipboard.
`Alt` `F6`	Switches between the document and the Find or Change dialog box.
`Alt` `F6`	Switches between the document and the Page Header or Page Footer dialog box.
`Shift` `→`	Selects a picture when the cursor is above the upper-left corner of the picture.
arrow keys	Moves the Size Picture cursor. Moves a selected picture after you choose Move Picture.
`Ctrl` `Shift` `-` (hyphen)	Inserts an optional hyphen.

Recorder Keys

Use the following keys in Recorder:

Key(s)	Function
`Ctrl` `B`	Stops recording or replaying a macro.
`Ctrl` `Esc`	Opens the Task List dialog box.
`Alt` `Esc`	Switches to the next application window or minimized icon, including full-screen applications.

Terminal Keys

Use the following keys in Terminal:

Key(s)	Function
`Ctrl` `Ins`	Copies the selection onto Clipboard.
`Shift` `Ins`	Sends the Clipboard contents to the remote system.
`Ctrl` `Shift` `Ins`	Sends the selected text to the remote system.
`Alt` `PrtSc`	Copies the entire screen onto Clipboard.

`Ctrl` `Esc`	Opens the Task List dialog box.
`Ctrl` `Alt` `F1` – `F8`	Executes one of 32 user-defined commands.

Notepad Keys

Use the following keys in Notepad:

MOVING THE INSERTION POINT

Key(s)	Function
`↑`	Moves up one line.
`↓`	Moves down one line.
`→`	Moves right one character.
`←`	Moves left one character.
`Ctrl` `→`	Moves right one word.
`Ctrl` `←`	Moves left one word.
`Home`	Moves to the beginning of the line.
`End`	Moves to the end of the line.
`PgUp`	Moves up one window.
`PgDn`	Moves down one window.
`Ctrl` `Home`	Moves to the beginning of the document.
`Ctrl` `End`	Moves to the end of the document.

SELECTING TEXT

Key(s)	Function
`Shift` `←` *or* `Shift` `→`	Selects text one character at a time to the left or right. Or, if the character is already selected, cancels the selection.
`Shift` `↓` *or* `Shift` `↑`	Selects one line of text up or down. Or, if the line is already selected, cancels the selection.
`Shift` `PgUp`	Selects text up one window. Or, if the previous window is already selected, cancels the selection.
`Shift` `PgDn`	Selects text down one window. Or, if the next window is already selected, cancels the selection.
`Shift` `Home`	Selects text to the beginning of the line.
`Shift` `End`	Selects text to the end of the line.
`Ctrl` `Shift` `←`	Selects the previous word.

Ctrl Shift →	Selects the next word.
Ctrl Shift Home	Selects text to the beginning of the document.
Ctrl Shift End	Selects text to the end of the document.

Calendar Keys

DAY VIEW

Key(s)	Function
↑	Moves to the time above.
↓ or Enter	Moves to the time below.
PgUp	Moves to the previous screen.
PgDn	Moves to the next screen.
Ctrl Home	Moves to the starting time.
Ctrl End	Moves to 12 hours after the starting time.
Tab	Moves between the appointment area and the scratch pad.
Shift Del	Cuts the selection and places it onto Clipboard.
Ctrl Ins	Copies the selection onto Clipboard.
Shift Ins	Pastes the Clipboard contents into the appointment area or scratch pad.

MONTH VIEW

Key(s)	Function
↑	Moves to the week above.
↓	Moves to the week below.
PgUp	Moves to the previous month.
PgDn	Moves to the next month.
Tab	Moves between a date and the scratch pad.
Enter	Changes to Day view.

Paintbrush Keys

Use the following keys in Paintbrush:

MOUSE EQUIVALENTS

Key(s)	*Function*
Ins	Clicking the left mouse button.
Del	Clicking the right mouse button.
F9 Ins	Double-clicking the left mouse button.
F9 Del	Double-clicking the right mouse button.

UNDO KEYS

Key(s)	*Function*
Backspace	Lets you undo all or part of what you have drawn since selecting a tool. Pressing Backspace just changes the pointer. You must then select that part of the drawing you want to undo.
Alt Backspace	Automatically undoes everything you have drawn since selecting a tool.

MOVEMENT KEYS

Key(s)	*Function*
Tab	Moves the pointer among the Toolbox, Line Size box, Palette, and Drawing Area in a counter-clockwise direction.
Shift Tab	Moves the pointer among the Toolbox, Line Size box, Palette, and Drawing Area in a clockwise direction.
arrow keys	Moves the pointer inside a window.
Shift Home	Moves to the left edge of the drawing.
Shift Enter	Moves to the right edge of the drawing.
PgUp	Moves up one screen.
PgDn	Moves down one screen.
Shift ←	Moves to the left one space.
Shift →	Moves to the right one space.
Shift ↑	Moves up one line.
Shift ↓	Moves down one line.

Cardfile Keys

Use the following keys in Cardfile:

Key(s)	Function
PgDn	Scrolls forward one card.
PgUp	Scrolls backward one card.
Ctrl Home	Brings the first card in the file to the front.
Ctrl End	Brings the last card in the file to the front.
Shift Ctrl + letter	Brings a card to the front of the file. Cardfile displays the first card whose index line begins with the letter.
Ctrl Esc	Opens the Task List dialog box.

Calculator Keys

STANDARD CALCULATOR FUNCTIONS

To use Calculator's standard functions, click the following buttons or press the keyboard equivalents:

Button	Key	Function
+	Shift = (plus)	Adds.
-	-	Subtracts.
*	Shift 8 (asterisk)	Multiplies.
/	/	Divides.
+/-	F9	Changes the sign of the displayed number.
.	. *or* ,	Inserts a decimal point in the displayed number. The period is the standard setting for a decimal separator. Use Control Panel to change the decimal separator.
%	Shift 5 (percent)	Calculates percentages.
=	= *or* Enter	Performs any operation between the previous two numbers. Choose again to repeat the last operation.
1/x	R	Calculates the reciprocal of the displayed number.
Back	Backspace	Deletes the rightmost digit of the displayed number.
	←	Deletes the rightmost digit of the displayed number.

C	[Esc]	Clears the current calculation.
CE	[Del]	Clears the displayed number.
sqrt	[Shift][@2] (apiece)	Calculates the square root of the displayed value.

MEMORY FUNCTIONS

To use Calculator's memory functions, click the following buttons or press the keyboard equivalents:

Button	*Key*	*Function*
MS	[Ctrl][M]	Stores the displayed value in memory.
M+	[Ctrl][P]	Adds the displayed value to any value already in memory.
MR	[Ctrl][R]	Recalls the value stored in memory.
MC	[Ctrl][L]	Clears any value stored in memory.

When you store a value in memory, the letter M appears in the box below the display area. If you store a zero in memory or if you add a value to memory that results in a value of zero, the letter M disappears. If you store a second value in memory, it replaces the current value in memory.

NUMBER BASE FUNCTIONS

To use Scientific Calculator's advanced number base functions, click the following buttons or press the keyboard equivalents:

Button	*Key*	*Function*
Bin	[F8]	Converts to the binary number system.
Byte	[F4]	Displays the lower 8 bits of the current number.
Dec	[F6]	Converts to the decimal number system.
Dword	[F2]	Displays the full 32-bit representation of the current number.
Hex	[F5]	Converts to the hexadecimal number system.
Oct	[F7]	Converts to the octal number system.
Word	[F3]	Displays the lower 16 bits of the current number.

OPERATORS

To use Scientific Calculator's advanced operator functions, click the following buttons or press the keyboard equivalents:

Button	Key	Function
(	Shift 9 (left parenthesis)	Starts a new level of parentheses. The current level appears below the display. The maximum number of levels is 25.
)	Shift 0 (right parenthesis)	Closes the current level of parentheses.
And	Shift 7 (ampersand)	Calculates bitwise AND.
Int	;	Displays the integer portion of a decimal value.
Inv, Int	I, ;	Displays the fractional portion of a decimal value.
Lsh	<	Shifts left. This operation is binary.
Inv, Lsh	I, <	Shifts right. This operation is binary.
Mod	Shift 5 (percent)	Displays the modulus, or remainder, of x/y.
Not	Shift ` (tilde)	Calculates bitwise inverse.
Or	Shift \ (pipe)	Calculates bitwise OR.
Xor	6	Calculates bitwise exclusive OR.

ADVANCED STATISTICAL FUNCTIONS

To use Scientific Calculator's advanced statistical functions, click the following buttons or press the keyboard equivalents:

Button(s)	Key(s)	Function
Ave	Ctrl A	Calculates the mean of the values displayed in the Statistics Box.
Inv, Ave	I, Ctrl A	Calculates the mean of the squares.
Dat	Ins	Enters the displayed number in the Statistics Box.
s	Ctrl D	Calculates the standard deviation with the population parameter as $n-1$.
Inv, s	I, Ctrl D	Calculates the standard deviation with the population parameter as n.
Sta	Ctrl S	Activates the Statistics Box and the Ave, Sum, s, and Dat buttons.

| Sum | Ctrl T | Calculates the sum of values in the Statistics Box. |

| Inv, Sum | I, Ctrl T | Calculates the sum of the squares. |

OTHER ADVANCED FUNCTIONS

To use Scientific Calculator's other advanced functions, click the following buttons or press the keyboard equivalents:

Button(s)	*Key(s)*	*Function*
cos	O	Calculates the cosine of the displayed number.
Inv, cos	I, O	Calculates the arc cosine.
Hyp, cos	H, O	Calculates the hyperbolic cosine.
Inv, Hyp, cos	I, H, O	Calculates the arc hyperbolic cosine.
Deg	F2	Sets trigonometric input for degrees. Use this function in decimal mode.
dms	M	Converts the displayed number to degree-minute-second format. Calculator assumes the displayed number is in degrees.
Inv, dms	I, M	Converts the displayed number to degrees. Calculator assumes the displayed number is in degree-minute-second format.
Exp	X	Allows entry of scientific notation numbers. The exponent has an upper limit of +307. You can continue to enter numbers as long as you only use keys 0–9. Exp can only be used with the decimal number system.
F-E	V	Toggles scientific notation on and off. Numbers bigger than 10^{15} are always displayed exponentially. F-E can only be used with the decimal number system.
Grad	F4	Sets trigonometric input for gradients when in decimal mode.
Hyp	H	Sets the hyperbolic function for sin, cos, and tan. The different functions automatically turn off the hyperbolic function after a calculation is completed.

Inv	I	Sets the inverse function for sin, cos, tan, pi, x^y, x^2, x^3, ln, log, Ave, Sum, and s. The different functions automatically turn off the inverse function after a calculation is completed.
ln	N	Calculates natural (base e) logarithm.
Inv, ln	I, N	Calculates e raised to the xth power, where x is the current number.
log	L	Calculates common (base 10) logarithm.
Inv, log	I, L	Calculates 10 raised to the xth power.
n!	Shift I (exclamation)	Calculates factorial of the displayed number.
pi	P	Displays the value of pi (3.1415…).
Inv, pi	I, P	Displays 2 * pi (6.28…).
Rad	F3	Sets trigonometric input for radians when in decimal mode.
sin	S	Calculates the sine of the displayed number.
Inv, sin	I, S	Calculates the arc sine.
Hyp, sin	H, S	Calculates the hyperbolic sine.
Inv, Hyp, sin	I, H, S	Calculates the arc hyperbolic sine.
tan	T	Calculates the tangent of the displayed number.
Inv, tan	I, T	Calculates the arc tangent.
Hyp, tan	H, T	Calculates the hyperbolic tangent.
Inv, Hyp, tan	I, H, T	Calculates the arc hyperbolic tangent.
x^y	Y	Computes x raised to the yth power.
Inv, x^y	I, Y	Calculates the yth root of x.
x^2	Shift 2 (apiece)	Squares the displayed number.
Inv, x^2	I, Shift 2 (apiece)	Calculates the square root.
x^3	Shift 3 (number sign)	Cubes the displayed number.
Inv, x^3	I, Shift 3 (number sign)	Calculates the cube root.

Sound Keys

To use Sound, click the following button or press the keyboard equivalent:

⌨Ctrl ⌨C   Copy

Object Packager Keys

To use Object Packager, click the following buttons or press the keyboard equivalents:

⌨Ctrl ⌨Z   Undo last command

⌨Ctrl ⌨X   Cut

⌨Ctrl ⌨C   Copy

⌨Ctrl ⌨V   Paste

C

Answers to Selected Review Questions

1-2. The recent success of Microsoft Windows 3.1 is attributable to the fact that it gives users of DOS computers a control program flexible and powerful enough to support applications of many kinds and levels of complexity and ambition. Also, an enormous range of Windows applications is available now. Windows users do not have to wait years for the kinds of applications promised, but not yet delivered, for other advanced operating systems. Furthermore, Windows runs on tens of millions of PCs. Windows can run on virtually any DOS-based machine with a suitable graphics adapter and monitor. Windows 3.1 is able to push any PC to its limit in ways that few other programs can. It exploits the power of a 386 or 486 machine by letting you multitask DOS sessions while you also run multiple Windows applications. On a 286 machine, Windows lets you multitask Windows applications and access up to 16MB of RAM.

1-3. Windows enables your computer to operate with greater efficiency, unhampered by memory restrictions of previous operating environments. Windows allows you to execute several programs simultaneously and to easily transfer information from one program to another.

Windows is the computer "cockpit" that permits you to control all of your computer's capabilities with the push of a button. It coordinates such high-powered, windows-based programs for desktop publishing, spreadsheets, word processing, and graphics as PageMaker, Excel, Word, and Paintbrush. Other features found in Windows 3.1 are the File Manager, which allows a full range of mouse maneuvers that enable you to copy and move files and directories by dragging their icons with your mouse; the Control Panel, which lets you connect to network printers, switch to additional ports, set multitasking options, and customize the appearance of your desktop; MS-DOS Prompt, which allows you to use many of the commands familiar to users of MS-DOS; Print Manager, which provides information about files that are printing and shows the operator network print queues; Clipboard, which is the temporary storage place for information being transferred from one application to another; and Windows Setup, which is used to change settings for the keyboard, mouse, and video display screen.

1-4. The steps required for starting Windows 3.1 are as follows:

    a. Turn on your PC and monitor. Enter the appropriate date and time if your computer asks for them.

    b. The monitor will display the DOS prompt C\>.

    c. At the DOS prompt, type WIN and press [Enter] to start Windows 3.1.

    d. The Microsoft Windows 3.1 copyright screen appears.

    e. After a short pause, the Windows desktop appears.

2-2. The chief advantage for using the keyboard for input versus using the mouse is that, occasionally, the keyboard allows you to use a single-key shortcut, replacing many mouse movements. The purpose of the [Alt] key or the [F10] (function) key in keyboard commands is to allow you to obtain menu names in the menu bar.

2-4. A menu command with an ellipsis (…) after the name means that a dialog box will appear when the command is chosen, asking for information the application requires to carry out the command. A grayed-out command is one that is not currently available as an option. When a menu command has a check mark next to the name, the command is active; this convention is used for commands that toggle between one state and another (for instance, the Clock can be set to either analog or digital display).

A key combination after the name is a shortcut for this command; one can use this key combination to choose the menu command without first opening the menu.

2-5. Windows utilizes a dialog box both to request information from the user and to provide information to the user. A dialog box appears whenever you choose a command that is followed by an ellipsis (…).

3-2. To avoid exiting Windows, you must press the Cancel button or [Esc].

3-3. A program group is a group consisting of icons called program items. Program items represent applications that you can run.

3-4. Program group windows can be arranged by the Cascade and Tile commands. The Cascade command layers the open program group window within Program Manager with each title bar appearing, as shown in Figure 3.3. On the other hand, the Tile command divides the Program Manager workspace into smaller windows of similar sizes for each program group window that is open, as shown in Figure 3.4.

3-5. The five typical program groups are: (1) Main group, which consists of the File Manager, Control Panel, MS-DOS Prompt, Print Manager, Windows Setup, Clipboard, and sometimes PIF Editor; (2) Accessories group, which includes Write, Paintbrush, Terminal, Notepad, Recorder, Cardfile, Calendar, Calculator, Clock, and PIF Editor; (3) Windows Applications group, which may contain such programs as Word for Windows (word processing) and Excel (spreadsheet)—although the programs in this group vary from one organization or system to another depending on what has been purchased, and are not included in the basic Windows package; (4) Non-Windows Applications group, which contains programs such as WordPerfect, Quattro Pro, dBASE IV, Lotus 1-2-3, and Norton Utilities—these also vary from one system to another; (5) Games group, which displays three games, Solitaire, Minesweeper, and Reversi (others might be added).

4-1. File Manager's principal role is to help you organize files and directories, by allowing you to view them and then build a structure for those files and directories in a fashion that makes sense to you. In other words, it is a shell program that permits you to convert abstract commands into understandable English.

To start File Manager, double-click on the File Manager program item icon, or if using the keyboard press ⬅ or ➡ to move the highlight to the File Manager program item icon. Then, press [Enter], or choose Open from the File menu. File Manager displays the Directory Tree window for your current disk drive.

If File Manager's icon is not found in the Main program group, you can start File Manager as follows:

a. Pull down the File menu and choose Run.

b. Next, type `WINFILE.EXE` in the dialog box.

If File Manager's icon is in the Main Program group, you can start File Manager by doing the following:

a. Double-click on its icon.

b. Insert a properly formatted disk in drive A:.

c. Click on the drive A: icon, and click the mouse.

d. Double-click on a directory to view its contents.

e. Browse a directory's contents by clicking on the scroll bars on the right border of the window.

f. Close File Manager by clicking on File, then on Exit.

4-3. Directories that have subdirectories are represented in the Directory Tree by a plus sign (+), if the system is set up to show expandable directories.

4-5. To list individual files in a particular directory (after double-clicking on it), you must choose Include from the View menu, then select the option that indicates the files you want to display (directories, programs, documents, other). To complete the selection, click or choose OK.

4-6.   **a.**   Directory icons represent directories, listed first and in alphabetical order.

   b.   Program file icons represent program files and batch files, with extensions .EXE, .COM, .PIF, and .BAT, which are executable files used to start up applications.

   c.   Document item icons represent document files, which are part of specific applications.

   d.   Data file icons represent other files.

4-9.   The maximum number of characters that a file name may contain is eight alphanumeric characters, plus an extension of three characters.

   The types of characters that can begin a file name are either a letter or a number.

   The reserved words that cannot be used as file names are: CON, AUX, COM1, COM2, COM3, COM4, COM5, LPT1, LPT2, LPT3, LPT4, PRN, and NUL. These words cannot be used as file names because they are commands intended to address hardware devices.

4-13.   When deleting files, you must be absolutely sure that you want to delete a particular file, especially since files being deleted will be erased from the disk directory and become virtually unrecoverable.

5-1.   Twelve icons are in the control panel. Below is a description of their functions:

   a.   The color icon allows you to set the color of the desktop.

   b.   The fonts icon allows you to add or remove fonts from your printer and monitor.

   c.   The ports icon allows you to set communications parameters.

   d.   The mouse icon allows you to set up the mouse, including speed.

   e.   The desktop icon allows you to customize patterns for the desktop and set the cursor blink rate.

   f.   The 386 Enhanced icon allows you to specify how applications are run.

   g.   The printers icon allows you to install and configure printers.

   h.   The international icon allows you to set international options, such as country and language, number and currency formats, time, and date.

   i.   The keyboard icon allows you to set keyboard speed.

   j.   The date/time icon allows you to change system date and time.

   k.   The sound icon allows you to disable the warning beep for error conditions.

   l.   The drivers icon allows you to install and configure drivers for devices such as sound cards and video players.

5-2. The color scheme can be changed using the mouse by:

a. Opening the Control Panel window from the Main program group in Program Manager by double-clicking on the Control Panel icon.

b. Double-clicking on the Color icon.

c. Clicking on the Color Palette box.

d. Clicking on the Application workspace.

e. Looking at the Basic Color palette on the right side of the screen and checking the color of the current Screen Element. Next, clicking on the arrow to the right of the Screen Element box and changing the current element to see the black frame will enable you to change the current color by clicking on the particular color of your choice.

The color scheme can be changed using the keyboard by:

a. Opening the Control Panel window from the Main program in Program Manager or highlighting the Control Panel icon by using the direction arrows and pressing [Enter].

b. Pressing [Alt][S] for the Settings menu, selecting Color, then highlighting the Color icon and pressing [Enter] to avoid going through a menu.

c. Pressing [Alt][P]; this will allow you to see the Color Palette.

d. Pressing [Alt][E] and using the arrow keys to change the current Screen Element. This will allow you to see the color change, if it is changed, in that particular area only.

e. Looking at the Basic Color palette on the right side of the screen, and checking the color of the current Screen Element. Change the current color by pressing [Alt][B]; enter the Basic Colors area by using the arrow keys to highlight a color, then press [Spacebar] to complete the selection.

5-3. A font is a graphic design that affects the appearance of numerals, symbols, and characters. Fonts allow you to give your work a professional or casual appearance. It is recommended that you remove any fonts that are not being used, since fonts take up valuable memory that may be required for other applications.

6-1. Printing in the background means that once you send a document to the printer, you can continue with another application. You do not have to wait until the print job is completed to continue with your work.

6-2. Print Manager has two types of print queues: local and network. The local queue means that a printer is connected with a cable directly to your computer. The network queue refers to the print queue on the network server. It is managed by a completely separate network print manager, which is different from the one found in Print Manager.

6-5. The problems that may occur while printing in Print Manager are as follows:

    a. Printer does not print.

    b. Printer advances the paper but does not print.

    c. Page prints but is formatted incorrectly.

    d. Printer output is garbled.

    e. Printer output from two files gets mixed.

    f. Laser printer does not print your cartridge or soft fonts.

    g. Printer loses text.

    h. Only part of a page prints.

7-2. To erase a large area of text efficiently, mark the text that you want erased. Position the cursor on the first character and drag to the last line of the text that you want erased. The block of text will be shaded in black. Press [Del] to erase this block of text.

7-3. Formats do transfer if formatted text is copied or moved to another location and/or Write document.

7-5. Text that is left-aligned will possess a straight edge on the left margin, but the right margin will be uneven or jagged. Text that is aligned at the middle of the page is centered. Text that is right-aligned is the opposite of text that is left-aligned, since the right edge is even and the left margin is jagged. Justified means that both margins (left and right) are straight.

8-1. The mouse actions and their keyboard equivalents are:

Mouse Action	*Keyboard Equivalent*
Drag, hold left button	Hold down [Ins] and use arrows
Drag, hold right button	Hold down [Del] and use arrows
Click left button	[Ins]
Click right button	[Del]
Double-click left button	[F9] [Ins]
Double-click right button	[F9] [Del]

8-3. The elements of the Paintbrush Window are the workspace, cursor, toolbox, palette, and the line size box.

    The workspace is the area where you will create your drawings.

    The cursor indicates where a line or other object will be placed when you begin your drawings. (The cursor shape may be different, depending on the tool that is being used.)

The toolbox contains the tools that you use to create drawings. These tools include Fill, Airbrush, Erase, Enter Text, Cut, and so on.

The palette contains the colors and patterns available.

The line size box contains the available drawing widths.

8-5. The Copy command will make an exact duplicate of the material designated to be copied, and place it at the desired destination. By contrast, Cut will remove the selected material from its present location and place it temporarily on the Clipboard.

8-7. Using the mouse to select a tool from the toolbox, click on the tool that you want. Using the keyboard, press [Tab] until the pointer is in the toolbox area, use the arrows to highlight the tool, and press [Ins].

9-1. **a.** A modem (modulator/demodulator) is a hardware device that is used to telecommunicate data. It converts digital signals (data) to analog signals that can be sent over telephone lines at the sending end. At the receiving end, analog signals are converted back into digital signals used by terminals and computers.

  b. Baud rate is the measure of the speed at which data are sent or received over a telephone line. The higher the rate, the faster the data are sent.

  c. Data bits are data sent through the modem in a series of ones and zeros (digits). The number of data bits equals the number of ones and zeros in a piece of data, such as a character sent via a telephone line. Two types of data bits are 7 bits (which represents all the letters of the alphabet, numbers, punctuation marks, and some special symbols) and 8 bits (which is large enough for the entire IBM-PC character set).

  d. Stop bits are used as a signal to tell the receiving computer where one character ends and another begins.

  e. Parity is a method of detecting errors in the data being transmitted. By adding a one or a zero after the data, the software alters the total number of ones into even or odd numbers. The choices for parity checking are Odd, Even, or None.

  f. Data flow control is designed to notify the remote computer when Terminal's buffer capacity has been reached. Terminal needs to notify the remote system to pause momentarily before sending any more characters; otherwise, incoming data will be lost.

  g. "Pause" and "resume" signals are known as handshaking. The method of handshaking used is determined by the Flow Control setting. Terminal's default choice (Xon/Xoff) is the method most commonly used.

9-4. The terminal Emulation setting reflects the type of terminal of the remote computer. The information on terminal type is available from the on-line service to which you are connecting. The choices for terminal type include TTY (Generic),

DEC VT-100 (ANSI), and DEC VT-52. The default terminal type is DEC-VT-100 (ANSI).

If you are not sure which terminal type to use, select TTY.

9-5. Configuring the communications settings will determine how your data are packaged and sent over the telephone line. Modem settings identify for Terminal what signals it needs to initiate a call, receive a call, dial the telephone, and hang up.

10-1. Once you have opened Calculator, you can switch from standard calculator to a scientific calculator by choosing View from the Calculator menu.

10-4. Calendar is a scheduling program that allows you to enter information on either a daily or monthly basis. Calendar reminds you of any scheduled appointment at any time you specify. With Calendar, you can enter appointments, display appointment days, set an alarm to remind you of appointments, and customize your Calendar so that it displays in other than 60-minute intervals. You can also add headers or footers to your appointments before you print with Calendar.

10-7. To avoid entering text beyond the right edge of the window, set Word Wrap from the Edit menu. This option automatically wraps text to the next line when you reach the right-hand border of the window.

10-8. A time-log file is created by entering .LOG in capital letters at the beginning of the file. Notepad will automatically add the current time and date to the file.

11-1. The Windows family of products includes the following:

    a. Word for Windows is a word processing application.

    b. Excel is a spreadsheet application.

    c. Project is an application for managing schedules and resources and for graphically communicating project planning.

    d. PowerPoint is an application that allows you to create and manage high-quality overhead and 35mm slide presentations.

11-3.   **a.** Microsoft Excel

    b. Microsoft PowerPoint

    c. Microsoft Word for Windows

    d. Microsoft Project for Windows

12-1. The shortcut key name is used to play back (run) a macro.

12-2. The basic purpose of a macro is to provide the user with a more efficient and time-saving way of executing the longer step-by-step sequence commands, such as (a) entering text, (b) saving files, or (c) entering applications.

12-4. A macro that is created for Write cannot be used in Calendar, because the command sequences are not identical for different applications. In other words, one application's commands are often dissimilar from another's.

12-6. Some properties of a macro that can be changed are shortcut key assignment, name of the macro, description, speed, and so forth.

The changes can be made in the following way:

a. Select a macro you want to modify from the Recorder window, using the Open command from the File menu.

b. Select Properties from the Macro menu. The drop-down dialog box will appear.

13-1. A program information file (PIF) is a file that contains special information regarding Windows' requirements to run an application.

13-4. The advanced options are organized into four groups as follows:

a. Multitasking refers to how the application will run in relation to other applications.

b. Memory options control how the application uses the computer's available memory. Memory options include EMS and XMS locked memory, High memory, and Locked Application Memory.

c. Display options determine how the application appears on the screen and how Windows manages memory for the application's display. Display options include Video Memory, Monitor Ports, Emulate Text Mode, and Retain Video Memory.

d. Other options permit the user to customize the way applications are run in Windows in the 386 Enhanced mode. These options allow for Fast Paste, Close When Active, Reserve Shortcut Keys, and application of shortcut keys.

14-1. The desktop is the area of the Windows screen that borders any particular window or icon. It is the background area where you create and work with windows applications.

14-2. The options available for customizing the desktop are as follows:

a. Pattern lets you cover your desktop with a repeating dot pattern. You can create the pattern yourself or use a pattern furnished by Windows.

b. Wallpaper provides a scenic design for your desktop.

c. Granularity options let you control the position of objects on your desktop.

14-6. You can determine that the sound is off when you select a command that is not valid and the warning beep does not come on.

15-1. **a.** Conventional memory is the first 640KB (kilobytes) of memory on any computer that uses an 8086, 8088, 80286, 80386, 80386SX, or 80486 microprocessor. It is used to load the Disk Operating System (DOS). Conventional memory may also be used with other device drivers, network software, and any other memory-resident program.

b. Extended memory is that beyond 640KB. It is an extension of the computer's conventional memory. Extended memory is needed to run Windows in Standard or 386 Enhanced mode. To use extended memory efficiently, you will need to install a special program called an extended memory manager.

c. Expanded memory exists apart from your system's conventional and extended memory. As is the case with extended memory, you must install a special program called expanded memory manager, which comes with the expanded memory board.

15-3. Determining disk space requires that you quit Windows and reset your computer by pressing Ctrl Alt Del or turning off the power and starting the computer again. At the DOS prompt, type CHKDSK and press Enter. On your screen, the last two lines in CHKDSK's report provide memory information. The "bytes total memory" number tells you how much conventional memory your system starts out with before you even turn on the computer. The "bytes free" number indicates how much conventional memory is available for Windows to use.

15-4. You can reduce network software, device drivers, memory-resident "pop-up" programs, and memory-resident DOS commands to increase the available conventional memory.

16-1. Clipboard is a utility program that acts as a temporary storage area for the information you are transferring between applications during a Windows session. Information can be copied or cut from an application onto the Clipboard and then transferred into other applications. Clipboard can be used to transfer information among Calculator, Cardfile, Notepad, Paintbrush, Terminal, and most non-Windows applications. Clipboard also provides a fast and convenient way to gather in one place at one time all the information required to complete a project. It can be used to move data between applications not specifically designed for Windows.

16-2. Copy puts the selected information in the Clipboard without removing it from the original document. Cut, on the other hand, puts the information on the Clipboard and at the same time deletes it from the source.

16-4. Multiple formats are important because when you are transferring data to the Clipboard you are allowed to identify which formats are available, by pulling down Clipboard's Display menu. In other words, you are given a broader range of formats from which to choose.

Index

ASCII
    character set, 158
    file, 158
ASSIGN, 221
Auto, 232
AUTOEXEC.BAT file, 214, 221
Automatic numbering, 172
Average, 143

B

Background, 143
    color, 110
    pattern, 198
    priority, 198
Basic Color, 75
Basic options, 195
Batch files, 168, 223
Baud rate, 128, 131
Binary, 143
    files, 134
    RX, 132
    transfer, 134
    TX, 132
Bitmap, 109, 232
BMP file, 115, 221
Bold, 100, 172
Bordeaux (color scheme), 77
Borders, 170, 199
Box, 112
Boxes (desktop pattern), 79
Browse, 209
Brush, 112
Buffer, 90, 91, 128, 134, 219
    line, 131
BUFFERS, 219
Built-in icon, 209
Built-in auditing tools, 170

Bullet, 174
Bytes free, 217

C

CAD, 145
Calculator, 6, 40, 140, 141
    button, 141
    icon, 140
Calendar, 40, 148, 152
CALENDAR.EXE, 222
Cardfile, 6, 40, 153
Carrier detect, 131
Cartridges, 120
Cascade, 37
Cascading menu, 20
Castle, 203
CD, 145
CE, 145
Changing directories, 54
Character at a time, 143
Character formats, 172
Character-based user interface, 4
Check box, 21
CHKDSK, 216
Click, 8,
Clipboard, 226
    viewer, 229
Clock, 40
Close command, 29
Color
    bitmap, 116
    palette, 73, 74
    scheme, 73
Command button, 22
Communications
    dialog box, 131
    protocol, 127

F

FASTOPEN.EXE, 220, 221
File
   information line, 90
   insert Excel chart, 174
   Manager, 45
FILE0001.CHK, 217
Flow control, 131
Fourescent (color scheme), 73
Font, 76
Footers, 151
Foreground, 87
   color, 110
   priority, 195
Formatting a document, 99
Fragmentation, 222
French, 205

G

Gantt charts, 168
GOTO, 221
Granularity, 199
Graphical user interface, 4
Graphics resolution, 120
GUI, 4

H

Handout, 173
Handshaking, 128
Hang-up, 132
Hard returns, 98
Hayes-compatible modem, 132
Headers, 151
High capacity disk, 116
High graphics, 193

High memory area, 194
Highlight, 8, 171
HIMEM.SYS, 216
Hotline, 221

I

I-beam, 97
Icon, 4
   spacing, 199
Indexing, 172
Insertion point, 97
International, 84
Italian, 205
Italic, 100, 172

J

JOIN, 221
Justified, 101

K

Keyboard layout, 205
Kilobyte, 217

L

Landscape, 120
Language, 205
LASTDRIVE=, 220
Legend, 170
Line
   size box, 110
   spacing, 101
List separator, 205

NOTES:

NOTES:

NOTES:

NOTES:

NOTES: